Praise for *Selling Online 2.0*

"*Selling Online 2.0* not only helps new and current eBay sellers better understand the pros and cons of the number of selling options within the 'Net's largest online marketplaces, but it is also useful for larger online retailers looking to new channels."

> —Linda Bustos, e-commerce analyst, Elastic Path/GetElastic.com

"Michael Miller's intriguing *Selling Online 2.0* is sort of an e-commerce version of *The Goose That Laid the Golden Egg*, asking if eBay can survive for long if it continues policy changes that are quickly alienating most of its hundreds of thousands of small sellers. If you're one of those sellers, this is an essential guide to surviving in the new eBay environment."

> —Evan Schuman, editor, StorefrontBacktalk.com,
> a retail technology and e-commerce newsletter site

"There is success to be found selling online beyond eBay, and *Selling Online 2.0* tells readers how to find it. This book is a must-read guide for anyone who wants to carve out a niche and make money online. It provides detailed explanations that both beginners and seasoned online sellers can learn from and immediately put into action."

> —Susan Gunelius, author, president and CEO of
> KeySplash Creative, Inc. (www.KeySplashCreative.com)

"Michael Miller has given small business owners looking to sell online a roadmap to success. From businesses looking to list via classifieds and eBay to those ready for their own shopping carts and store, Miller offers the goods."

> —Tim Peter, e-commerce executive, author of *"thinks"* blog

"Few books offer more directly usable information for web marketers than *Selling Online 2.0*. It can make an expert out of a novice in short order...make that in a short online order."

> —Tom Inglesby, *M2M Magazine* and *ConstrucTECH Magazine*;
> former contributing editor, *e-com Magazine*

"As an online entrepreneur, I know there's a lot to think about when you're starting an e-business, from building a site to marketing to the right customers. This book is a valuable tool for new businesses looking to position themselves in the right online space."

> —Michelle Madhok, CEO, White Cat Media Inc.,
> publisher of SheFinds.com and MomFinds.com

"Michael Miller gives compelling reasons why it's time for sellers to move away from online auctions and then gives easy-to-follow instructions on how it's done."

—Jerry Karpe, www.catalogbuildersonline.com

"*Selling Online 2.0* is an accessible, practical guide for small and medium online auction sellers who wish to transition their businesses to alternative marketplaces or establish their first stand-alone e-commerce websites."

—Jonathan D. Frieden, Esq., Odin, Feldman, and Pittleman, P.C.; author of *E-Commerce Law* blog (www.ecommercelaw.typepad.com)

"This book is a great match for sellers who are getting ready to take the leap and branch out into the Ecom-verse. Michael Miller not only introduces the different choices sellers will face, but really gives an honest opinion of the benefits and pitfalls of the different options. It's obvious that Miller has a good deal of knowledge and experience. I would recommend this book to anyone who is worried about the future of their eBay business. I'd also say it's a must-read for the small business owner just starting out selling online."

—Adam Morris, CEO, redstage networks llc

SELLING
ONLINE 2.0:

Migrating from **eBay**® to **Amazon**®, **craigslist**®, and Your Own **E-Commerce Website**

Michael Miller

 800 East 96th Street,
Indianapolis, Indiana 46240 USA

Selling Online 2.0: Migrating from eBay® to Amazon®, craigslist®, and Your Own E-Commerce Website

Copyright © 2009 by Pearson Education, Inc.

ISBN-13: 978-0-789-73974-2
ISBN-10: 0-789-73974-7

Library of Congress Cataloging-in-Publication Data

Miller, Michael, 1958–
  Selling online 2.0 : migrating from eBay to Amazon, Craigslist, and your own e-commerce website / Michael Miller.
    p. cm.
  ISBN 978-0-7897-3974-2
  1. Electronic commerce. 2. Selling. 3. Internet. 4. Amazon.com (Firm) 5. Craigslist.com (Firm) I. Title.
  HF5548.32.M538 2009
  658.8'72--dc22
                    2009003467

Printed in the United States of America

First Printing: April 2009

Trademarks

Warning and Disclaimer

Bulk Sales

Que Publishing offers excellent discounts on this book when ordered in quantity for bulk purchases or special sales. For more information, please contact

U.S. Corporate and Government Sales
1-800-382-3419
corpsales@pearsontechgroup.com

For sales outside the U.S., please contact

International Sales
international@pearsoned.com

Associate Publisher
Greg Wiegand

Acquisitions Editor
Michelle Newcomb

Development Editor
Kevin Howard

Managing Editor
Kristy Hart

Project Editor
Betsy Harris

Copy Editor
Kitty Wilson

Indexer
Ken Johnson

Proofreader
Dan Knott

Technical Editor
Matthew S. Thomas

Publishing Coordinator
Cindy Teeters

Book Designer
Anne Jones

Compositor
Nonie Ratcliff

Contents at a Glance

Table of Contents

About the Author

Michael Miller has written more than 90 nonfiction how-to books over the past two decades, including Que's *Absolute Beginner's Guide to eBay, Making a Living from Your eBay Business,* and *Tricks of the eBay Business Masters.* He also wrote *Teach Yourself Business Plans in 24 Hours* and *The Complete Idiot's Guide to Search Engine Optimization* for Alpha Books and *Online Marketing Heroes: Interviews with 25 Successful Online Marketing Gurus* for Wiley.

Mr. Miller has established a reputation for clearly explaining complex topics to the average reader and for offering useful real-world advice. Find more information at his website, www.molehillgroup.com.

Dedication

To Sherry—you keep me warm on the cold days.

Acknowledgments

Thanks to the usual suspects at Que, including but not limited to Greg Wiegand, Michelle Newcomb, Kevin Howard, Betsy Harris, Kitty Wilson, and technical editor Matthew Thomas.

We Want to Hear from You!

As the reader of this book, *you* are our most important critic and commentator. We value your opinion and want to know what we're doing right, what we could do better, what areas you'd like to see us publish in, and any other words of wisdom you're willing to pass our way.

As an associate publisher for Que Publishing, I welcome your comments. You can email or write me directly to let me know what you did or didn't like about this book—as well as what we can do to make our books better.

Please note that I cannot help you with technical problems related to the topic of this book. We do have a User Services group, however, where I will forward specific technical questions related to the book.

When you write, please be sure to include this book's title and author, as well as your name, email address, and phone number. I will carefully review your comments and share them with the author and editors who worked on the book.

Email: feedback@quepublishing.com

Mail: Greg Wiegand
           Associate Publisher
           Que Publishing
           800 East 96th Street
           Indianapolis, IN 46240 USA

Reader Services

Visit our website and register this book at informit.com/register for convenient access to any updates, downloads, or errata that might be available for this book.

Introduction

Selling online isn't quite as simple as it used to be. In the good old days, just about anybody could create an eBay listing and let the online auction site do the bulk of the work. All you had to do was wait for the auction to end to see what the final price was and who to ship to. This model created a lot of successful sellers.

All things change, however, and online selling is in the process of some major changes. The eBay auction site isn't near as friendly to small sellers as it used to be; sellers are finding that it's harder and harder to make a decent profit selling exclusively on eBay.

If you made your mark as an eBay seller but find eBay an increasingly unfriendly environment, what do you do next? It's all about migrating your sales to the next-generation selling model—what I like to call Selling Online 2.0.

Selling Online 2.0 doesn't completely abandon eBay—at least, it doesn't have to. But it does embrace alternative marketplaces and channels, opening up the opportunity for you to sell your merchandise on sites such as craigslist and Amazon, as well as on your own e-commerce website.

Here's the bottom line: If you want to maintain or grow your current level of sales, you have to move beyond eBay auctions. To do this, you have to learn some new skills and fine-tune some old ones; you may even have to spend some money setting things up. But the upside is that your online sales can be even more profitable than before—and you may be able to attract a completely new base of customers.

If all you know is selling on eBay, how do you learn what you need to know to sell in other marketplaces and channels? Well, you've come to the right place; that's what this book is all about. While selling on Amazon or craigslist or your own online store might seem daunting at first, it's something you can do if you have the motivation and the knowledge. You'll have to supply your own motivation, of course, but the knowledge you can get from reading this book.

What's in This Book

As you can probably tell from the title, this book tells you everything you need to know to migrate your current eBay business to other online marketplaces and channels. You'll learn how sites such as Amazon and craigslist work, how to plan for success on these sites, and how to create listings, manage sales, accept payments, and even migrate your existing eBay sales to the new marketplaces. You'll also learn how to plan for and launch your own e-commerce website and how to promote and manage that site on a day-to-day basis. Some of the information presented will be familiar to you (both craigslist and Amazon share some similarities with eBay, after all), and some will be completely new. That's the nature of the beast.

There are 22 chapters in this book, divided into five major parts. Each part deals with a different online selling channel, walking you through everything you need to know to get your business up and running in that channel:

- **Part I, "Beyond Online Auctions: Creating a Successful Online Business,"** is the part you want to read before you get into all the details in the rest of the book. Here is where you learn about how eBay is changing and how to plan for online sales success outside eBay.

- **Part II, "Fixed-Price Selling on eBay,"** shows that there is life on eBay beyond the auction format. You'll learn how to migrate your auction listings to fixed-price listings, how to open an eBay Store, how to sell on Half.com, and how to promote your fixed-price sales on the eBay site.

- **Part III, "Selling via craigslist Online Classifieds,"** presents the first alternative to eBay: local online classified ads. craigslist is the biggest online classifieds site, and in this section you learn how and what to sell on craigslist, how to migrate your eBay listings to craigslist, and how to promote your online classifieds business.

- **Part IV, "Selling on the Amazon Marketplace,"** details how to sell your merchandise on the Amazon.com website. You'll learn what types of items sell best on Amazon, how to create and price your listings, how to migrate your existing eBay listings to Amazon, and how to promote your new Amazon business.

- **Part V, "Selling on Your Own Website,"** is the section for any seller who wants to launch a standalone online store. You'll learn how to plan your online presence, set up an e-commerce website, manage your store's sales, promote your online business, migrate your eBay business to your own store, and sell items in multiple channels.

That's a lot to cover—because there's a lot you need to know to be successful. While you can skip around a bit, particularly if you have no intention of selling in a specific channel or marketplace, my recommendation is to start with Chapter 1 and read the whole way through the book. There's a logical process to migrating from eBay to these other channels, and what you learn in one chapter will be applied in following chapters.

Who Can Use This Book

I assume that if you're interested in Selling Online 2.0, you're not a newbie to selling online. You have some experience as an eBay seller under your belt, and you have a handle on what you sell and how.

In other words, I'm not going to teach you how and what to sell. If you're looking for the magic product that will make you rich, look someplace else. This book is for serious and experienced sellers who are ready to move to the next level of online selling.

That said, you don't have to be a large seller to move beyond eBay. This book is written for all levels of sellers, large and small; all you need is some online selling experience and the willingness to make the next move. It also doesn't matter *what* you sell; all types of sellers can be successful selling beyond eBay.

How to Use This Book

This book is easy enough to read that you really don't need instructions. But there are a few elements that bear explaining.

First, there are several special elements in this book, presented in what we in the publishing business call "margin notes." There are different types of margin notes for different types of information, as you see here:

---

note

This is a note that presents information of interest, even if it isn't wholly relevant to the discussion in the main text.

---

tip

This is a tip that might prove useful for whatever it is you're in the process of doing.

---

caution

This is a caution that something you might accidentally do might have undesirable results.

Because many of the solutions presented in this book involve various websites on the Internet, there are lots of web addresses in the text. When you see one of these addresses (also known as a URL), you can go to that web page by entering the URL into the address box in your web browser. I've made every effort to ensure the accuracy of the web addresses presented here, but given the ever-changing nature of the web, don't be surprised if you run across an address or two that's changed.

For that matter, some of the products and services (and corresponding prices) presented here are likely to change by the time you read this text. I apologize in advance, but that's the way the online world works.

There's More Online...

When you need a break from reading, feel free to go online and check out my personal website, located at www.molehillgroup.com. Here you'll find more information on this book and other books I've written. And if you have any questions or comments, feel free to email me directly, at sellingonline@molehillgroup.com. I can't guarantee that I'll respond to every email, but I will guarantee that I'll read them all.

Making the Move

With all these preliminaries out of the way, it's now time to get started. Put on your reading glasses, put on your best business thinking cap, and get ready to migrate to the next level—Selling Online 2.0!

Beyond Online Auctions: Creating a Successful Online Business

1

The Problem with Online Auctions

If you're a small or medium-sized eBay seller, your world is changing—and not for the better. For years, sellers like you have relied on eBay auctions to sell all manner of merchandise, and have done so successfully and profitably. But eBay is in the process of changing its business model, and in the process it is abandoning you and other similar sellers.

Over the past year or so, eBay has changed its fee structure, altered its seller feedback policies, given larger sellers more prominence in its search results, and even done deals with large retailers such as Buy.com to put their merchandise on the eBay site without paying listing fees. It certainly appears as if eBay is abandoning both its traditional online auction model and its mom-and-pop base of sellers in favor of fixed-priced sales and larger, more professional retailers.

So what's *really* going on at eBay—and how does it affect your online auction sales?

What eBay *Used* to Be Like...

For many sellers, eBay was the route to, if not riches, at least reasonable prosperity. eBay's online auctions created a multi-billion-dollar economy where virtually any item could be bought and sold to somebody; the rarer your item (or the more gullible the buyer), the more money you could make per transaction.

eBay enabled hundreds of thousands, if not millions, of casual sellers to evolve from selling odds and ends to running profitable online businesses. It was relatively easy for people to start selling items found in their basements or attics, via eBay's online auction format. Then, once you got the hang of it—or got bitten by the bug, as the case may be—you could ramp up your volume to dozens or even hundreds of auctions each week. Before you knew it, you were running a real business, based entirely on eBay auctions.

Back in the day, eBay was very seller friendly—to a degree. The early eBay site didn't include a lot of seller tools; sellers had to resort to hand-coded HTML if they wanted fancy listings, and invest in third-party services to manage large sales volumes. But still, the focus of the site was to provide a marketplace where buyers and sellers could connect to trade just about any type of merchandise; to do this, eBay had to court lots of individual sellers, which it did.

This focus on connecting individual buyers and sellers was evident from the very beginning. In fact, it's how eBay came about, back the fall of 1995.

Founder Pierre Omidyar launched what he then called Auction Web as part of his own personal site. It was intended as a place for people to buy and sell used and collectible merchandise. This small site quickly became a big site. Pierre started charging users a small fee to list items, to help pay his expenses. The day that Pierre opened his mailbox and saw $10,000 worth of fees—all from individual sellers—was the day he quit his day job and made eBay a full-time proposition.

---

note

Omidyar later renamed Auction Web eBay—short for Echo Bay, the consulting firm that Omidyar ran at the time.

---

eBay evolved from that small trading site into the e-commerce behemoth that it is today. As the company grew, it survived (and arguably brought about) a shakeout that caused dozens of smaller online sites to close their doors. It also survived the dot-com implosion of the early 2000s that destroyed many promising e-commerce businesses.

During its heady early years, eBay's business was doubling year over year. Not surprisingly, the company went public (in 1998), and it now has a boatload of shareholders (and Wall Street analysts) to answer to. In its most recent fiscal year (2007), eBay facilitated the trading of $59 billion worth of merchandise from more 2.3 billion individual transactions. At the end of 2007, eBay had 83.2 million active users worldwide. During the 2007 holiday season, eBay was the number-one e-commerce site in the United States, United Kingdom, and Germany. That's right, more customers bought merchandise from the eBay marketplace than they did from Amazon.com and similar purely retail sites. That's big business, folks.

And, at least in the early years, the vast majority of this business was centered around the online auction concept. If you've ever bought or sold anything on eBay, you know how it works: A seller lists an item for sale at a minimum bid price. Potential buyers start bidding on the item, starting with that minimum price and going upward from there. At the end of the auction (typically seven days), the user with the highest bid wins the auction and buys the item.

The online auction model can be a lot of fun, and it's a great way to let the market value used, rare, or collectible items. But it's a somewhat inefficient process for buying and selling commodity products. After all, if a given model of printer ink cartridge sells day-in, day-out for $20 at Office Depot and Staples, why should a potential buyer have to wait seven days to see if his $20 bid for that item is the high bid? Commodity buyers want their purchases faster—and they want to make sure they actually purchase the item, as opposed to placing a losing bid.

With that in mind, several years ago eBay established two alternatives to its auction sales. First, it let sellers offer a Buy It Now option, which effectively puts a fixed price on an item listed for auction; a buyer can opt to skip the bidding and end the auction by paying the specified fixed price. Second, eBay started offering traditional fixed-price listings, no bidding involved, primarily through its eBay Stores. Both of these alternatives provided buyers with a way to buy products without going through the auction process.

Even with these fixed-price options, traditional online auctions still accounted for the bulk of eBay's sales—and the bulk of these auction listings came from smaller sellers. I'm talking folks like you and me, people selling onesies and twosies out of their garages and attics, as well as folks who got a little larger and had turned their eBay sales into full- or part-time businesses. What these sellers have in common is that they aren't big businesses with warehouses full of products, automated back-office operations, and professional shipping processes. These sellers do pretty much everything by hand—which is great if you like the personal touch but sometimes leaves buyers in the lurch. After all, a guy selling a used Tonka truck for five bucks isn't likely to have a customer relations department, money-back returns policy, or sophisticated packing and shipping.

In fact, some small sellers aren't all that good at it. They sometimes offer inferior or misrepresented merchandise, pack poorly, and ship slowly. And if a buyer has a question or a problem, they may respond slowly—if at all. A buyer who has a few transactions with these questionable sellers quickly sours on the whole eBay experience, which is not good for the rest of us sellers—or for eBay itself.

It's interesting. Over the years, eBay has tried to walk a thin line, doing its best to make both its buyers and sellers happy. But the interests of buyers and sellers aren't always in sync. Buyers want low prices, free shipping, money-back return policies, and no-questions-asked protection against fraudulent sellers; sellers want high prices, as much free back-end support as they can get, and protection against deadbeat buyers. It's a tough line to straddle, and one that ensured that eBay would eventually disappoint one or both sides.

For the first decade or so of eBay's existence, it appeared to many that the company was in strong support of its seller community. It continually introduced new services intended to support its sellers and make the selling process easier. The company did its best to communicate with sellers, especially its most active sellers, even to the point of hosting local seminars and educational sessions, as well as the immensely popular eBay Live yearly event. Not all sellers were completely happy (you can't please all the sellers all the time, to borrow an old phrase), but it generally worked out okay for all concerned.

However, a year or so ago, eBay's growth began to slow. That's when the changes started to come.

Why Is eBay Abandoning Smaller Sellers?

With slowing growth from its traditional auction business, eBay had to do something to keep its shareholders happy. And because shareholders are only interested in the money, that meant finding new ways to increase the company's revenues and profits.

One surefire way to increase short-term profits, of course, is to raise prices. Which eBay did—several times. The company also found ways to earn additional money from its auctions by offering a variety of optional features and services, most of which involved sprucing up the look of individual item listings by adding pictures, subtitles, boldfaced search result listings, and the like. eBay even purchased PayPal, the firm that many sellers used to accept credit card payments, so it could include PayPal fees as part of its revenue stream.

But you can only increase prices so much. After a point, higher fees start driving sellers away, resulting in fewer overall listings. That was not a good thing.

Added to the need to increase revenues was the constant harping from some buyers that they wanted a more professional shopping experience. Bidding in online auctions from individual sellers was fine the first few times they did it, but after awhile, buyers just wanted to buy what they wanted to buy. In addition, many potential buyers were scared off by the unprofessional purchasing experience offered by some small sellers; some buyers flat out had bad experiences that drove them away from eBay into the arms of Amazon, Buy.com, and other large retailers.

So, to both appease its current buyers and attract a larger base of new buyers, eBay decided to clean up its act —or, more precisely, offer its buyers a more professional shopping experience. To do that, eBay had to do several things.

First, the company had to attract more sellers offering more merchandise. Buyers had to be assured that they could always find whatever they were looking for on the eBay site; eBay couldn't let the whims of individual sellers dictate its merchandise inventory. Ultimately, it had to offer more items for sale day-in and day-out.

Second, eBay had to shift more of its sales to larger, more professional sellers. These sellers had to be encouraged to offer (if they didn't already) large amounts of merchandise for sale at reasonable prices, consistent and affordable shipping/handling fees (or, ideally, free shipping/handling), professional communications and back-end operations, quick and professional packing and shipping, and money-back return policies. eBay wanted buyers to get exactly the same shopping and pur-chasing experience from its sellers as they would receive from Amazon, Lands' End, and other large online merchants.

Finally, the company had to encourage a shift from items offered via online auction to those sold at a fixed price. More and more buyers were not willing to suffer through the traditional seven-day auction process, so eBay had to evolve from an auction site to a traditional fixed-price retail-ing site.

Here's how eBay put its new efforts in an April 2008 release to share-holders: "[eBay] continues to focus on customer-facing initiatives designed to make transactions on the eBay platform safer and its various global sites easier to use, while enhancing selection in a uniquely eBay way." In non-eBay speak, this means eBay wanted to become less like eBay and more like Amazon—which meant pushing out smaller hobbyist sellers in favor of larger professional retailers.

Changes Are Afoot—and You Probably Won't Like Them

Recognizing its new goals, eBay set about affecting a series of changes to the way it does business—including changing its fee structure, implementing a series of new rules and regulations, and doing some deals with large retailers to ensure a steady flow of popular merchandise.

Many of these changes, unfortunately, adversely affected smaller sellers. Oh, if you only sold a half-dozen items a year, it wasn't a big deal; you paid a little more in fees, but you could still sell the junk you wanted to sell. But if you sold a half-dozen or more items a week, these changes put a big squeeze on your business. Not only did your costs go up, these changes had the effect of making you less competitive than you used to be.

The bottom line is that the changes eBay made in 2007 and 2008 resulted in its large base of smaller sellers selling less merchandise and with higher costs. That's not an equation for long-term success.

Emphasizing Fixed-Price Sales over Auction Sales

Many of eBay's policy changes have the intended effect of shifting its mix from traditional auction sales to fixed-price sales. Let's look at some numbers.

At the end of 2005, fixed-price sales represented 34% of eBay's total gross merchandise value. By the end of 2006, fixed-price sales were up to 38% of the mix; by the end of 2007, they had increased to 42% of the mix, and by the third quarter of 2008 (the most recent data available at this writing), that number was up to 46%. That's right, by the end of 2008, almost half of all eBay transactions were fixed-price sales. When half your sales are fixed price, are you still an online auction site? Well, maybe not—but eBay's goal is to switch from auction to fixed-price sales.

Changes to the Fee Structure

Let's look at the most noticeable of eBay's recent changes: the company's revamped fee structure. This new fee schedule took effect September 16, 2008, with the goal of encouraging more fixed-price item listings.

The most notable change in the fee schedule concerns fees for fixed-price listings. eBay reduced the fixed-price listing fee to a flat $0.35, a significant reduction from the previous schedule, based on the listing price of the item, that ran up to $4.80 per listing. In the process, eBay also extended the length of its fixed-price listings, from seven days to one month.

The listing fee is even lower for media products, such as music, movies, books, and video games. In these categories, the fixed-price listing fee is just $0.15 per item.

eBay's listing fees for auction items, on the other hand, are still based on the item's starting price and range from $0.15 (for items priced under $1) to $4 (for items priced $500 or more). Table 1.1 details eBay's insertion fee schedule for auction items, as of February 2009.

Table 1.1   eBay Auction Insertion Fees

Starting Price	Insertion Fee (General Items)	Insertion Fee (Media Items)
$0.01–$0.99	$0.15	$0.10
$1.00–$9.99	$0.35	$0.25
$10.00–$24.99	$0.55	$0.35
$25.00–$49.99	$1.00	$1.00
$50.00–$199.99	$2.00	$2.00
$200.00–$499.99	$3.00	$3.00
$500.00 or more	$4.00	$4.00

If you're selling a $30 item, for example, you'll pay $1.00 to list it for a one-week auction, or just $0.35 to list it for a month at a fixed price. As you can see, this puts the auction seller at a distinct financial disadvantage compared to a fixed-price competitor.

---

note

Naturally, both fixed-price and auction sellers still have to pay a final value fee (FVF) when an item sells. For auction items, this fee starts at 8.75% of the final selling price. For fixed-priced items, the final value fee varies by product category; for example, the FVF fee for fixed-price consumer electronics items starts at 8%, while it's 12% for clothing and 15% for media items.

Adding insult to injury, eBay offers its largest sellers discounts on the fees they pay. PowerSellers with high customer ratings qualify for discounts on their FVFs of between 5% and 20%. Think of that: You could be competing with sellers who are paying 20% less than you are whenever they sell an item. That's 20% more in their pocket, and nothing more for you. Is that fair?

---

note

To obtain a fee discount, a seller must be a member of eBay's PowerSeller program and maintain a rating of 4.6 or higher on all four of eBay's detailed seller ratings (DSRs), which buyers use to rate sellers on specific aspects of a transaction.

Not surprisingly, eBay's traditional seller community is up in arms about these fee changes—and the discounts offered to their largest competitors. The fee changes alone are driving many sellers from eBay to Amazon and other online marketplaces. But, unfortunately, that's not where the changes end.

Changes to the Payment System

eBay enacted another major policy change in October 2008. No longer can sellers accept personal checks, money orders, and cashier's checks as payment for their transactions. Instead, all sellers must offer some form of credit card payment.

For small and medium-sized sellers, that effectively means using PayPal for all their sales transactions—which means more fees flowing to the eBay mothership. (Remember: eBay owns PayPal.) Larger sellers who have their own credit card payment services can use them instead of PayPal, but few smaller sellers have that sort of setup.

Payments have been shifting from checks and money orders to credit cards for some time now, but in many product categories, sellers still did a significant amount of business via paper payments—which had no fees attached. You now have to shift all your payments to PayPal and pay PayPal fees (typically 2.9% plus $0.35 per transaction) on all those payments. For some sellers, this is a significant increase in the fees they pay—and a corresponding decrease in their profits.

eBay says that it's making this change to increase buyer protection. (Credit card purchases are protected from fraud by the credit card companies themselves, while buyers have little protection if they pay using paper.) And, to be fair, it's difficult to make a purchase from a large online retailer by check. But if you're a small seller, being forced to use PayPal not only affects your bottom line, it also affects the freedom you have to run your business your own way. If you don't like PayPal, you're out of luck.

Changes to the Feedback System

Here's another buyer-focused change that really dings eBay's seller community: eBay no longer lets sellers leave negative feedback about bad buyers.

You have to understand, eBay's feedback system, while less than perfect, is a decent way to learn more about the buyers and sellers you deal with in the eBay marketplace. Buyers know that a seller with a low feedback rating is probably to be avoided; sellers know that they might not want to transact with a buyer who has numerous negative feedback comments.

However, eBay has eliminated the ability for sellers to leave negative or neutral feedback about buyers. (They can still leave positive feedback, however.) This removes one of the weapons that sellers used to protect themselves against malicious buyers.

The old feedback system had a self-policing nature to it. In the old days, if a buyer threatened to leave negative feedback if a seller didn't take back an item or issue a refund, the seller could counter by threatening to leave negative feedback about the buyer. Now that the seller can't counter one threat with another, malicious buyers can theoretically hold sellers hostage post-sale. If a buyer has a beef with a seller, the seller has no recourse if the buyer leaves unwarranted negative feedback.

While this change doesn't necessarily favor large sellers over smaller ones, it does favor buyers over sellers—which many eBay sellers take issue with.

Changes to Search Results

It used to be that when a buyer searched for an item on eBay, items from all sellers were listed in the order of when the items' listings expired. It didn't matter whether you were a large seller or a small one: Your items were equally listed in the mix.

That all changed in September 2007. eBay's new Best Match system returns search results that emphasize sellers with high feedback ratings, which tends to discriminate against lower-volume and newer sellers who haven't yet built up high feedback numbers. As a result, many smaller sellers find their items getting buried deep in the back of search results pages. With Best Match, bigger sellers get their items listed first; mom-and-pop sellers get their items listed last.

> **note**
>
> eBay's Best Match system also favors sellers who offer free shipping and handling on their items—more common among larger sellers than smaller ones.

The result is that for many sellers, potential buyers never see the items they have for sale. Some sellers have found their sales decrease by 50% or more based on eBay's new search algorithm. It's a definite bias toward larger sellers—and is driving many smaller sales out of the eBay marketplace.

eBay's Deal with Buy.com

There's one last thing that eBay has done that is really torquing off its established sellers. That thing is a special deal that eBay has made with Buy.com to flood the eBay marketplace with fixed-priced items for sale.

This deal, which took effect in spring of 2008, enables Buy.com to sell millions of DVDs, CDs, video games, books, and electronics items on eBay, directly competing with eBay's traditional seller community. To make matters worse, Buy.com gets to place these listings without paying any listing fees. That's a competitive advantage that no current eBay seller can match, and it creates something less than a level playing field.

Why did eBay do this deal with Buy.com? The company says that this deal helps to fill gaps in its product offerings, while presenting a more predictable shopping experience to its buyers. (Buy.com offers money-back returns, toll-free telephone support, and, in many cases, free shipping.) That's probably true, but it's yet another signal that eBay sees its future lying with large, professional sellers instead of the mom-and-pop sellers who helped grow the company.

How Do eBay's Changes Affect You?

If you weren't already aware, you now know all about eBay's recent changes to its fees and policies, and you're probably not happy about them. Here's the bottom-line question: How do all these changes affect you as an eBay seller?

First things first. If you continue to sell most of your merchandise via the online auction format, expect to see your profits decrease due to eBay's higher listing fees and FVFs for auction listings. If you stick with online auctions, you'll be generating less profit than your competitors who sell primarily fixed-price items.

Second, expect to see fewer sales. That's because eBay is introducing more competition (via its deal with Buy.com—and presumably others in the future) and promoting larger competitors over smaller businesses like yours. The big guys not only get a price break, they get favorable placement in eBay's product search results. The upshot is that fewer potential customers will see your listings, and you'll sell fewer items. Not a good thing.

So how do you respond? The lower listing fees for fixed-price items mean that even if you stay with eBay, you want to shift your selling from the traditional auction format to fixed-price listings. If you don't, you'll be selling similar items for a lower profit than your fixed-price competitors, which is not a good thing.

Finally, you probably want to investigate moving some or all of your sales off eBay and onto an alternative online marketplace. Let's face it, eBay is favoring your larger competitors, and they're going to keep grabbing more and more of what used to be your sales. There's no reason for you to put up with an environment that puts you at such a competitive disadvantage.

So if you're a small or medium-sized eBay seller, you need to change the way you do business in order to stay in business. How do you do that? Well, that's what we start to discuss in the next chapter, so read on to learn more.

Are Buyers Tiring of Online Auctions?

Looking at the shift in eBay's auction versus fixed-price sales mix brings up the reality-check question: Is this shift being forced by eBay, or are buyers tiring of online auctions?

Unfortunately, there's no good research to answer this question, but I think it's a bit of each. eBay's changes are definitely pushing sellers to offer more fixed-price merchandise, and you can see this by searching eBay's listings. But many buyers I know aren't as enamored of the auction process as they used to be. Yeah, bidding on an online auction can be fun, and auctions are a good way to pick up some bargains if you're good at it, but when you just want to buy something, doing the seven-day auction thing can be a bit of a hassle.

Personally, I think eBay reached the limits of popularity with the online auction format. To break further into the general consumer population (and thus continue growing its business), eBay has to offer consumers a more traditional and professional shopping experience. And that doesn't come from mom-and-pop auction sales.

Not that I think eBay's online auctions will ever completely go away—unless eBay deliberately kills the format sometime in the future, that is. The auction format is still the best way to value and trade collectible and rare items, such as stamps, coins, antiques, and the like. It's also probably a good way to trade used merchandise, including clothing, toys, and the like. But it's a horrible way to sell new and commodity products that are available on competing sites at fixed prices for immediate shipment.

For eBay to compete in the marketplace for new clothing, electronics, household goods, and the like, it must offer a consumer experience that is similar if not superior to that offered by Amazon, Buy.com, and other competing sites. eBay knows this, and this is what's driving the company's recent changes. The real question, though, is how does all this affect *your* business? For many sellers, it means shifting business from eBay to other online marketplaces—which is what this book is all about. ■

2

Planning for Selling Success

If you're a small or medium-sized eBay seller, you're no doubt feeling the squeeze. Continue doing business via online auction like you've always done, and you're likely to see both your sales and your profits shrink. It's change or perish; you have to change the way you do business to survive.

Before you change your business model, however, you need to plan for the change. Without careful planning, you're liable to make the wrong changes and end up worse off than you were previously. Planning is key to building a successful business—even if you've already tasted success on eBay.

Planning for Life Beyond eBay Auctions

Here's a fact I really don't like to admit: In the past, it's been possible to obtain short-term success on eBay without doing a whole lot of planning beforehand. I hate to admit this because I am, by nature, a planner, and I know the value of planning when building a successful business of any kind. But eBay auctions, in the past, were just too easy to do, and many sellers found themselves making lots of money without actually planning for it. Put another way, it was easy to get lucky.

That was the past, of course; going forward, it's going to be much, much harder to build a lasting business based solely on eBay online auctions. Luck won't factor into things as much; building a next-generation online business will require planning and skill and probably a little financing—the same things required to build any other type of successful business. In other words, you need to know what you're going to do before you actually do it.

That means thinking through all your options, doing a little research, and then sitting down and writing a detailed plan for how to achieve what you want to achieve. You have to do your homework and figure out where you want to go and how you're going to get there.

If you *don't* plan your next moves in advance, chances are you'll run into more than a few surprises. Unpleasant surprises. You don't want to get six months into your business and then find out that you're losing money on every sale you make. Far better to think through everything beforehand, so you'll know what to expect. No surprises—that's my motto.

Asking—and Answering—Key Questions

The easiest way to begin the planning process is to ask yourself a series of questions. When you can comfortably answer these questions, you'll have the framework of your business plan—and a roadmap for how to implement the necessary changes to ensure the continued survival and success of your business.

What Type of Merchandise Do You Want to Sell?

The first question is the most important: What type of merchandise do you want to sell?

Now, you may already have this question answered, especially if you have an established eBay business. But already selling a specific type of product on eBay doesn't mean you want to continue selling this type of product beyond eBay. In fact, what you sell on eBay may not be that profitable on other online marketplaces.

But let's start at the top. Are you happy selling what you currently sell on eBay? Is it something you like? Is it something you're good at? Is it something that has widespread selling appeal? Is it a product category that's large enough or growing enough to make you think that it will continue to be viable in the years ahead?

Note that I said *category*, singular. Not every eBay seller specializes in a specific category; some sellers have seen success with sort of a garage sale approach, selling whatever products they can obtain at a reasonable cost. I'll say it right here: A multi-category model, while workable on eBay, is unlikely to be successful outside eBay. Most successful online businesses specialize in a particular product category, for many good reasons.

First, specializing in a single category (or several related categories) helps you get to know that category better; you become an expert at one thing rather than a dilettante at many. And the better you know that one thing, the better you can sell it.

Second, specializing in a category means you'll be purchasing bigger quantities of those things you sell, as opposed to smaller quantities of a wider base of inventory. And the bigger the quantities you purchase, the lower your purchase price is likely to be—which means bigger profits in the long term.

Finally, specializing in a specific type of item makes it easier to set up a selling, packing, and shipping "factory." Sell one SKU, and you have to stock only one type of box or envelope; you can get really good at packing and shipping that one thing, over and over and over. The fewer SKUs you sell, the less reinventing of the wheel you have to do post-sale. It's a simple business model—and simplicity can be profitable.

That said, you have to decide *which* product category you want to specialize in. Ideally, you want to sell items with which you are familiar, that have a strong profit margin, that have a large (and hopefully growing) base of potential customers, that can be simply and efficiently packed and shipped, that can be sourced at a reasonable cost, and that aren't widely available from bigger, better-financed competitors. It sounds like a tall order, but that's part of what business planning is about.

The point is that you have to know what you're going to sell before you can figure out how to sell it. That's why this step is so crucial to putting together your business plan.

How Much Money Do You Want to Make?

Knowing what you want to sell is one thing. Knowing how much money you want to make is another. And, unfortunately, sometimes they don't match up. (This is why planning is important—so you'll know what works before you're hip-deep in things.)

Start from the top down. For your business to be successful, you have to generate an income on which you can comfortably live—unless, of course, you're looking for your online business to supplement an existing income. In any case, you need to set a monetary goal that you want to achieve. This number will determine how many items you need to sell.

What you *don't* want to do is set up your business first and then ask how much money you'll make with it. Successful businesses start out with a specific goal in mind and then work toward that goal. Unsuccessful businesses open their doors (figuratively speaking, of course) without knowing where they'll end up—and, more often than not, end up going pretty much nowhere at all.

This type of financial goal-setting may be new to you. Many eBay sellers buy something for $5, sell it for $10, and then pay their eBay fees at the end of the month without ever calculating just how much profit they're making. That's not the way real businesses work, however; building a business for the long run involves setting sales goals and expense budgets and making sure that the business sticks to the plan.

Let's work through an example. You've talked it over with your family and decided that you would be extremely happy if you could take home $30,000 a year from your online activities. That means building a business that can generate $2,500 a month in profit; your job, then, is determining how you're going to hit that profit target.

For the purposes of this example, let's say that you're selling gift baskets that have an average selling price of $20. So you do some quick math and determine that you need to sell 125 of these $20 gift baskets every month to reach your $2,500/month goal. (That's $2,500 divided by $20.)

Stop right there! There's something wrong with this calculation. I hope you know what it is.

Here's the problem: This simple calculation fails to take into account any of your expenses! That $20 per item represents your gross revenue, *not* your net profit. So you have to go back and figure out the costs involved with the sale of each item.

The first cost you have to take into account is the actual cost of the merchandise. Let's say that you pay $5 for each gift basket. Subtract that $5 product cost from your $20 selling price, and you have a $15 profit for every item you sell.

But that's not your only expense. Depending on which marketplace you're using to sell your products, you probably have some sort of commission or selling fee to pay for every item you sell. If you accept credit card payments, you'll pay a percentage for all purchases made with plastic, just as you do with PayPal on eBay. And if you're selling on your own website, you'll need to add in some advertising and promotion costs, as well.

Altogether, these non-product costs can add up to 10% to 20% of your total revenues. Let's use the top figure—20%—and subtract $4 for each $20 sale.

Now let's do the new math. Take your $20 selling price, subtract your $5 product cost and $4 for selling fees and such, and you have a net profit of $11. To generate $2,500 a month in profit, you have to sell 228 gift baskets each month. (That's $2,500 divided by $11.) That's your sales goal.

Of course, there may be other options available. What if you could find a better-quality gift basket that you could sell for $40 instead of $20? Assuming that you could keep the rest of your costs in line, that would cut in half the number of sales you would have to make every month. Or what if you decided you could live on $20,000 a year instead of $30,000? That would reduce your financial nut by a third.

You see where we're going with this. By working through these types of details ahead of time, you can fine-tune the amount of money you expect to make and the amount of effort you have to expend. Want to make more money? Then find a higher-priced (or lower-cost) item to sell or plan on somehow increasing your monthly sales volume. It's all related—plan where you want to go, and then you can figure out how to get there.

How Do You Intend to Manage Your Business?

Deciding what to sell and for how much is just a small part of the planning process. You also need to think through every aspect of your new business—from purchasing your inventory through packing and shipping the items you sell.

Let's walk through the details that you have to deal with.

First, there's the inventory. In order to sell an item to a customer, you first have to purchase the item to sell. That means identifying a supplier for the items you sell, typically a distributor that offers these items for sale in bulk, at wholesale pricing. For some items, you may deal directly with the manufacturer, although you'll typically be required to make larger purchases than from a distributor. There's also the option of working with a dropshipper—a distributor who handles all the stocking and fulfillment for you, at a price.

So you have to determine what type of supplier you want to deal with and then find one or more suppliers. I find it safer to have a primary supplier and a secondary one; the secondary supplier is used as backup if the primary supplier is out of stock or has other issues. In any case, you should compare prices between suppliers and look for those that offer the best deals, in terms of both pricing and payment terms.

---

tip

It helps if you can get extended terms, so that you don't have to actually pay for your inventory in advance. If you play your cards right and get net 30 (payable 30 days after the order) or longer terms, you may be able to sell the item and get paid by your customer before you have to pay the supplier.

Then there's the matter of managing that inventory. Assuming that you have to buy in larger quantities, you have to figure out where to store all that merchandise until you sell it to your customers. If you sell small stuff and have a large basement or garage, you may not have any issues. But if you sell larger items that you have to buy in bulk, you may have to look at some sort of supplemental warehouse space. That might mean placing a POD in your driveway or renting a storage locker; it might also mean leasing part or all of an actual warehouse. It all depends on what you sell and how much you have to keep in stock.

Once you have merchandise to sell, you have to start selling it. In many cases, this will involve some sort of advertising or promotion. This might mean purchasing online ads via Google AdWords or some similar service, it might mean purchasing larger display ads, or it might mean more of a guerilla marketing approach via blog and email marketing. In any case, you have to include your promotional efforts in your business plan—and account for them in your business budget.

After you make a sale, it's nice to get paid. When you sell on eBay, eBay takes care of that—typically via the PayPal online payment service. Outside eBay, you'll have to make your own arrangements. While some online marketplaces, such as Amazon, have their own payment services, if you run your own website, you'll have to find your own payment service in order to accept credit card payments. It's a necessary part of the business.

The other thing that happens after a sale is that you pack and ship the items you sell. This is pretty much the same process no matter where you sell, so you can probably port your eBay packing/shipping operation to your new business.

Dealing with customers, however, is going to be different when you move beyond eBay. Let's face it, eBay does a good job of managing the customer communications process for you; when you branch out on your own, you need to set up your own email contact system. You may even want to establish toll-free telephone customer support; your customer support and communications have to be at least on par with those offered by your competitors.

Finally, you have to manage the progress of your business, which means setting up an inventory management/sales tracking/financial accounting system. I recommend that you consult an accountant before you get too far in this process, as you'll probably want to supplement computer-based systems (such as QuickBooks) with the services of a real-live number cruncher.

Does all this sound a little daunting? It's meant to. eBay provides a nice little support cocoon for even the most inexperienced sellers; when you go off on your own, you break free of this cocoon and have to start doing all this yourself. Remember to plan for not only the processes involved but also the costs of all these processes.

Where Do You Want to Sell?

I've left one key question until last: *Where* do you intend to sell your merchandise? It's not an easy question to answer—which is probably one of the reasons you bought this book.

I've identified, in no particular order, four types of marketplaces you can use to sell your products:

- **eBay fixed-price sales.** eBay auctions are part of your past, not your future. But you can migrate your auction listings to fixed-price listings on the general eBay site, in an eBay Store, or on eBay's Half.com sister site. Of course, you'll still be competing at a disadvantage against some much larger sellers, but at least you won't be financially penalized by running auctions instead of fixed-price sales. (Learn more about fixed-price selling on eBay in Part II, "Fixed-Price Selling on eBay.")

- **Online classifieds sites.** Online classifieds are probably the closest cousins to eBay online auctions. You can set a desired price for your items but still leave room for negotiation, or a "best offer." Of course, the best-known online classified site is craigslist; while other sites exist, craigslist is the big dog in many cities. (Learn more about selling via online classifieds in Part III, "Selling via craigslist Online Classifieds.")

- **The Amazon marketplace.** eBay's biggest competitor for smaller sellers is Amazon. Yes, Amazon sells tons of merchandise on its own, but it also offers a marketplace where small and medium-sized sellers can offer their own products for sale. In many ways Amazon costs less and offers more services than does eBay, although it's not without its drawbacks—chiefly, that you're competing against

Amazon itself. That said, this is the preferred new venue for many former eBay sellers. (Learn more about selling on Amazon in Part IV, "Selling on the Amazon Marketplace.")

- **Your own e-commerce website**. For many sellers, this is the holy grail—your own online store. This option requires a lot more work than using the services of an existing online marketplace, and it involves more upfront costs. But, theoretically anyway, this should be a more profitable channel after you crack the initial nut, as you aren't nickel-and-dimed to death with post-sale fees. (Learn more about setting up your own website in Part V, "Selling on Your Own Website.")

Of course, you're not limited to selling in just a single marketplace. You may decide to continue selling on eBay while also expanding to craigslist or Amazon. Or you may move your eBay business to Amazon while also building your own e-commerce website. It's not unusual to sell in multiple channels, although it does require a bit more business management on your part. (Learn more about multichannel selling in Chapter 22, "Selling in Multiple Channels.")

Determining where you want to sell is essential to how you run your new business—which is why the balance of this book is devoted to selling in these various channels. You probably want to read through the entire book before you put this part of your plan on paper.

Conceiving a Business Plan

The act of figuring out what kind of business you'll be running is best done by preparing a written *business plan*. If that sounds terribly formal and complicated, don't stress out—it doesn't have to be. The plan for your business can be as simple as some bullet points written out in longhand, or as sophisticated as a professional-looking desktop-published document. Your plan is simply a formal declaration of what you want to do and how you want to do it. The key thing is to set down on paper the details about the business you want to create and then follow the steps in your plan to build that business.

You may think that a business plan has to be a complex document, full of long sentences, overly technical terms, convoluted legalese, lots of pie charts, and detailed financial data. Nothing could be further from the truth. If you can talk about your business—and you no doubt can, at length—then you can create an effective business plan.

The best business plans are conversational in tone, are easy to read and understand, avoid as much legalese as possible, and include only the numeric data necessary to paint an accurate picture of your business's potential. In fact, you could probably dictate the bulk of your business plan in a single sitting, based on your inherent knowledge of what you're trying to accomplish and why.

I like to look at it this way: Imagine you're sitting in a restaurant or a coffeehouse, and someone you know comes up and asks you what you're up to these days. You answer that you're in the process of moving your eBay sales to another marketplace, and then you start to tell a little story. You tell this person what your business is all about, why you've decided to move away from eBay, the opportunity you see by selling in another channel, and how you intend to exploit that opportunity. If you're on good terms with the person you're talking to, you might even share the revenues and profits you hope to generate.

Here's the type of story you tell:

> Let me tell you about what I plan to do. You see, for the past few years I've been selling computer cables on eBay. I typically run 100 auctions a month and have a 50% success rate. So I end up selling 50 cables every month, at an average sales price of $20.
>
> I buy my cables for $5 apiece from a distributor in Iowa. That means I make $15 per cable, or about $750 per month—before eBay and PayPal fees, of course. Those fees run about $3.35 per item, so that puts my gross profit at $580 or so each month. I spend another $75 or $80 for shipping boxes and supplies, so my net profit ends up being about $500 per month.
>
> The problem is, I'm seeing my eBay sales go down every week. I'm competing with a lot of larger sellers who are selling their cables at a fixed price, which means their costs are lower than mine. Plus, eBay is giving them favorable treatment in their search results, and it's really hurting my business. Unless I do something fast, I may have to close down.
>
> So I've been researching other ways to sell online, and I've decided to move my business to the Amazon marketplace. On Amazon, I can sell my cables for the same $20 per item, but at a fixed price, no auctions involved. Amazon also has a lower fee structure, so that's a good thing for me. In fact, I think I can increase my sales by at least 10% by moving to Amazon, which also helps my costs—I can purchase my inventory at a 5% additional discount.

I ran the numbers, and here's what I came up with. I still sell the cables for $20 apiece, but now I'm selling 55 units per month. My new cost is $4.75 per item, so that's $838 gross profit per month, a lot higher than the $750 I made on eBay. Amazon charges a 6% commission for each item sold, plus a $.50 closing fee. There's no credit card or PayPal fee; that's all included in the commission. So that comes to $1.70 per item in Amazon fees, plus a $39.99 monthly subscription fee, plus my normal $80 or so in packing supplies. I do all the math and end up making a net profit of about $625 per month—$125 more than I've been doing on eBay. That's money in my pocket.

And the best part is, I'm pretty sure I can keep up that level of sales on Amazon, where my eBay sales had been decreasing. I also think I'll be able to expand my product mix, so the future looks brighter—without much more work on my part. That's why I'm making the change.

As you can see, this short story (fewer than 500 words) tells your audience everything they need to know about your new business. They know why you're moving from eBay to Amazon, they see the opportunity presented, they understand how you expect to profit from that opportunity, they sense the unique things that you intend to do, and they learn how much money you expect to make. It's all there, presented in a logical order; everything important is included, with nothing extraneous added.

In short, you've just created your business plan—orally. Now all you have to do is put it down on paper.

Understanding the Components of a Useful Business Plan

Now that you have the outline of your business plan in your head, let's look at how to translate your story into a written document.

In essence, you take your oral story and write it down, in a logical order. The typical business plan is divided into several distinct sections—each of which maps to a part of your business story. You have to take the story you just told and sort it out into short sections that help the reader understand just what your business is about.

---

note

This chapter presents the type of bare-bones business plan you need for a small online business. If you want to create a really serious business plan—or a plan for a larger business opportunity—check out my companion book, *Teach Yourself Business Plans in 24 Hours* (2001, Alpha Books).

Of course, your particular business plan can contain more or fewer or different sections than presented here, but it should contain the same information—because this information will describe and drive your new business. If you were writing a business plan for a big corporation, each section might be several pages long. For the purposes of your online business, though, think along the lines of a few sentences or paragraphs.

You see, the length of your business plan document depends entirely on your particular circumstances. If your business plan is solely for your own personal use, you don't need to make it any longer or fancier than it needs to be. It's even okay to write in bullets rather than complete sentences. If you expect to present your business plan to others, then by all means go a little fancier and use proper grammar and punctuation. The key thing is to include all the information necessary to get your points across.

Mission

The Mission section of a business plan, typically just a sentence or so long, describes your dream for your business—why you're doing what you're doing. Although this is the shortest section of your plan, it is sometimes the most difficult section to write. That's because many people find it difficult to articulate the reasons they do what they do.

Sometimes called a *mission statement*, this section describes the *what*— what your business does and what you're trying to achieve. Someone reading your Mission section should know immediately what your business does—and what it *doesn't* do.

A relevant mission statement might be something like this: "I intend to sell high-quality gift baskets to targeted buyers via the Amazon marketplace." It should *not* be "I plan to make a lot of money on Amazon." That isn't a very specific mission, and it certainly isn't market driven.

---

note

A mission is different from a goal in that a mission defines a general direction, while a goal defines a specific target. A business has but a single mission but can have many individual goals.

Opportunity

The Opportunity section, sometimes called the *market dynamics* or *market analysis* section, describes the compelling reason for your business to exist; in other words, it presents the market opportunity you've identified. Typically, this section starts out by identifying the target market, sizing it, and then presenting growth opportunities.

The goal of this section is to describe the market opportunity you seek and, for larger businesses, to pursue and to convince potential investors that it's a significant enough opportunity to be worth pursuing. This section should include narrative text (you have to tell a story about the market) and some amount of numeric data. Which data you choose to present, how you choose to present them, and how you weave the data into your narrative will determine the effectiveness of this section.

When the Opportunity section is complete, the reader should understand the basic nature of the market you choose to pursue, the size of that market, the market's growth potential, and the types of customers who comprise the market. You can obtain most if not all of these data by searching Amazon or eBay for similar types of merchandise or by doing a little creative Googling for your product category.

Why do you need to present market data in your business plan, anyway? The answer is simple: to help you sell prospective lenders and investors on your specific business strategy. (That's assuming that you need investors; you may be able to finance inventory purchases out of your own pocket or bank account.) You also need to realistically size the opportunity for your own needs; you don't want to pursue merchandise categories that aren't big or robust enough to achieve your financial goals.

Strategy

The Strategy section of your plan details how you'll exploit the market opportunity described in the Opportunity section and puts forward your potential selling activities. This section typically includes information about the products you'll be selling, as well as how you plan to obtain and market these products. In essence, you want to describe the business you're in, what you plan to sell, and how you'll make money. You'll probably want to include some sort of time line that details the major milestones you will likely face in successfully implementing your new business.

This section of your plan should also detail *where* you intend to sell your merchandise. This means describing the online marketplace(s) you've selected and perhaps explaining why you're moving your business from eBay.

Organization and Operations

The Organization and Operations section describes your company structure as well as the back-end operations you use to bring your products and services to market. If your employee base consists of you and no one else, state that; if you have plans to hire an assistant or two, throw in that information. The key thing in this section is to describe your "back office," how you plan to get things done. This means describing how you'll create your item listings, how you'll warehouse your inventory, and how you'll pack and ship your merchandise.

In short, the Organization and Operations section of your business plan is where you detail how your business is structured and how it will work.

Strengths and Weaknesses

The Strengths and Weaknesses section is the last text section of your business plan. A lot of businesses don't include this section, but I think it's well worth writing. In essence, this section lays bare your core competencies and the challenges you face—which are good to know *before* you actually go into business.

I like including strengths and weaknesses in a business plan for several reasons. First, summarizing your competitive advantages serves to highlight those unique aspects of your business strategy. In addition, ending the text part of your plan with a list of your strengths is a great way to wrap things up; in essence, you provide a summary of the key points of your plan. Finally, by detailing potential challenges you might face, you get a chance to reassess the reality of what you're about to attempt—and to proactively address those issues before they become real problems.

Remember, when you answer potential challenges with distinct strategies, you turn your weaknesses into strengths—and present yourself as being both realistic and proactive.

Financials

The final section of your business plan is the Financials section. This is the place where you present the financial status of and projections for your business. Put simply, these are the numbers—at minimum, an income statement and a balance sheet. You'll want to include your current statements (from your existing eBay business) and projections for the next three years.

If you're borrowing money or trying to attract investors, your potential business partners will want to know what size of a business you're talking about, how profitable that business is likely to be, and how you expect to grow revenues and profits over the years. Your financial statements provide that critical information. In addition, this section of the plan helps you come to grips with the financial realities of what you plan to do.

tip

Although everyone will want to see a few common financial statements, different lenders and investors will have different requirements in this regard. You may want to enlist the assistance of a qualified accountant or financial advisor to help prepare these financial statements—and to prepare for any financial questions that may be asked of you.

You use the Financials section to define the goals you have for your new online business. The revenues and profits you project for future years *are* your company's financial goals; they're the yardstick with which you'll measure the success of your business strategy over the next several years.

When you're making your projections, you should make sure that the numbers you forecast actually make sense. Is there a logic to the revenue buildup over the period? Do the projected expenses make sense in relation to the projected revenues? Are these numbers realistic? Are they achievable? Are they *comfortable*—to you and, if applicable, your investors? Bottom line, do the numbers feel right?

Remember, the numbers you put together quantify your financial goals. Once you accept them, you're committing yourself to running a successful online business.

Writing Your Business Plan

As daunting as writing your business plan may sound, it isn't that difficult. The hardest part is sitting down and getting started. Carve out a few hours of an evening or over a weekend, close the door, turn off your music, and disconnect the telephone and the Internet. Concentrate on the task at hand, starting with a rough outline and filling in the details as if you were telling them to a friend. Take as much time as you need—a few hours, a few evenings, or a few weeks. Don't overthink it; just start writing and worry about editing later.

Once you have a rough draft down, reread it as if you were a stranger to the story. Even better, give it to someone else to read and see if it tells that person everything he or she needs to know about your business. See what questions the person has and incorporate answers to them into any changes you need in your second draft.

After all the words are right, you can spend a few minutes making your document look pretty. Print it out, give it a final proofreading, and you're done. Then, and only then, you can start *using* the plan—to get your eBay business up and running.

Implementing Your Business Plan

You can talk the talk, but sooner or later you have to walk the walk. That's the hard part—implementing your plan.

As I've said, I view a good business plan as a blueprint or roadmap to business success. You need to follow that roadmap, step by step, and put into action all the pieces and parts you've outlined. You have to actually do what you say you're going to do, in the way you said you'd do it.

So if you said you're going to migrate your business from eBay auctions to the Amazon marketplace, you have to do it. Your plan should outline details on how you plan to do it and in what timeframe; follow your own instructions to put the plan into place.

Once you've done that, you can start measuring your success. Track your actual sales against your forecast sales; measure your actual profits against your planned profits. If you're falling short of plan, you need to figure out why and see if you can rectify the situation. And if you're exceeding plan, good for you—you're doing better than you thought possible.

In either instance, 6 or 12 months down the road, you should evaluate your performance and then rewrite your plan for the next two to three years accordingly. Take what you've learned from your experience and use that knowledge to build a more realistic plan. A business plan, after all, is a living thing; it should be adapted to the reality of changing business conditions to provide even better planning in the future.

Doing Your Research

You shouldn't make any major business move without doing your homework first. It's important to know what you're getting yourself into before you get yourself into it, to minimize unpleasant surprises. This means, of course, that you need to do a little research. Don't assume that you know what's going on without first verifying what's going on.

This is especially important as you move from eBay into other online marketplaces. Just because you thought you had eBay figured out doesn't mean you know half as much about other selling channels. Not only are you less familiar with those other marketplaces, chances are they have subtly different dynamics than the eBay marketplace.

Just because a category is big on eBay doesn't mean that it's equally big on craigslist or Amazon. Just because people flock to your eBay auctions in a given category doesn't mean they'll hunt down your e-commerce website that focuses on the same category. In other words, what works in one place doesn't necessarily work in another.

This is why, of course, you need to do your research. Use whatever tools you can find to determine the size and shape of key product categories in the marketplaces you're interested in. Detail the best-selling products and what they sell for. Learn who your competitors are. Figure out what they're doing well—and what they're not.

Then use this research to inform the decisions you make as you plan to move beyond eBay auctions. You can't assume that you can operate your business the same way in another marketplace; use your research to determine how you need to change the way you do business. There's no need to fly blind—you can learn from what others have done in the past. ∎

Fixed-Price Selling on eBay

3

Migrating to Fixed-Price Listings

As far as eBay is concerned, the online auction format is a thing of the past; the future revolves around fixed-price listings. That's what more and more buyers presumably want, and it's certainly what eBay is pushing and incentivizing.

While some sellers might be so ticked off at eBay's changes as to completely abandon the eBay marketplace, other sellers see value in staying (at least partially) with eBay but migrating their merchandise from the online auction format to the fixed-price format. There are many advantages to switching from online auctions to fixed-price sales, and even with eBay's embrace of larger sellers, there are still many advantages that small and medium-sized sellers can recognize on the eBay site.

So if you want to stay on eBay, moving to fixed-price listings is a viable option—as you'll learn in this chapter.

Why Fixed-Priced Sales Are the Way to Go

As you learned in Chapter 1, "The Problem with Online Auctions," eBay is trying to move its business from online auctions to traditional fixed-price sales. There are many reasons for this, but the main one is that this is apparently what most buyers want. People are no longer willing to wait seven days for an auction to end and then risk losing the auction; they want to buy something today and have it shipped out immediately.

Let's put it another way. There are more potential customers who are used to buying straight out at Amazon than there are who are comfortable bidding in online auctions. While there may be a base of previous buyers who like the online auction format, there is a larger base of potential buyers who don't; for eBay to grow, it has to meet the needs of that larger, non-auction customer base. This is why eBay has changed its fees and policies to favor fixed-price sales.

No, the online auction isn't going away anytime soon (auctions still account for about half of eBay's total transactions), but eBay is working to make auctions less profitable for sellers. In other words, you can still sell your items via auction, but you'll make less money doing so than if you sell them at a fixed price.

Comparing Fees

eBay's fees are much different for fixed-price sales than for auction sales. In general, you pay much lower listing fees for fixed-price items than you do for auction items. You also pay lower final value fees (FVFs) for fixed-price items *in some categories*; in other categories, FVFs are actually higher for fixed-price items. See Tables 3.1 and 3.2 for the (somewhat complex) details.

Table 3.1   eBay Insertion Fees

Starting Price or Fixed Price	Auction Listings for Books, Music, DVDs, and Video Games Categories	Auction Listings for All Other Categories	Fixed-Price Listings for Books, Music, DVDs, and Video Games Categories	Fixed-Price Listings for All Other Categories
$0.01–$0.99	$0.10	$0.15	$0.15	$0.35
$1.00–$9.99	$0.25	$0.35	$0.15	$0.35
$10.00–$24.99	$0.35	$0.55	$0.15	$0.35
$25.00–$49.99	$1.00	$1.00	$0.15	$0.35
$50.00–$199.99	$2.00	$2.00	$0.15	$0.35
$200.00–$499.99	$3.00	$3.00	$0.15	$0.35
$500.00+	$4.00	$4.00	$0.15	$0.35

Table 3.2 eBay Final Value Fees

Selling Price	Auction Listings	Fixed-Price Listings for Computers and Networking Categories	Fixed-Price Listings for Consumer Electronics and Photo Categories	Fixed-Price Listings for Clothing and Shoes Categories	Fixed-Price Listings for Books, Music, DVDs, and Video Games Categories	Fixed-Price Listings for All Other Categories
$0.01–$25.00	8.75%	6%	8%	12%	15%	12%
$25.01–$50.00	8.75% of first $25 + 3.5% of balance	6%	8%	12%	15%	12%
$50.01–$1,000.00	8.75% of first $25 + 3.5% of balance	6% of first $50 + 3.75% of balance	8% of first $50 + 4.5% of balance	12% of first $50 + 9% of balance	15% of first $50 + 5% of balance	12% of first $50 + 6% of balance
$1,000.01+	8.75% of first $25 + 3.5% of $25–$1,000 + 1.5% of balance	6% of first $50 + 3.75% of $50–$1,000 + 1% of balance	8% of first $50 + 4.5% of $50–$1,000 + 1% of balance	12% of first $50 + 9% of $50–$1,000 + 2% of balance	15% of first $50 + 5% of $50–$1,000 + 2% of balance	12% of first $50 + 6% of $50–$1,000 + 2% of balance

Admittedly, it's a bit confusing looking at these complicated fee schedules. Different types of products at different price points come with different fees, so you can't make sweeping statements about what type of listing is always best. With that in mind, Table 3.3 compares actual fees for a few different products in a few different scenarios; the results are interesting.

Table 3.3 Sample Fee Comparisons

Item	Starting Auction Price	Selling Price	Total Auction Fees	Total Fixed-Price Fees
Used book	$1	$2	$0.28	$0.45
Laptop computer	$200	$400	$18.31	$16.48
DVD player	$25	$50	$4.06	$4.35
Digital camera	$100	$200	$10.32	$11.10
Men's shirt	$5	$10	$1.23	$1.55
Vintage toy	$15	$30	$2.91	$3.95

What can you tell from looking at these comparisons? First, fixed-price sales don't always cost you less; it all depends on the category and the pricing. In general, lower-priced items cost a little more to sell via fixed-price listings, while higher-priced items (or at least items that have a higher starting auction price) cost less to sell via fixed-price listings. This is more often (but not always) true if you're selling electronics hardware—computers, cameras, and other consumer electronics goods, all of which have significantly lower fixed-price FVFs than they do auction FVFs.

But that's not the entire story. Where fixed-price listings really make sense is for those categories where you have a low sell-through rate. Let's say, for example, that you stock a large number of used books, and you end up successfully closing only about 25% of your auctions. (And that number might be high for this particular category...) This means you'd need to list a particular title for auction four times to make a single sale. If you listed the item for $5, you'd pay $1 in auction listing fees (4 times $0.25), versus $0.15 for a single month-long fixed-price listing fee. There's where the real savings comes in.

And the listing fee savings aren't just for large SKU categories. Most eBay auction categories these days have a close rate in the 50% range—that is, about half the auctions end with no sales. Look at the example, then, of a $100 audio/video receiver that you have to list twice to sell via auction. You'll end up paying $4.00 in auction listing fees (2 times $2.00) compared to just $0.35 for a single fixed-price listing fee. You see the savings.

note

SKU is short for *stock keeping unit*. Each individual item you sell is a single SKU.

The bottom line, when it comes to fees, is that you need to get out your calculator or spreadsheet program and do some very precise calculations based on the specific products you sell. While you may find that the auction format is still a good deal for you, it's possible that you can make at least a little more profit if you shift to fixed-price sales.

Comparing Listing Lengths

The fees themselves don't tell the entire story. Remember, a fixed-price listing is good for 30 days, while an auction listing is good for only 7 days. So if you're selling something that won't necessarily sell in a week, you end up paying far less in listing fees with fixed-price listings than for auction listings.

This factor is significant if you sell in a large SKU category, such as books, CDs, or DVDs. If you're a bookseller, for example, you're likely to list thousands of items for sale at any given time, even though only a small fraction will sell in a given week. If you multiply the auction format's $0.10 listing fee (for a $0.99 book) by 4, that's $0.40 for a full month's listing compared to $0.15 for a single one-month fixed-price listing; the difference is even more pronounced the higher the book's listing and selling price.

Let's look at a real-world example. Say that you're a used bookseller with 500 individual titles to list. You need to list these titles day-in, day-out, so you're looking at a full month's worth of listings at a time. These titles sell for $5 apiece on average; if you're selling via auction, you start the bidding at $2.50 apiece.

For 500 auction listings starting at $2.50 apiece, four weeks each, you'll pay a total of $500 in insertion fees alone. For 500 similar fixed-price listings (priced at $5 apiece), you'll pay a measly $75 in insertion fees for a 30-day period. That, my friends, is more than enough reason to switch from auction to fixed-price listings.

Factoring in Customer Demand

The final reason to consider switching from auction to fixed-price listings is more straightforward: It's what the customers want.

Why do you think eBay is pushing the fixed-price format? It's not necessarily because the company can make more money per transaction. (Although sometimes it can.) It's because eBay thinks it can make more money by increasing the number of transactions—by attracting more customers, particularly those who might otherwise be turned off or scared off by the auction format.

Let's face it: Most people in the real world buy just about everything at a fixed price. You don't go into the grocery store and start bidding on a pound of ground beef (and wait around a week to see if you won the auction); you pay the price asked and walk out with the package.

It's the same thing online; eBay's online auction marketplace is an anomaly (albeit rather large) in terms of how people buy things. Amazon, Buy.com, Lands' End, you name it, are all fixed-price marketplaces. It's what people are used to and what they're comfortable with.

That's not to say, of course, that fixed-price sales are best for all types of products. I would argue that the online auction format is still the best way to go for rare, collectible, one-of-a-kind types of items, items that have fluctuating market value based on the number and the whims of potential buyers interested in any particular item on any particular day. So if you have a comic book collection to sell, or like to trade stamps or coins or vintage stemware, you'd actually be doing yourself a disservice by putting a fixed price on your items; you need to let interested buyers decide what your items are worth, and they can do that by bidding in online auctions.

That doesn't mean that all new items should be sold at a fixed price and all used items via auction, however. First off, some new items are immediately collectible, especially limited-run items in short supply; these items can bring a higher price via auction bidding. Second, not every used item is a collectible; used baby clothing, for example, is probably best sold by assigning a reasonable fixed price rather than forcing buyers to bid on low-dollar items.

Think of it this way: If what you're selling is truly unique, without much direct competition, then stay with the online auction format. But if you're selling a commodity—something that buyers can easily find elsewhere— then you should be selling in the fixed-price format, with your pricing determined in part by what your competitors are charging.

Different Ways to Sell at a Fixed Price

There are lots of ways to sell fixed-price merchandise on the Internet; we will discuss many throughout this book. But for now, let's focus on the eBay marketplace and the several ways that eBay lets you sell at a fixed price.

eBay offers four primary ways to sell fixed-price merchandise—simple fixed-price listings, traditional auctions with the Buy It Now option, listings in an eBay Store, and listings on eBay's Half.com website. We'll look at each option separately, but Table 3.4 compares them for you upfront.

Table 3.4   eBay's Fixed-Price Selling Options

Pricing Option	Pros	Cons
Fixed-price listing	Traditional selling format appeals to majority of potential buyers; listings appear alongside auction listings in eBay search results; lower cost for longer listings.	Reduces the upside of unrestrained bidding.
Auction with Buy It Now option	Lets you "advertise" a lower price (starting bid price) while still enabling immediate fixed-price purchasing; familiar to buyers who prefer the auction format.	Comes with the risk of selling below the fixed price (if bidding takes place without reaching the fixed price); doesn't have the selling price upside found in traditional online auctions; can be confusing to non-auction buyers; higher costs than either auction or fixed-price listings.

Pricing Option	Pros	Cons
Fixed-price listing in an eBay Store	Even lower fees than fixed-price listings; a good way to make high-profit add-on sales to traditional fixed-price or auction sales.	Items are not as visible as they are on the main eBay site (don't appear in standard search results); need to pay monthly eBay Store subscription fee.
Fixed-price listing on Half.com	No listing fees; ease of listing products (by UPC or ISBN).	Payment is only twice a month; site isn't nearly as popular as the main eBay site; offers only limited product categories: Half.com dictates shipping charges.

Which type of fixed-price listing should you use? It depends, to some degree, on the type of product you sell and the costs you want to incur. Read on to learn about each type of listing.

Understanding eBay's Fixed-Price Listings

The simplest way to sell items on eBay at a fixed price is by creating a fixed-price listing. A fixed-price listing is good for 30 days (or until the item sells), costs just $0.35 ($0.15 if you're selling a book, CD, DVD, or video game), and—most importantly—appears on the eBay site alongside the millions of eBay's traditional auction listings.

This last point is important. Some types of fixed-price listings, notably those in eBay Stores and on Half.com, do not show up in eBay's default search results, which makes them difficult for buyers to find. Simple fixed-price listings, however, *do* appear in eBay's search results. So when you create a fixed-price listing, anyone searching the eBay site for that item will see your listing in their search results.

Managing a fixed-price listing is very similar to managing an eBay auction, which helps when you're transitioning your business from one to the other. Buyers see an item listing that looks just like an auction listing, as shown in Figure 3.1, but without the auction terms and bidding instructions. Instead, there's just a Buy It Now button; when buyers click the button, they're taken to PayPal for checkout. Your management of the listing is almost identical to management of an auction listing.

As described previously, one of the big advantages of a fixed-price listing is the cost—at least the initial insertion fee, which is good for a 30-day listing. You still pay an FVF when the item sells, of course; this fee varies by product category and selling price, as detailed in Table 3.2.

FIGURE 3.1

An eBay fixed-price listing.

For most sellers of most types of products, this is the preferred way to sell items at a fixed price on the eBay site. You get maximum visibility at a lower initial price than with traditional auctions. And, while other fixed-price formats may have lower insertion fees, the fact that they don't show up in eBay search results is a major negative. eBay's simple fixed-price listings, then, offer the best of both worlds: low cost and high visibility.

Understanding eBay's Buy It Now Auctions

If you don't want to jump into fixed-price listings all at once, consider running traditional auctions with the Buy It Now (BIN) option. The BIN option lets you offer a fixed-price option—in addition to traditional auction bidding—to potential buyers.

With BIN, you stipulate both a starting bid price and a desired fixed price for your item; the fixed price is higher than the minimum bid price. As you can see in Figure 3.2, the listing looks like a traditional auction listing, but with both Place Bid and Buy It Now buttons. A potential buyer can choose to start the bidding process by bidding the minimum bid or, if he or she wants to purchase the item immediately, pay the fixed price instead.

note

The BIN price is active only until a bid is placed. If the first bidder places a bid lower than the BIN price, the BIN price is removed, and the auction proceeds normally.

FIGURE 3.2

An eBay auction listing with the Buy It Now option.

For buyers, the advantage of an auction with the BIN option is that they have a choice. If they like bidding and don't mind the risk of losing an auction, they can go the traditional auction route—and hopefully, on their part, pay less than the fixed price you're asking. If they prefer to purchase something now at a known price, they can click the Buy It Now button and pay the fixed price.

As a seller, you also get the best of both worlds—sort of. Your listing appears in all eBay search results, which provides maximum visibility. And you appeal to both auction and fixed-price buyers. But you don't have all the upsides of a traditional auction; your item probably won't sell for more than the Buy It Now price.

You also have to pay more for the BIN option. Your insertion fee is based on the starting bid price in eBay's auction fee schedule, but then you pay an additional fee for the BIN option (based on the BIN price you set), as detailed in Table 3.5. Your FVF is based on the final selling price, using eBay's auction fee schedule (not the fixed-price fee schedule).

Table 3.5   eBay's Buy It Now Fees

Buy It Now Price	Fee
$1.00–$9.99	$0.05
$10.00–$24.99	$0.10
$25.00–$49.99	$0.20
$50.00+	$0.25

Let's work through an example. If you list an item with a $20 starting bid price and a $40 BIN price, you'll pay a $0.55 insertion fee and $0.20 BIN fee, for a total of $0.75 in initial fees. If you had listed this as a simple fixed-price listing, you instead would have paid only a $0.35 insertion fee, with no BIN fee. Of course, if the item sells, the picture changes somewhat; depending on the category, you may pay more in FVFs than you save in listing fees. But your initial fees are still significantly less with simple fixed-price listings than with the auction/BIN combination.

Understanding eBay Stores

Another fixed-price listing option involves creating an eBay Store, your own storefront on the eBay site. Your store includes all your current auction and fixed-price items on the eBay site, as well as items you list specifically within the eBay Store at a fixed price.

There are many pros and cons to having your own eBay Store, which we'll discuss in due time. One of the pros is cost; as you can see in Table 3.6, eBay Store insertion fees are significantly lower than fees for either auction or fixed-price listings on the eBay site, and they are good for 30 days. (You still have to pay FVFs on the items you sell, of course; eBay Store FVFs start at 12% of the selling price.)

Table 3.6   eBay Store Insertion Fees

Item Price	Fee
$1.00–$24.99	$0.03
$25.00–$199.99	$0.05
$200.00+	$0.10

These lower listing fees mean that an eBay Store is a great place to list tons of products. This is especially useful if you are in a high-SKU category, such as CDs or DVDs or books, or even clothing with a multitude of colors and sizes.

However, there are a few downsides to relying on eBay Store listings for the bulk of your online sales. First, you have to pay a monthly subscription fee to keep your eBay Store open. At the Basic level (which works for most sellers), you pay $15.95 per month. Premium Stores cost $49.95/month, and Anchor Stores cost $299.95/month.

Second, and most importantly, none of the listings in your eBay Store show up in eBay's default search results. So if eBay users are looking for whatever it is you're selling, they won't see you. That is a major downside as well as a challenge: How do you drive traffic to your eBay Store when no one knows that you're selling?

Once users find your eBay Store, however, your item listings look identical to eBay fixed-price listings. That's because they *are* fixed-price listings, of course; a customer purchases an item by clicking the Buy It Now button, and the rest of the process continues as expected.

Given the low visibility of eBay Store listings, why would any seller choose this route? Well, you probably wouldn't go the Store route *exclusively*; if you did, no one would ever see your listings. Instead, many sellers use an eBay Store to *supplement* their main fixed-price or auction listings or to sell add-on or accessory products to active buyers. They drive sales to their eBay Store via their other listings; potential buyers see the eBay Store link and a few Store listings when they view the traditional listing, and they see even more Store listings when they go through the item checkout process when purchasing. That is, the fixed-price and auction listings serve to promote the higher-profit goods available in the seller's eBay Store.

Remember, you pay only a few pennies to create an eBay Store listing. This makes for high-profit Store sales—when you can get them.

note

Learn more about eBay Stores in Chapter 4, "Fixed-Price Selling in an eBay Store."

Understanding Half.com

The last way to sell items at a fixed price takes place away from the main eBay site. You see, eBay runs a separate site called Half.com (www.half.com), which exists purely to sell books, music, DVDs, and video games. If this describes the types of items you sell, Half.com may be worthy of your attention.

First, a description of the Half.com site: I look at it as eBay's attempt to mimic Amazon, at least for these core media product categories. The Half.com home page looks a lot like Amazon's home page, and the shopping experience for buyers is a little like Amazon's—except with multiple sellers for each item.

Here's the deal: When a potential buyer searches for an item on Half.com, he or she receives a results page like the one in Figure 3.3. As you can see, this page describes the product and offers a list of sellers who have that item for sale. Pick a seller you want to buy from, and the transaction is processed.

FIGURE 3.3

A Half.com product page, complete with multiple sellers.

All items offered for sale on Half.com are at a price fixed by each seller; there are no auction transactions. A buyer can purchase from multiple sellers and use a single checkout and payment system. Sellers are then paid individually by Half.com.

Selling on Half.com is easy; because the site provides all the product info (based on each item's UPC or ISBN), you don't even have to create item listings with descriptions and photos. All you have to do is list your items for sale.

And here's an even better thing: All Half.com listings are free; there are no insertion fees. You don't even have to pay a monthly subscription or membership fee. All you owe is an FVF (accurately called a *commission* by Half.com) for each item that sells. The commission is based on the item's final selling price, as detailed in Table 3.7.

I like Half.com's commission schedule. It's not complicated; there aren't different fees for different product categories, as with eBay's fixed-price listings; and the commission decreases the higher the selling price, which means you make more money by selling higher-priced items, as it should be. Add that to the lack of listing fees, and Half.com can be a very profitable channel for sellers.

Table 3.7 Half.com Commissions

Selling Price	Commission (Final Value Fee)
$0.75–$50.00	15%
$50.01–$100.00	12.5%
$100.01–$250.00	10%
$250.01–$500.00	7.5%
$500.01+	5%

Let's compare using Half.com with using eBay's fixed-price listings for a few different products. If you sell a $5 book on eBay, you pay $0.90 in fees, compared with $0.75 on Half.com. If you sell a $20 DVD on eBay, you pay $3.15 in fees, compared to $3.00 on Half.com. If you sell a $60 video game on eBay, you pay $8.15 in fees, compared to $7.50 on Half.com. In every instance, Half.com is the better deal.

There are a few drawbacks to selling on Half.com, however. First is the payment schedule. Whereas you receive payment immediately on eBay, via PayPal, Half.com pays sellers just twice a month, on the 15th and the last day of the month. So you have to wait longer to receive your funds.

Second, Half.com dictates the shipping/handling charges for each item, automatically adding a default charge to each customer's order. The seller then gets a "shipping reimbursement" from Half.com for that amount. Theoretically, this should be a wash, but it isn't necessarily so. If your handling costs are higher than Half.com figures, you get hosed. Same thing if your actual shipping (for a heavier-than-normal item, for example) is higher than the default reimbursement; you could end up in the lurch.

The final drawback is that few customers seem to know about Half.com. The site simply doesn't have the visibility of the main eBay site, and Half.com listings do not appear in eBay search results. So even though Half.com sales may be more profitable, you'll probably have less traffic to draw from.

That said, with zero cost to list an item, it's probably worth your while to at least experiment with the Half.com site—if you sell the types of media items that Half.com specializes in, of course.

> **note**
>
> Learn more about Half.com in Chapter 5, "Fixed-Price Selling on Half.com."

Creating an eBay Fixed-Price Listing

We'll discuss eBay Stores and Half.com in more depth in the next two chapters, so let's keep our focus here on the ways to sell fixed-price items on the eBay site. First up is the straight fixed-price listing, probably the best approach for most sellers.

As noted previously, an eBay fixed-price listing looks and feels pretty much like a standard auction listing, with a few exceptions. First, the listing runs for 30 days, not just 7. Second, the listing doesn't have a Place Bid button, just a Buy It Now button. Other than that, the listing is identical.

To launch a fixed-price listing, start by creating a new item listing. When you get to the Choose How You'd Like to Sell Your Item part of the Create Your Listing page, select the Fixed Price tab, shown in Figure 3.4. Enter the item's fixed selling price into the Buy It Now Price box and then enter the quantity available and the duration of the listing. Complete the rest of the listing as normal, and you're ready to go.

FIGURE 3.4

Creating an eBay fixed-price listing.

Note the following about the options presented here:

- The Buy It Now price you enter is the price that the item is listed for and the price that it will sell for. There will be no bidding on the item.

- You have the option of allowing buyers to make a "best offer" for your item. Unless you want to take less than what you entered as the BIN price, ignore this option.

- You can list multiple quantities of any item you list. You'll be charged $0.35 (or $0.15 for media items) for each item you offer. So, for example, if you list 10 tee shirts for sale, your insertion fee for this listing is $3.50 (10 × $0.35). That said, the *maximum* insertion fee charged is $4.00, so if you listed 20 tee shirts, you wouldn't pay $7.00, you'd be charged only $4.00 in fees.

- eBay lets you choose a duration for your fixed-price listing of from 3 days to 30 days. The price for the listing is the same, no matter the duration; it costs the same $0.35 to list for 30 days as it does to list for 3 days. You can also choose the "Good 'Till Cancelled" option, which essentially relists your item (for another $0.35) if it is unsold at the end of the first 30 days.

Beyond these options, a fixed-price listing looks similar to and works very much like a traditional auction listing. It also shows up in eBay's default search results, alongside auction listings—which helps drive traffic to your listings.

Creating an Auction Listing with a Buy It Now Price

eBay's BIN option lets you add a fixed-price option to your auction listings. It's therefore an interesting bridge between traditional online auctions and fixed-price sales.

The way BIN works is that you name a fixed price for your item in addition to the starting auction bid price; if a user opts to pay the fixed price (by clicking the Buy It Now button), the auction is automatically closed, and that user is named the high bidder. Note, however, that the BIN price is active only until the first bid is placed. If the first bidder places a bid lower than the BIN price, the BIN price is removed, and the auction proceeds normally.

You activate the BIN when you're creating your item listing. When you get to the Choose How You'd Like to Sell Your Item part of the Create Your Listing page, make sure the Online Auction tab (*not* the Fixed Price tab) is selected. As shown in Figure 3.5, enter the item's starting bid price into the Starting Price box and then enter the fixed selling price into the Buy It Now Price box. Complete the rest of the listing as you would normally.

FIGURE 3.5

Adding the BIN option to an auction listing.

tip

The BIN price you specify for an item should be *higher* than the starting price.

Know, however, that using the BIN option costs more than running a traditional auction. Adding a BIN price to your auction costs anywhere from $0.05 to $.0.25 extra, depending on the BIN price you set. (BIN fees are detailed in Table 3.5.)

Also know that because this is, at heart, an auction listing, you have to work within eBay's shorter auction durations. That means choosing a 1-, 3-, 5-, or 7-day duration, or paying an extra $0.40 for a 10-day auction. You don't have the option of 30-day listings, as you do with fixed-price listings.

Managing Fixed-Price Sales

How easy is it to switch from traditional auction sales to fixed-price sales on eBay? The differences are on the front end and the back end.

Before the Sale: Setting the Price

Probably the hardest part of switching from traditional auction sales to fixed-price sales on eBay is determining your selling price. Unlike with auction sales, you have to state the final selling price up front rather than have it decided via the bidding process.

This means you need to do a little research. It shouldn't be too hard if you're selling a commodity product; just check and see what your competitors are charging for that item. If you charge more than the going price, you won't make many sales; if you charge much less than this price, you're throwing away profits (or perhaps selling unprofitably).

Another approach is to use "cost plus" pricing. This is where you take your cost for an item and then mark it up by a certain percentage or by a certain dollar amount. For example, you might calculate that you need a 40% profit margin to make selling the item worth your while. To mark the item up to provide a 40% markup, you multiply your cost by 1.4; if the item costs $4, you specify a selling price of $5.60 ($4 × 1.4).

tip

To mark up an item to achieve a certain profit margin, multiply the cost of the item by 1 plus the profit margin percentage. For example, to achieve a 25% profit margin, multiply the cost by 1.25.

If you prefer to think in terms of dollar margins, you simply add your desired profit margin to the unit's cost. So, for example, if you want to make a $5 profit on a $20 item, you price the item at $25.

tip

You may want to include in the item cost your costs for related services and materials. For example, if you spend $3 in boxes and packing materials for an item with a unit cost of $10, you'd view the item's total cost at $13.

After the Sale: Payment and Shipping

Whether you choose a simple fixed-price listing or an auction listing with the BIN option, managing the purchase process is similar. When a buyer decides to buy what you're selling at the fixed price, he or she clicks the Buy It Now button. The buyer is then prompted to pay (via PayPal); most buyers pay at this time.

When an item is sold, you receive two emails from eBay. The first email notifies you that the item has been sold. The second email comes when the payment is made, notifying you that funds have been deposited in your PayPal account.

After you receive notice of payment, it's time to pack and ship the item. You can also take this opportunity to withdraw the funds for the payment from your PayPal account.

What's different about a fixed-price sale as compared to a traditional auction sale is that it can occur at any time. With an auction sale, you know that the sale will happen at the end of the auction, typically seven days from when you first listed the item. (Of course, you're not guaranteed of a sale when you list an auction item; you may receive notice of an unsold item resulting from zero bids.) With a fixed-price sale, the sale can come at any time during the duration of the item listing. So you need to check your email daily and be prepared to act quickly when an item is sold.

Staying with eBay: Pros and Cons

You know how you can convert your eBay auction sales into fixed-price sales. Should you do it?

There are advantages to staying with eBay, as opposed to moving to another online marketplace or selling on your own website. The chief advantage is visibility; eBay has more than 83 million active users who could be interested in what you're selling. It's tough to find another marketplace that has that many potential customers.

In addition, eBay is where you got your start, and it's what you're familiar with. If you've been selling on eBay for any length of time, you have an established reputation, and you might not want to throw that away. It's tough to leave home, especially when it's been so good to you over the years.

The downside, of course, is that eBay isn't quite as good to you today as it used to be. Yes, you can migrate from auction sales to fixed-price sales on the eBay site, but you're still at a significant competitive disadvantage compared to larger sellers. eBay offers larger sellers more visibility and lower costs (in the form of FVF discounts), neither one of which remotely works in your favor. If you can stomach being treated as a second-class citizen (and can work with eBay's continually changing rules and regulations), then by all means keep selling on the site.

Lots of small and medium-sized sellers remain on eBay and have found ways to stay profitable. That doesn't mean they couldn't make more money elsewhere, just that they've managed to work with eBay's recent changes. If you're a smart seller, you can change with the times and continue selling profitably on eBay. But if you want to maximize your sales and profits, you may want to expand your business beyond eBay into other online marketplaces—as you'll discover as you continue to read through this book. ■

4

Fixed-Price Selling in an eBay Store

In the previous chapter we discussed how to convert traditional eBay auction listings to fixed-price listings. But as you also learned, eBay offers two other ways to sell items at a fixed price, via eBay Store listings and on eBay's sister site, Half.com.

We'll leave Half.com for Chapter 5, "Fixed-Price Selling on Half.com," and focus in this chapter on opening and selling in an eBay Store. It's quite easy—and very cost-effective.

What Is an eBay Store?

An eBay Store, like the one shown in Figure 4.1, is a web page where you can sell fixed-price inventory specific to the Store. You can list as few or as many items in your Store as you like; the Store also contains all your current auction and fixed-price listings on the normal eBay site.

As you can see in Figure 4.2, merchants on the eBay Stores home page (stores.ebay.com) are organized by the same categories as the eBay auction site: Antiques, Art, Books, and so on. Buyers can also search for a specific Store or a Store selling a certain type of item, or they can view an alphabetical list of all Stores.

For a buyer, purchasing an item from an eBay Store retailer offers the benefits of the eBay marketplace (including PayPal checkout) and the benefits of dealing directly with an individual retailer. Purchasing is done on an item-by-item basis within a Store, with each item generating its own PayPal checkout page.

FIGURE 4.1
The author's Molehill Group eBay Store.

FIGURE 4.2
The home page for eBay Stores.

Benefits of Opening Your Own eBay Store

There are more than a half million eBay Stores, and for good reason. Hosting an eBay Store lets sellers offer large inventories of fixed-price merchandise to eBay users, at a relatively low listing cost.

Why would you want to open your own eBay Store? Well, it certainly isn't for casual sellers; you have to set up your own web page and keep the Store filled with merchandise, both of which take time and energy.

But if you're a high-volume seller who specializes in a single category (or even a handful of categories), there are many benefits to opening your own Store. They include being able to sell more merchandise (through your Store) than you can otherwise list on the traditional eBay site, being able to offer more merchandise for sale at a lower cost (due to the dramatically lower listing fees), and being able to generate repeat business from future sales to current purchasers.

Opening an eBay Store is a good way to get into fixed-price sales, especially if you offer a lot of similar SKUs. You can put items in your eBay Store before you offer them for sale on the general eBay site, and you can thus have more merchandise for sale than you might otherwise. An eBay Store is also a good place to "park" merchandise that hasn't sold on the eBay site before you choose to relist it.

A huge benefit is that you can use your eBay Store to sell more merchandise to your existing customers. And, because eBay Store insertion fees are lower than eBay's traditional listing fees, you'll be decreasing your costs by selling direct rather than through the eBay marketplace.

Another benefit of selling merchandise in an eBay Store is that eBay will automatically advertise items from your Store on the Bid Confirmation and Checkout Confirmation pages it displays to bidders and buyers in your regular eBay auctions and fixed-price listings. These "merchandising placements" help you cross-sell additional merchandise to your eBay customers.

In addition, eBay provides robust reporting to all eBay Store owners, including the monthly Sales Report Plus report. This report provides a variety of data to help you track your Store activity, including total sales, average sales price, buyer counts, and metrics by category, format, and ending day or time.

You'll also receive live Traffic Reports that show the number of page views for each of your listings and Store pages, as well as a list of keywords used by buyers to find your listings. An owner of a Featured or Anchor Store also receives an additional path analysis that shows how buyers navigate within the Store, as well as bid/BIN tracking. And all eBay Store owners can export their Store data to QuickBooks, using eBay's Accounting Assistant program, for personal financial management.

note

Accounting Assistant is a software program that enables you to export eBay and PayPal data directly into the QuickBooks accounting program. The program is free to download and use for all eBay Store subscribers. Find out more at pages.ebay.com/help/sell/accounting-assistant-ov.html.

To drive traffic to your Store, eBay offers a variety of promotional services to Store owners. You get your choice of customized promotional email newsletters, marketing widgets you can add to blogs and other web pages, printable promotional flyers, RSS listing feeds to send to comparison shopping sites, and keyword management help to optimize your Store for search engine placement.

Finally, all eBay Store owners get a free subscription to eBay Selling Manager or Selling Manager Pro. If you'd planned on using one of these tools anyway, getting them free helps to defray the costs of running your eBay Store.

Challenges of eBay Store Selling

Of course, it isn't all milk and honey in the land of eBay Stores. Back in 2006, eBay released data which showed that, on average, items listed in eBay Stores took 14 times longer to sell than did items listed in normal eBay auctions—and, in some media categories (books, CDs, and DVDs, for example) up to *40 times* longer. And, while eBay Stores merchandise accounted for 83% of all listings across the eBay empire, they contributed only 9% of eBay's total gross merchandise value. Now, this research is a few years old (and eBay hasn't provided updated numbers), but it's fair to assume that there's still a lot of merchandise listed in eBay Stores that just isn't selling.

To explain why this is the case, eBay originally blamed the low listing fees charged for Store merchandise. Back then, it cost only $0.02 to list an item for 30 days; at such a low listing fee, too many sellers (according to eBay) were just "parking" unwanted merchandise in their Stores. This led to eBay dramatically increasing its Store listing fees, to discourage the listing of less desirable merchandise.

---

note

Things change. eBay's unpopular 2006 increase in eBay Stores insertion fees was rolled back somewhat in 2008, when minimum insertion fees dropped from $0.05 per item to $0.03 per item. (That's still higher than the previous $0.02 per item, of course—but not quite as bad as the fees had been.)

This price increase led to the predictable uproar from Store sellers, who blamed eBay's other policies on low Store sell-through rates. The chief complaint to this day is the way Store listings are included in eBay's search results—by default, they're not. That's right; none of the items you list in your eBay Store will appear in the search results when potential buyers search eBay for those items. Your Store listings are invisible to most eBay users, unless the users are specifically searching the eBay Stores site.

The exclusion of eBay Store listings from eBay's main inventory is a major disadvantage to running an eBay Store. Instead of relying on eBay to promote the items you have for sale in your eBay Store, you have to come up with alternative promotional methods—which increases your overall costs, of course.

---

note

Learn more about how to promote your eBay Store listings in Chapter 6, "Promoting Your Fixed-Price eBay Sales."

Understanding eBay Store Subscription Levels

There are three types of costs associated with selling items in an eBay Store. (Four, if you count PayPal costs.) You have to pay a monthly subscription fee to keep your Store open, you have to pay an insertion fee to list each item in your Store, and you have to pay a final value fee (FVF) when you sell an item from your Store.

Let's examine the Store subscription fees first. eBay offers three levels of Store subscriptions. The Basic level costs $15.95 per month; the Featured level costs $49.95 per month; and the Anchor level costs $299.95 per month.

What are the differences between the three subscription levels? It's primarily a matter of services offered, as detailed in Table 4.1.

Table 4.1   eBay Stores Subscription Levels

	Basic Store	Featured Store	Anchor Store
Subscription fee	$15.95/month	$49.95/month	$299.95/month
Number of product pages per Store	Unlimited	Unlimited	Unlimited
Number of custom pages per Store	5	10	15
eBay header reduced on Store pages	No	Yes	Yes
Sales management	eBay Selling Manager	eBay Selling Manager Pro	eBay Selling Manager Pro
Markdown Manager for discounted listings	250 listings/day	2,500 listings/day	5,000 listings/day
Picture Manager image hosting	1 MB free	1 MB free and $5 off subscription	1 GB free and free subscription
Email marketing	5,000 emails/month	7,500 emails/month	10,000 emails/month
Printable promotional flyers and business collateral templates	Yes	Yes	Yes
RSS listing feeds	Yes	Yes	Yes
Store name appears in "Shop eBay Stores" area of search results	Occasionally	Sometimes	Frequently
Rotating placement on eBay Stores home page	No	Text link at center of page	Store logo at top of page
Traffic reports	Basic data	Advanced data	Advanced data
Accounting Assistant software	Yes	Yes	Yes
Customer support	6 a.m. to 6 p.m. PST	24/7	24/7

eBay says that a Basic Store is designed for sellers moving between 10 and 50 items per month, or between $100 and $500 in sales volume. A Premium Store is better for sellers moving between 50 and 500 items per month, or between $500 and $5,000 in sales volume. And an Anchor Store is best for larger sellers moving more than 500 items per month, or more than $5,000 in sales volume.

In reality, a Basic Store works for sellers of virtually any size. There may be some slight value (primarily in terms of customer support and reporting) from moving up to a Premium Store subscription, but you'll get little in the way of returns from the much more expensive Anchor Store level. In any case, it makes sense to start with a Basic subscription and see how it goes; if you find you need the additional features, you can always upgrade to Premium at a later time.

Understanding Insertion Fees and FVFs

As with traditional eBay item listings, you have to pay when you list and sell items in your eBay Store.

eBay Stores insertion fees are good for 30 days; you can opt for a "good 'till cancelled" listing which automatically renews (for an additional monthly fee) at the end of each 30-day period.

The insertion fees associated with an eBay Store are relatively simple, as detailed in Table 4.2. These insertion fees compare favorably to the $0.35 insertion fee for eBay's traditional fixed-price listings.

Table 4.2   eBay Store Insertion Fees

Item Price	Fee
$1.00–$24.99	$0.03
$25.00–$199.99	$0.05
$200.00+	$0.10

In addition, for each item you sell in your eBay Store, eBay charges an FVF. Table 4.3 lists these selling charges.

Table 4.3   eBay Stores FVFs

Closing Value	Fee
$1.00–$25.00	12%
$25.01–$100.00	12% of the initial $25, plus 8% of the remaining balance
$100.01–$1,000.00	12% on the first $25 *plus* 8% on the part between $25 and $100, *plus* 4% on the remaining balance
$1,000.01+	12% on the first $25 *plus* 8% on the part between $25 and $100, *plus* 4% on the part between $100 and $1,000 *plus* 2% on the remaining balance

eBay Stores also offers a full assortment of listing upgrades, just like the ones you can use in regular eBay listings. These enhancements—bold, highlight, and so on—are priced according to the length of the listing. You can also offer multiples of the same item in a listing.

How to Open an eBay Store

Opening your own eBay Store is as easy as clicking through eBay's setup pages. There's nothing overly complex involved; you'll need to create your

Store, customize your pages (otherwise known as your *virtual storefront*), and list the items you want to sell. Just follow the onscreen instructions, and you'll have your own Store up and running in just a few minutes.

To open your eBay Store, follow these basic steps:

1. Go to pages.ebay.com/storefronts/start.html and click the Open a Store Now! button.

2. When the Choose Your Subscription Level page appears, as shown in Figure 4.3, select a subscription level, enter a name for your Store, and then click the Continue button.

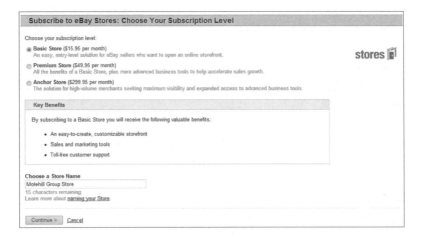

FIGURE 4.3

Choosing a subscription level.

3. When the Select Additional Products page appears, check to receive all the available free options you want (the options differ by Store level) and then click the Continue button.

4. When the Review & Submit page appears, accept the user agreement and click the Subscribe button.

5. Your Store is now created, and you're shown a Congratulations page. Now it's time to customize your Store; click the Start Quick Store Setup button to begin.

6. The Quick Store Setup page, shown in Figure 4.4, displays recommendations for the look and feel of your Store. To accept all the recommendations as-is, click the Apply Settings button. If you prefer to personalize your Store, continue to step 7.

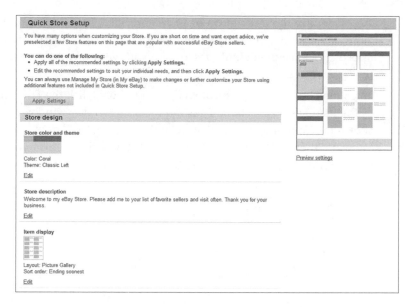

FIGURE 4.4
Configure the look and feel of your eBay Store.

7. To change the color scheme and design of your Store, click the Edit link in the Store Color and Theme section. This displays the Change Store Color and Theme window, as shown in Figure 4.5; select the theme you want and click the Save button.

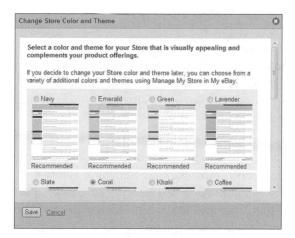

FIGURE 4.5
Selecting a color scheme for your eBay Store.

8. To personalize the description of your Store, click the Edit link in the Store Description section. The Change Store Description window appears; replace the default description with your own text then click the Save button.

9. To change how items are displayed in your Store, click the Edit link in the Item Display section. The Change Item Display window, shown in Figure 4.6, appears. Select either Picture Gallery or List View and then pull down the Sort Order list and choose how you want to sort your items. Click the Save button when you're done.

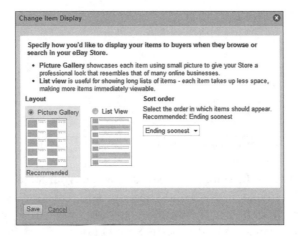

FIGURE 4.6

Selecting how you want your Store items displayed.

10. To display various promotion boxes on your Store pages, click the Edit link in the Promotion Boxes section. Click the Four Promotion Boxes option to display Newly Listed, Ending Soon, Shipping & Payment, and Newsletter Sign-Up boxes on your pages. Click the Save button.

11. To add navigation links to your Store from your other eBay listings, click the Edit link in the Custom Listing Frame section. The Change Custom Listing Frame window, shown in Figure 4.7, appears. You can choose to display a header with links to your Store, a left-hand navigation bar with links to your Store categories, or both. Click the Save button when you're done.

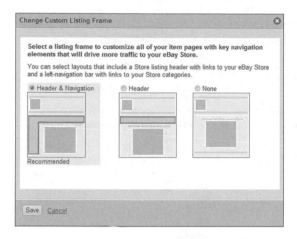

FIGURE 4.7

Adding Store promotional links to your other eBay listings.

12. To take advantage of eBay's email marketing function, scroll to the Email Marketing section and select the marketing emails you want to send to your customers.

13. When you're done making all these changes, click the Apply Settings button.

Further Customizing Your eBay Store

The selections you just made are just a few of the customization options offered for your eBay Store. You can make further changes at any time, from the Manage My Store page.

Follow these steps to make additional changes:

1. Go to your Store page and click the Seller Manage Store link at the bottom of the page.

2. When the Manage My Store page appears, click the Store Design link in the Store Management panel.

3. When the Store Design page appears, click the Change link in the Display Settings section; the Display Settings page, shown in Figure 4.8, appears.

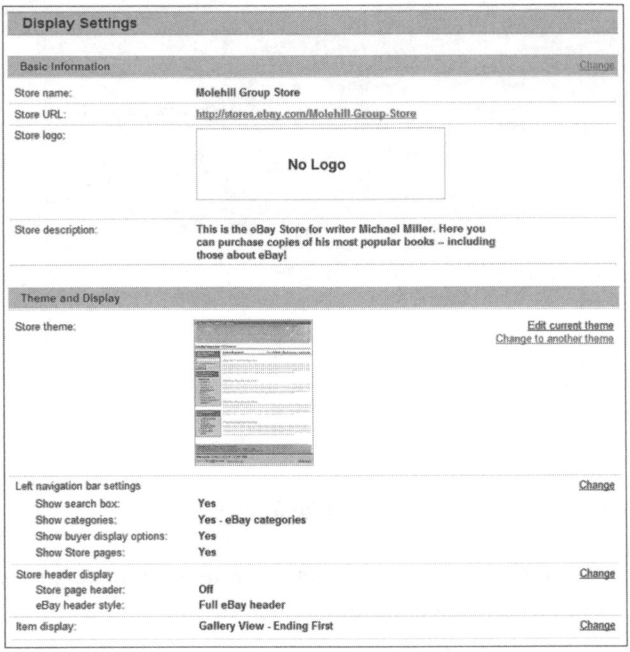

FIGURE 4.8

Editing your Store's display settings.

4. To change your Store name or description, or to select or upload an image for your Store's logo, click the Change link in the Basic Information section and make your changes on the next page.

5. To edit your current theme, click the Edit Current Theme link in the Theme and Display section. To select a different theme, click the Change to Another Theme link.

6. To edit the settings for the navigation bar, click the Change link in the Left Navigation Bar Settings section.

7. To edit the settings for the Store header, click the Change link in the Store Header Display section.

8. To change the way items are displayed on your Store pages, click the Change link in the Item Display section.

Managing Your eBay Store

You handle the day-to-day management of your eBay Store from the Manage My Store page, shown in Figure 4.9. You access this page by clicking the Seller Manage Store link at the bottom of your Store's home page or from your My eBay Summary page.

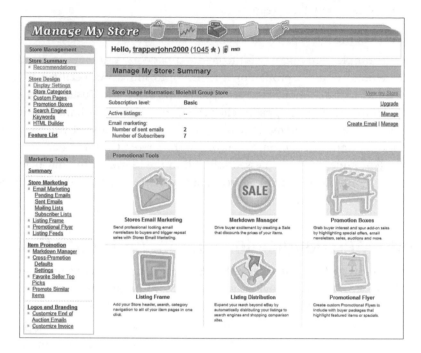

FIGURE 4.9

Managing your eBay Store.

From here, you can do the following:

- Change the look and feel of your Store pages
- Customize individual pages in your Store
- Manage your Store subscription
- Put your Store on "hold" while you go on vacation
- Specify which Store items you want to cross-promote in your auction listings
- Edit the keywords used to search for your eBay Store
- Send promotional emails to your customers
- Create promotional flyers and listing feeds
- Use Markdown Manager to create sales in your Store

- Manage your Store item listings
- Register your domain name
- Access eBay Store reports

Just click the appropriate link for the action you want to perform.

For example, you might want to create a page in your Store to detail your Store policies, to list promotional items, or to showcase specific merchandise. Go to the Manage Your Store page and select the Custom Pages link. When the next page appears, click the Create New Page link. The Create Custom Page: Select Layout page appears; select the layout you want and click the Continue button. You now see the Create Custom Page: Provide Content page, where you essentially fill in the blanks with your new page's content—text and pictures. Continue on to preview the new page and load it into your Store.

Listing Merchandise for Sale in Your eBay Store

Now that you've created your eBay Store, you need to add some merchandise to sell. As noted previously, all your Store-specific listings are fixed-priced listings with listing fees of a low $0.03 to $0.10 per 30 days.

To add an item to your Store inventory, click the Sell link at the top of any eBay listing page to begin the listing process. When you get to the Create Your Listing page, the Choose How You'd Like to Sell Your Item section now includes a Store Inventory tab, as shown in Figure 4.10. Select this tab then enter the selling price into the Buy It Now box. Complete the rest of the listing as normal, and this new listing is added to your eBay Store.

FIGURE 4.10

Creating a new eBay Store item listing.

As you can see in Figure 4.11, an eBay Store listing looks almost identical to a regular eBay fixed-price or auction listing. There's no Place Bid button, of course, just a Buy It Now button; for the buyer, it's a similar purchasing experience as with items on the main eBay site.

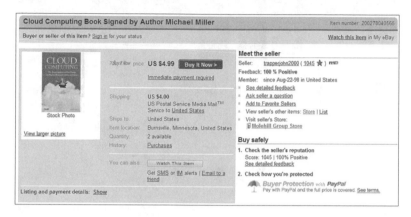

FIGURE 4.11

A fixed-price item for sale in an eBay Store.

Handling eBay Store Sales

Handling eBay Store sales is identical to handling fixed-price sales from the eBay site. You receive an email when an item is sold, plus another email when the item is paid for; if the buyer pays at the time of sale, these emails are sent almost simultaneously. You then pack and ship the item and collect your funds from PayPal.

What's different about eBay Store sales is that you can manage the whole process from eBay Selling Manager, which you get free as part of your eBay Stores subscription. Selling Manager is a web-based auction management tool you use to keep track of all your current item listings, as well as all your closed sales. You can use Selling Manager to send emails to winning bidders, print invoices and shipping labels, and even leave feedback. When Selling Manager is active, the All Selling page in My eBay is transformed into a Selling Manager page. As you can see in Figure 4.12, the main Selling Manager page provides an overview of all your active and closed auctions. Selling Manager lets you manage all your post-sale activities.

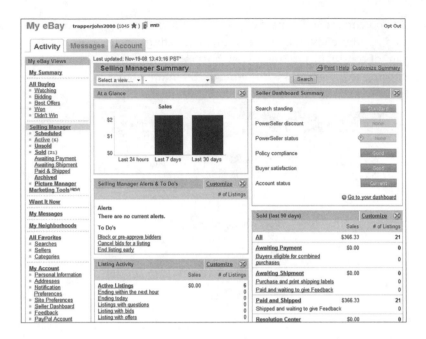

FIGURE 4.12
Managing your sales with eBay Selling Manager.

Marking Down Your Merchandise

Here's a neat feature that eBay has added to eBay Stores: the ability to mark down merchandise for quicker sale. This is great if you want to offer a short-term discount to encourage movement on particular items.

You make your markdowns by using eBay's Markdown Manager. Just go to your Manage My Store page and click the Markdown Manager icon; when the next page appears, click the Create Sale button.

You now see the Create Your Sale page, shown in Figure 4.13. From here you enter a name for your sale; choose the start and end dates for the sale; enter the amount of the discount you're offering (or free shipping, if that's what you want to do); select which listings are part of the sale; and choose how you want to promote the sale. Click the Create Your Sale button, and the sale prices go into effect as you've specified. (Figure 4.14 shows a sale listing created with Markdown Manager.)

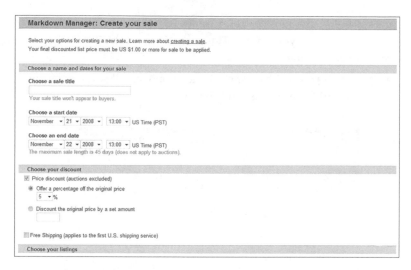

FIGURE 4.13

Creating an online sale with eBay's Markdown Manager.

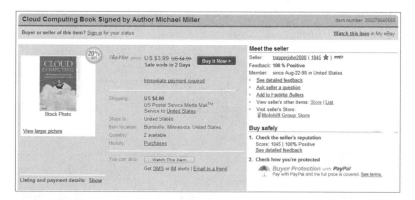

FIGURE 4.14

An item discounted with Markdown Manager—note the 20% off icon.

Viewing eBay Store Reports

Another benefit of an eBay Store subscription is detailed reporting. eBay offers two different reports, both included with all subscription levels:

- **Traffic Reports.** These include data on page views, visits, daily unique visitors, referring domains, referring search engines, search

keywords, the most popular pages in your Store, and the most popular listings in your Store. (Figure 4.15 shows the Traffic Report's My
Summary page.)

• **Sales Reports.** These include data on overall sales, sales by category, and format, fees, and the like.

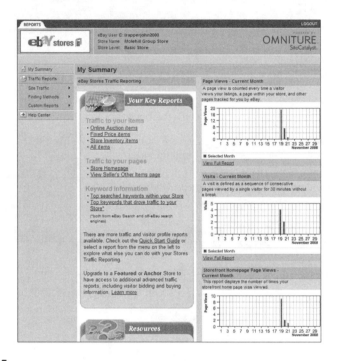

FIGURE 4.15

Tracking eBay Store traffic.

Use these reports to track the performance of your eBay Store—and to
fine-tune its performance going forward.

Should You Open an eBay Store?

I admit to being conflicted on the value of selling via an eBay Store. On the one hand, hundreds of thousands of sellers do it, and have been doing it for a number of years. On the other hand, it just doesn't seem like that good a deal. I'll explain.

The pluses of selling via an eBay Store are primarily financial. Your listing costs are considerably lower in an eBay Store than they are for creating similar fixed-price listings on the main eBay site. The lower insertion fees mean you can list more items for a longer period of time—which makes using an eBay Store a good way to sell slower-selling items.

The minuses have to do with visibility. Yes, you can stock your eBay Store with hundreds or thousands of items, but few eBay users will see them. That's because eBay doesn't include Store listings in its default eBay search results. It's like eBay Store owners are second-class citizens, not worthy of being listed alongside eBay's traditional sellers. And that kind of sucks.

What you end up with are eBay Stores with big inventories and low sell-through rates. That's not necessarily a recipe for certain failure, but it's certainly a much different business model than I'm used to. And when you add in the cost of the Store subscription itself and the time it takes to manage the Store, I'm not sure it's a business model I want to get used to.

But that's just my opinion; reasonable minds may disagree. ■

5

Fixed-Price Selling on Half.com

So far in Part II, "Fixed-Price Selling on eBay," you've learned how to offer a fixed-price option in traditional auction listings, create straight fixed-priced listings, and sell fixed-price items in an eBay Store. That leaves one more way to sell fixed-price items on eBay. However, the final way to sell fixed-priced items on eBay isn't on the eBay site itself. eBay runs a sister site, Half.com, that lets you sell specific types of items in a format that not-coincidentally resembles that of the Amazon Marketplace.

Getting to Know Half.com

Half.com (www.half.com) specializes in media products. Specific categories include the following:

- Books (including textbooks)
- Audiobooks
- CDs
- DVDs
- VHS videotapes
- Video games
- Video game systems

Merchandise is offered from individual sellers, although information about each item is provided by Half.com. In this manner, Half.com works a little like the Amazon marketplace—in fact, it's the closest that eBay comes to duplicating the Amazon experience, for both buyers and sellers. And, as you can see in Figure 5.1, the Half.com home page even looks a lot like Amazon's home page.

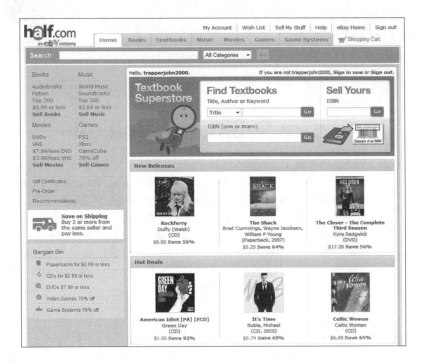

FIGURE 5.1

Half.com: eBay's fixed-price marketplace for books, CDs, DVDs, and other media products.

For sellers, using Half.com doesn't require a lot of work. Unlike running an eBay Store, which requires a lot of setup and maintenance of the Store itself, listing on Half.com is much easier; all you have to do is enter the item's UPC or ISBN and then describe the item's condition. Half.com provides the item description and picture and presents this information to buyers.

The Half.com experience, for both buyers and sellers, is quite a bit different from the traditional eBay experience. Buyers deal with multiple sellers via a single product page and checkout; sellers essentially provide inventory information only to the site, instead of full listings. That means less work for both buyers and sellers, which is a good thing.

Understanding the Half.com Shopping Experience

A listing you create on Half.com isn't like a listing you create on eBay. What you create, instead, is a data point in the Half.com product database—and that drives the entire Half.com shopping experience.

When a customer searches for a specific item on Half.com, the site returns a product page like the one in Figure 5.2. As you can see, this page includes a description of the product at the top, and at the bottom it shows a list of sellers who have the item for sale. The list is sorted into sellers offering new and used items, with the used items further sorted by condition—like new, very good, good, acceptable, and so on.

FIGURE 5.2

Viewing items for sale on Half.com.

The buyer can read more about the condition of an individual item by clicking the More Info link next to that listing—although most sellers don't include any information beyond the basic product description supplied by Half.com. To make a purchase, the customer simply clicks the Buy button, and that item is added to his or her Half.com shopping cart.

As noted previously, a Half.com buyer can purchase items from multiple sellers and have all his or her purchases consolidated into a single shopping cart and checkout. The buyer makes a single payment to complete the checkout; individual sellers are then notified of their respective sales.

While the Half.com experience is very Amazon-like, it's different from Amazon in one crucial aspect: When a Half.com user purchases from multiple sellers, he or she doesn't pay a single shipping charge; instead, the buyer pays for shipping on each individual item ordered. That's because each item purchased comes from a different seller, of course. But the buyer at least has the benefit of knowing the shipping charges up front—and knowing those charges are the same from seller to seller.

Understanding Half.com Fees

For sellers, one of the primary advantages of selling on Half.com is that the initial investment is much lower than elsewhere on eBay. As you may recall, Half.com differs from the main eBay site in that it doesn't charge any listing fees. You can list as many items as you like for absolutely no charge. Table 5.1 details the Half.com commission rates as of February 2009.

Table 5.1   Half.com Commissions

Selling Price	Commission (Final Value Fee)
$0.75–$50.00	15%
$50.01–$100.00	12.5%
$100.01–$250.00	10%
$250.01–$500.00	7.5%
$500.01+	5%

Instead of a buyer paying you directly, as you're used to with other eBay sales, Half.com collects the buyer's payment as part of its aggregated checkout process. (Remember, buyers can purchase from multiple sellers and use a single checkout page for all those purchases.) The site sends you your payments every two weeks, typically via direct deposit to your bank account.

tip

Half.com's free listings make the site a better place to sell hard-to-sell items than the eBay site itself. You're not out a listing fee if the item doesn't sell.

Listing on Half.com

You don't create your Half.com listing via the normal eBay process. Instead, you list merchandise for sale directly from the Half.com site.

> **caution**
>
> To sell an item on Half.com, that item must have an ISBN or UPC number or code. You cannot sell items that do not have ISBN or UPC identification.

To sell on Half.com, follow these steps:

1. Go to the Half.com home page and click the Sell My Stuff link at the top of the page.

2. When the Sell Your Items on Half.com page appears, as shown in Figure 5.3, enter the item's UPC, ISBN, or model number in the Quick Sell box and click the Continue button.

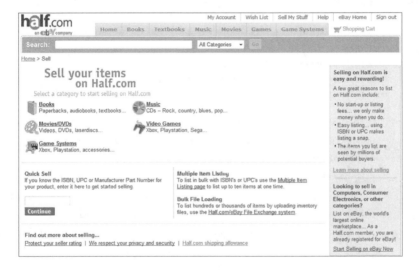

FIGURE 5.3

Getting ready to list an item for sale on Half.com.

3. You now see the Sell Your Item page, as shown in Figure 5.4. Select the condition of the item, enter any comments about the item, and enter an optional longer description if necessary. Click the Continue button when you're done.

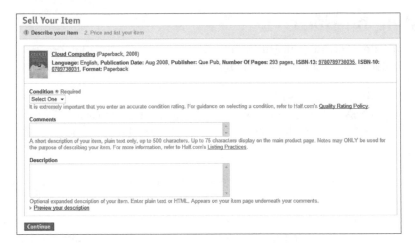

FIGURE 5.4

Describing the item for sale.

---

tip

Because Half.com provides the item description for each product, you don't have to describe items. However, you should describe each item's *condition*— especially if it's a used item.

---

4. If this is your first time listing, you'll be asked to place a credit or debit card on file, for security reasons. Do so and then click the Continue button to proceed.

5. Next, if this is your first time listing, you'll need to provide bank account information so that Half.com can deposit your payments. Do so and then click the Continue button to proceed.

6. If you're a first-time lister, you're now prompted to select which shipping methods you support, as well as enter your shipping location.

7. When you see the page shown in Figure 5.5, enter the selling price of the item and the quantity that you have to sell.

8. Click the List Item button to submit your listing.

When you've completed this process, Half.com lists your item in its inventory. As you can see, it's a much quicker listing process than on the eBay site (after the initial signup, anyway). And remember, creating a listing is free.

FIGURE 5.5
Entering price and quantity information.

Pricing Your Half.com Items

Given that you don't really have an opportunity to promote your own business on Half.com, any competitive advantage you may have boils down to price. If you have the lowest price, chances are you'll get the sale; if your price is too high, buyers will purchase from another seller.

So how should you set your Half.com prices? This is where a little research comes in; you need to know how competitors are pricing similar items and put your price right in the middle of that pack. So it pays to look up your items on Half.com to determine the going rates before you begin the listing process.

Know, however, that when you're listing an item for sale, Half.com recommends a price based on the item's condition. Half.com calculates its suggested price as a percentage of the best available retail price for a new item, based on the item's condition. Table 5.2 shows the schedule that Half.com uses.

Table 5.2   Half.com Pricing Recommendations

Item Condition	Suggested Price (as a Percentage of the Best Available New Retail Price)
Like new	50%
Very good	45%
Good	40%
Acceptable	35%

This is as good a pricing scale as you can get without actively researching the actual selling prices of similar-condition items.

Calculating Shipping and Handling Charges

Remember that buyers pay the same shipping charge for an item whether they purchase from you or from another seller. That's because Half.com dictates these charges—to both buyers and sellers.

You see, Half.com automatically adds a default shipping charge to each customer's order, based on its own schedule. You can't determine your own shipping charges; you have to accept what Half.com says.

That said, as a seller, you get a "shipping reimbursement" from Half.com. However, this charge is less than what Half.com charges the buyer; the site takes its own cut of the proceeds. (It's good to be the guy running things!)

How much do you charge for shipping a Half.com item? Table 5.3 details the customer shipping charges and your corresponding shipping reimbursements.

Table 5.3   Half.com Shipping Charges and Reimbursements

Product Category	Shipping Method	Customer Shipping Charge (per Item)	Seller Shipping Reimbursement (per Item)
Hardcover books	USPS Media Mail	$3.99	$3.07
Paperback books	USPS Media Mail	$3.49	$2.64
Audio books	USPS Media Mail	$3.49	$2.64
Music CDs	USPS Media Mail	$2.99	$2.39
VHS movies	USPS Media Mail	$2.99	$2.14
DVD movies	USPS Media Mail	$2.99	$2.39
Video games	USPS Media Mail	$3.49	$2.89
Video game consoles (large)	Ground	$14.95	$13.50
Video game consoles (small)	Ground	$7.95	$7.00
Video game controllers	Ground	$7.95	$7.00
Flash cards	Ground	$4.95	$4.00
Other accessories	Ground	$5.95	$5.25

note

Half.com specifies charges for additional item shipments and for expedited shipping. See the Half.com site for a detailed list of charges.

As you can see, Half.com makes a nice profit on these shipping charges. For example, if you sell a DVD, Half.com charges the customer $2.99 for shipping and pays you $2.39. Hopefully you can ship the item for $2.39 or less and make a little profit yourself.

The shipping reimbursements are paid as part of your normal payment from the Half.com site. In most instances, the shipping reimbursement should be equal to or higher than the actual shipping you incur for each item.

tip

If you think your actual shipping costs will be higher than the Half.com's default charges, increase the selling price of your item to compensate for the shortage.

Managing Half.com Sales

The post-sales process at Half.com is similar to the process at the main eBay site. You are notified via email when a buyer makes a purchase, and then you pack and ship the item.

note

To ensure consistent quality of service for buyers, Half.com stipulates that you must ship an item within 72 hours (excluding weekends and holidays) of notification of sale.

Unfortunately, you don't get your Half.com payments immediately. Half.com pays sellers only twice a month (via direct deposit to your bank account), which means you'll be shipping some items before you receive your payment. Get used to it; that's just the way it works.

You can view all current and past sales from your My Account page, shown in Figure 5.6. To access this page, just click the My Account link at the top of any Half.com page. This page is a summary page, like My eBay on the eBay site, that lets you click to display more detailed information on items you are currently selling and have recently sold. You can also use this page to track items you've purchased and to manage your Half.com account.

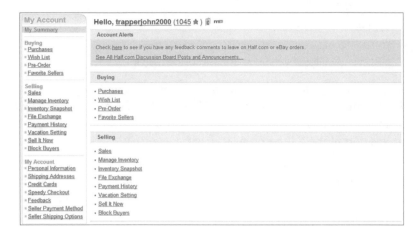

FIGURE 5.6

Managing your account and sales activity from Half.com's My Account page.

Pros and Cons of Selling on Half.com

Half.com is an interesting site, not quite eBay and not quite Amazon. Is it a good site for you to use to sell your merchandise?

In many ways, Half.com is a pretty good site to use. First off, your initial upfront investment, in both time and money, is minimal. Free is always a good listing price, and the fact that you don't have to take product photos and write item descriptions and all that cuts down on the time you have to spend on each listing. That means you can list more items in less time (and for lower cost) than you can on eBay, which should encourage you to put large amounts of inventory into the Half.com database.

On the flip side, Half.com doesn't have nearly the traffic that eBay (or Amazon, for that matter) has, so your chances of selling a particular item are lower than what you're probably used to. So even though your costs are lower, be prepared for a lower sell-through rate than with your eBay listings. You get what you pay for, I guess.

Of course, none of this matters if you don't sell what Half.com specializes in. If you don't sell CDs, DVDs, video games, or similar media items, you can forget all about Half.com—and concentrate on either the main eBay site or the Amazon Marketplace. ■

6

Promoting Your Fixed-Price eBay Sales

If you've decided to migrate your business from online auctions to fixed-price listings on one of eBay's sites, you're now facing the challenge of how to promote your new fixed-price business. Not all of eBay's sites provide the same visibility for sellers that you're used to with the main online auction site; in fact, some of eBay's sites do a pretty good job of hiding sellers and their merchandise from potential buyers.

How do you cut through this anonymity and promote your listings to the same level of visibility you'd have with online auctions? That's the focus of this chapter, so read on to learn more.

Promoting Your Fixed-Price Listings on the eBay Site

Let's start with what most sellers do when they move away from online auctions: sell via fixed-price listings on the main eBay site.

The good thing about selling in this fashion is that you don't have to do a lot of promotion. That's because regular fixed-price listings receive the same visibility in eBay search results as do traditional auction listings. So if you were satisfied with the visibility and sell-through of your previous auction listings, you shouldn't notice much of a change in traffic when you move to fixed-price listings. That said, there are some things you can do to maximize the performance of your fixed-price listings, as we'll now discuss.

---

tip

Because fixed-price listings are not penalized in eBay search results (as eBay Store listings are), many sellers who are migrating from auction-type listings prefer the fixed-price option.

Optimizing Your Listings for eBay Search

The most important thing you can do to promote your eBay fixed-price listings is to make them easier for potential buyers to find. You do this by optimizing your listings for search; the better your listings match buyers' search queries, the more buyers you'll have clicking through to your listings.

---

note

Optimizing your eBay listings for search involves many of the same techniques used in website search engine optimization (SEO). Learn more in my companion book, *The Complete Idiot's Guide to Search Engine Optimization* (Alpha Books, 2009).

Here's the deal: Fully 90% of eBay buyers find items by using eBay's search function. If you optimize your listings so that your items show up when customers are searching for similar items, you'll increase your listing traffic—and your resulting sales.

And there's another reason you want to optimize your listings for search. You see, your listings show up not only in eBay search results but also when web users use Google, Yahoo!, and other sites to search the Web. If your listings are heavy with the right keywords, they'll show up in Google and Yahoo! search results—which is free publicity for your items.

For eBay's search results, it's the title you need to focus on. That's because eBay's search function, by default, searches only listing titles. (There's an advanced option to search the listing description, but not all buyers use it.) So you'll need to cram as many relevant keywords into the listing title as you can.

Web search engines, on the other hand, search your entire listing—title *and* description. So you have more to work with there. How do you optimize your listings for web search engines? Here are a few tricks:

- **Include appropriate keywords.** Your listing title and description have to include the keywords and phrases that potential buyers are searching for. If someone is searching for "jewelry" and you don't mention that word in your item title or description, your listing won't show up in that person's search results. So you need to include any and all keywords a potential buyer for your item might use to search for that item. If you're selling a drum set, for example, make sure that your description includes words such as *drums, drumset, percussion, cymbals, snare,* and the like. Try to think through how *you* would search for this item and work those keywords into your content.

- **Create a clear organization and hierarchy in your description.** This is not terribly important for eBay's search results, but if you want your listings to rank high on Google and Yahoo!, you need to pay close attention to what you put into your item description. The crawler programs used by the major search engines can find more content on a web page if that content is in a clear hierarchical organization. For this reason, you should think of your item description as a mini-outline. The most important information should be in major headings, with lesser information in subheadings beneath the major headings. One way to do this is via standard HTML heading tags or just normal first-, second-, and third-level headings within your listing.

- **Put the most important information first.** Think about hierarchy and think about keywords and then think about how these two concepts work together. That's right, you want to place the most important keywords higher up in your item description. Search crawlers crawl only so far, and you don't want them to give up before they find key information. In addition, search engine page rank is partially determined by content; the more important the content looks to be on a page (as determined by placement on the page), the higher the page rank will be.

- **Make the most important information look important.** Many search engines look to highlighted text to determine what's important on a page. Therefore, you should make an effort to format keywords in your description as bold or italic.

- **Use text instead of or in addition to images.** Here's something you might not think about. Today's search engines parse only text content; they can't figure out what a picture or graphic is about unless you describe it in the text. So if you use graphic buttons or banners (instead of plain text) to convey important information, the search engine simply won't see it. You need to put every piece of important information somewhere in the text of the page—even if it's duplicated in a banner or graphic.

---

tip

If you use images in your description (and you should), make sure that you use the <ALT> tag for each image, and assign meaningful keywords to the image via this tag. Search engines will read the <ALT> tag text; they can't figure out what an image is without it.

Linking from Other Sites to Your eBay Listings

Don't rely on eBay alone to promote your fixed-price listings. You can link to a page that includes all your current listings from any web page or email message by using a bit of simple HTML code.

To include a text link to your listings, insert this code:

```
<a href="http://cgi6.ebay.com/ws/eBayISAPI.dll?
    ViewSellersOtherItems&amp;userid=USERID&amp;include=0&amp;since=-
    1&amp;sort=3&amp;rows=50&amp;sspageName=DB:OtherItems"
    target=_blank>
Your anchor text here.
</a>
```

If you prefer something a little more visual, you can embed a graphic eBay button on a web page or blog, like the one shown in Figure 6.1. When visitors click this button, they go to your items-for-sale page.

FIGURE 6.1

Embedding a clickable eBay button to link to your eBay fixed-price listings.

To add this button, go to the Link Your Site to eBay page, located at pages.ebay.com/services/buyandsell/link-buttons.html. Check the box next to the My Listings on eBay button, enter the URL of the page where you want to display the button, scroll to the bottom of the page, and click the I Agree button. When the next page appears, copy the generated HTML code and paste it into the code for your web page.

Promoting Your eBay Store

One of the disadvantages of selling via an eBay Store is that Store listings do not appear in eBay's default search results. A potential buyer searching for the merchandise you sell won't be able to find you unless he or she searches from the eBay Stores main page. Because of this, you need to work hard to draw attention to your Store and your Store listings. If you don't, the merchandise you offer for sale may go unnoticed by potential buyers.

note

Naturally, to promote the listings in your eBay Store, you can use the same techniques discussed for promoting individual eBay listings. In particular, make sure you optimize each listing for search—for those buyers who *do* search eBay Store listings.

Seeding Listings into the Traditional eBay Marketplace

One sure-fire way to get noticed in eBay's search results is to utilize a mix of eBay Store and normal fixed-priced listings. Yes, you keep the bulk of your merchandise in your eBay Store (where items cost a lot less to list), but you also post a few listings each week into the traditional eBay marketplace. These listings, few as they may, will appear in eBay's default search results. You can then use these listings to draw attention to the other merchandise you have for sale in your eBay Store.

The key here is to list main items in the eBay marketplace and balance that with add-on or accessory items in your Store. People will buy the main item via fixed-price listing but then be led to your Store, where they can augment their sale.

To do this, you must include links to your Store or to specific Store items within your fixed-price listings. That means working with underlying HTML to include these links and thinking smartly about what you should be linking to. When you do this right, you can turn a $20 fixed-price sale into a $40 total sale with items from your eBay Store.

Enabling Cross-Promotions

One way to take advantage of seeded fixed-price listings is to enable cross-promotions in your listings. Cross-promoting is a powerful tool for driving potential customers to the other items you have for sale in your eBay Store.

If you have an eBay Store, you can scroll down to the bottom of any of your eBay listings and see a cross-promotion box like the one shown in Figure 6.2. This box displays four other items you have for sale and serves as a powerful advertisement for those items.

FIGURE 6.2

Cross-promoted items at the bottom of an eBay listing.

This cross-promotion box is available to all eBay Store sellers, and you manage it via the Cross-Promotions Tool. You use the Cross-Promotions Tool to determine which items display with specific listings.

To manage your cross-promotions, go to your My eBay Summary page, scroll to the Shortcuts section, and click the Manage My Store link. When the Manage My Store page appears, go to the Marketing Tools section and click the Cross-Promotion Settings link. From there you can turn on or off cross-promotion, determine how you want to cross-promote, choose how your cross-promoted items appear, and so on.

In addition to these settings, you can configure what items display on your listing pages, based on product categories within your Store. To do this, click the Cross-Promotions Defaults link on the Manage My Store page. When the next page appears, click the Create New Rule link to link the display of products in a given category to the type of product viewed by a customer. For example, if you're a bookseller, you might want to display your active mystery books when someone is looking at or bidding on another book in the mystery category.

Creating an Email Mailing List

Email marketing is part and parcel of most online retailers' marketing mix. The good news is, eBay makes email marketing almost a one-click operation for eBay Stores owners.

Recall that email marketing is one of the freebies that eBay offers as part of its eBay Stores package. eBay lets you add a Sign Up for Store Newsletter link to each of your listings, and then you can create up to five different mailing lists to target different types of customers or product categories. You can even use eBay's email marketing tools to measure the success of your email newsletters, which makes it easier to fine-tune your promotions in the future.

An eBay Basic Store owner can send a total of 5,000 free emails a month to subscribers; Premium and Anchor Stores get 7,500 and 10,000 emails a month, respectively. If you want to send more than your allotted number of messages, you'll pay a penny per email for each additional message.

To create a new email mailing list, go to your Manage My Store page and click the Email Marketing link (in the Marketing Tools box). When the Marketing Tools: Summary page appears, click the Email Marketing link in the Store Marketing section. When the Email Marketing: Summary page appears, as shown in Figure 6.3, click the Create Mailing List button. When the next page appears, enter a name for this mailing list and then click the Save button. Your new mailing list now appears on the Email Marketing: Summary page.

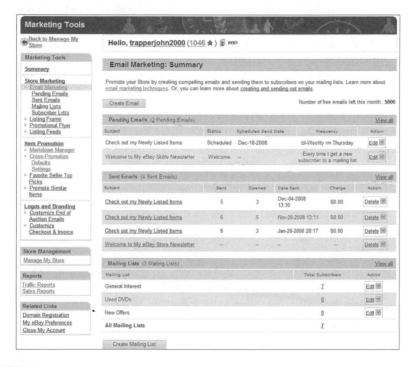

FIGURE 6.3

Managing your email mailing lists.

Of course, a mailing list isn't much of a list without subscribers. Unfortunately, you can't manually add subscribers to your mailing lists.

Instead, subscribers have to opt in of their own accord, which they do from your item listings and eBay Store pages. When users add you to their favorite sellers list, they have the option of subscribing to your email newsletter. In addition, they can sign up when they visit your eBay Store by clicking the Sign Up for Store Newsletter link at the top of the page.

---

tip

Once someone has subscribed to your newsletter, that user appears in the sub-scriber list at the bottom of the Email Marketing: Summary page. You can man-age the list of subscribers by clicking the Email Marketing Subscriber Lists link; the resulting page lets you block subscribers from receiving emails, in case you want to target your mailing to specific customers.

To create an email newsletter and send it to your subscriber list, return to the Email Marketing: Summary page and click the Create Email button. When the Select a Template page appears, pull down the Type of Email list and select the type of newsletter you want to send, select a template for your email newsletter, and click the Continue button. When the Create Email page appears, enter the necessary information: which mailing list(s) you're sending to, whether to send emails on an automatic sched-ule, whether to display your Store header, the subject of the newsletter, the message of the newsletter, which items you want to showcase or list, and whether to display your feedback. When you're finished, click the Preview & Continue button; if you like what you see on the preview page, click the Send Email button to send the email to your selected recipients.

Linking to Your eBay Store

Email marketing lets you promote to previous customers; to attract new customers, you have to move off eBay and spread the news of your Store near and far.

One of the easiest ways to do this, of course, is to place a link to your eBay Store on your website or blog, or perhaps make it part of your email signature. To do this, just insert the following HTML code:

```
<a href="http://stores.ebay.com/StoreName" target=_blank>
Your text here
</a>
```

Obviously, replace *StoreName* with your eBay Store name, and replace *Your text here* with your own anchor text.

Adding a Stores Widget to Your Blog or Website

You can add an eBay Stores To Go widget to your website or blog. This widget, as shown in Figure 6.4, displays a selected category of products and lets users search your Store inventory directly.

FIGURE 6.4

Displaying a widget to promote your eBay Store.

Here's how it works: Go to the eBay To Go home page (togo.ebay.com) and click the OK, Let's Go! button. On the next page, select the Store widget and click the I Want This One button. Next, enter your seller ID and click the Search button. When your Store is found in the search, click the Next button. Finally, enter a query for a particular type of product you sell; this product will be featured in the widget. eBay now displays the HTML code for the widget; copy this code and paste it into your blog or web page.

Creating a Listing Feed

Another way to drive traffic to your eBay Store is to create an RSS listing feed, which lists all the new items in your Store. You can then syndicate or distribute this feed so that anyone subscribing to the feed will automatically be notified of new items in your eBay Store.

To create an RSS feed for your Store listings, go to your Manage My Store page and click the Listing Feeds link (in the Marketing Tools box). From there, check the option Distribute Your Listings via RSS and then click Apply. The feed is created.

Once you've created the feed, you have to distribute it. One of the best ways to do this is via the FeedBurner service. Here's how to do it: Start by going to your eBay Store page. Scroll down to the bottom of the page and click the orange RSS box. The RSS feed for your site appears. Write down or copy the URL for this feed, which appears in your browser's Address box.

Now go to the FeedBurner site (www.feedburner.com). You'll need to create an account (no charge) and then follow the onscreen instructions to "burn" a feed. You next enter the URL that you copied for your eBay Store RSS feed and continue following instructions to save and distribute the feed. FeedBurner then makes sure your feed is syndicated across the web.

Whenever you add a new item to your eBay Store, your RSS feed is updated, and any subscribers to the feed are notified. This is a great way to attract repeat business to your Store.

tip

Because updates to your feed go out only when you add new items to your Store, you should list something new in your Store every few days. There's no need to add a lot of items at a time; the key is constant addition of merchandise, so that subscribers receive almost-daily updates.

Exporting Your Listings to Search Engines and Shopping Sites

There's another promotional opportunity available on the Listing Feeds page: eBay lets you export your Store listings to third-party search engines and price comparison sites.

When you check the Make a File of Your Store Inventory Listings Available option, eBay creates a special file of your Store listings and posts that file to a web page. This is an XML-format file that contains the following information for each item listed in your Store:

- Item title
- Item description
- URL of the item page
- Whether the item is orderable
- Current price
- Availability

- Item number
- Shipping cost (if specified ahead of time)
- Gallery picture (if available)
- Quantity
- Currency

You can then submit the URL for this file to your favorite search engines (Google, Yahoo!, MSN Search, and so on), as well as to various price comparison sites (Shopping.com, Yahoo! Shopping, BizRate, NexTag, and the like). While eBay creates the file for you (and keeps it updated with your latest listings), it's your responsibility to submit the file's URL to whatever sites you choose. Naturally, you should follow the submission instructions for each particular site.

When you submit your eBay Store listings to a web search engine, your listings appear in the search engine's search results. When you submit your Store listings to a price comparison site, your Store appears as an option whenever someone is price shopping for a particular item. It takes a little work on your part, but the result is much wider exposure—and wider exposure means more sales.

Advertising on the eBay Site with AdCommerce

There's a new way to promote your eBay Store—by advertising on the eBay site itself. eBay's new AdCommerce program offers pay-per-click (PPC) advertising to all eBay Store owners, which lets you put your ads in front of eBay users searching for similar merchandise.

The way it works is simple: You purchase one or more keywords, and then your advertisement appears on results pages when users search for those keywords. You don't pay anything until someone clicks on your ad.

More precisely, you don't purchase a keyword but rather bid on it—by specifying how much you're willing to pay for each click. (This is known as the cost-per-click [CPC].) If you bid $0.10 per click, you pay this amount every time someone clicks on your ad.

note

Your ad will not appear on every search results page for the keywords you purchase. Several factors, including the number of other bidders for that keyword and the amount of your bid, influence which ad appears when.

The ads you create are basically text ads, each with a title, short description, and an optional image, like the one in Figure 6.5. Ads appear in a Sponsored Links section at the bottom of relevant search results pages.

FIGURE 6.5

A typical AdCommerce ad.

Let's work through an example. If you're selling iPod accessories, you start by creating an ad for one of your accessories and bid $0.05 for the word "iPod." When a user searches for "iPod," your ad appears at the bottom of the user's search results page. You're not charged anything for this display; if the user clicks on your ad, however, you pay $0.05 —and hopefully make a sale.

Bidding on a keyword is a lot like bidding in an eBay product auction. You state the maximum amount you're willing to pay, and that's the maximum you'll be charged. If a competing advertiser bids a higher price, his or her ad gets displayed instead. If other bidders are lower, you'll pay $0.01 more than the next-highest bid.

To sign up for AdCommerce, go to www.adcommerce.com. Once you've signed up (it's free), you see the AdCommerce dashboard, shown in Figure 6.6. To create a new ad (what AdCommerce calls a "campaign"), select the Campaigns tab and then click the Create Campaign link.

On the Create Campaign page, enter a name and description for the campaign. Select whether you want to bid on a keyword (your ad appears on keyword search results pages) or category (your ad appears on category pages) and then select the target country and language. Select the start and end dates for your campaign and then enter the amount of money (total) you want to spend per day. Click the Continue button when you're ready.

Next, you're prompted to create an "ad group"; this essentially details the keywords or categories you're purchasing. Enter an ad group name and description, followed by the maximum cost per click you're willing to pay. Enter the keywords or select the categories you're bidding on and then click the Continue button.

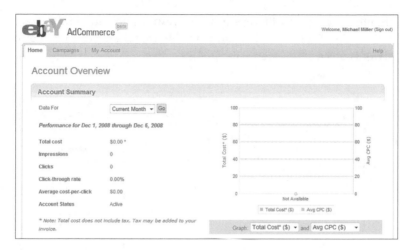

FIGURE 6.6

The AdCommerce dashboard.

> **note**
>
> A keyword can actually be a phrase of multiple words. Enter the phrase within quotation marks for an exact match.

Now you're prompted to create your ad. Enter a headline, one or two lines of description, and the URL for your eBay Store (in the Display URL box). For the Destination box, enter the URL of a specific product or category in your Store. Then, if you want to include an image in your ad, click the Browse button to upload that image. Click the Continue button when you're ready.

You now get to preview your ad. If you like what you see, click the Submit button, and your campaign is launched.

Advertising Across the Web with Google AdWords

AdCommerce is great, but it doesn't reach any potential customers outside the eBay site. Fortunately, there's nothing to stop you from advertising your eBay Store or listings on other websites.

Perhaps the best way to do this is with a web placement service, such as Google AdWords. Like AdCommerce, AdWords lets you "buy" keywords, and then it displays a "sponsored link" text ad on the Google search results pages for that keyword. For example, if you buy the word

"Hummel," your ad will appear on the results page anytime a Google user searches for the word "Hummel." (Figure 6.7 shows some typical AdWords ads on the Google site.)

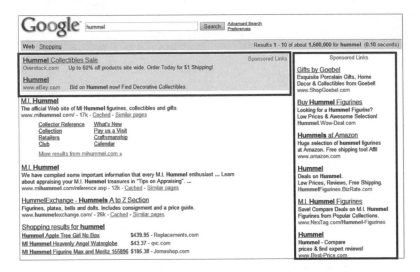

FIGURE 6.7

AdWords ads on a Google search results page—at the top and on the side.

note

In addition to the sponsored links on its own website, the AdWords program also places ads on third-party websites that feature similar content.

You can purchase ads for your eBay Store or for individual item listings. To do so, you first have to sign up for the AdWords program, which you do at adwords.google.com. You pay a one-time $5.00 activation fee and then are charged either on a CPC or cost-per-thousand-impressions (CPM) basis. (You can choose either method.) You control your costs by specifying how much you're willing to pay (per click or per impression) and by setting a daily spending budget. Google will never exceed the costs you specify.

How much does AdWords cost? As with eBay's AdCommerce program, that's entirely up to you. If you go with the cost-per-click method, you can choose a maximum CPC click price from $0.01 to $100. If you go with the CPM method, there is a minimum cost of $0.25 per 1,000 impressions. Your daily budget can be as low as a penny, up to whatever you're willing to pay.

note

If you go the CPC route, Google uses AdWords Discounter technology to match the price you pay with the price offered by competing advertisers for a given keyword. The AdWords Discounter automatically monitors your competition and lowers your CPC to $0.01 above what they're willing to pay.

You can opt to prepay your advertising costs or to pay after your ads start running. With this last option, Google charges you after 30 days or when you reach your initial credit limit of $50, whichever comes first. Google accepts payment via credit card, debit card, direct debit, or bank transfer.

It's surprisingly easy to create and activate an AdWords ad. All you have to do is follow these general steps:

1. Write the ad (a title line and two lines of text).

2. Enter the URL on your site that you want to link to.

3. Choose the keyword(s) you want to purchase—up to 20 keywords or phrases.

4. Set the maximum you're willing to pay per click.

5. Set your monthly AdWords budget. (Google recommends a $50 monthly minimum.)

It all starts on the Google AdWords home page, when you click the Start Now button. After your ad campaign is under way, you can monitor performance from this same main AdWords page by selecting the My Ad Campaign tab. You can view the performance of each keyword you selected, in terms of impressions, clicks, and total cost to date.

If you buy the right keywords, you should be able to drive significant traffic to your eBay Store or individual listings. That said, the cost of this advertising is such that you probably want to use it only with higher-priced items—or to advertise entire categories within your Store.

Promoting Your Store in the Real World

Finally, let's not neglect all the traditional means of advertising available offline, in the real world. The key to advertising in the real world is to use your eBay Store URL and plaster it everywhere:

- On business cards
- On letterhead
- In flyers you post locally

- On promotional materials you hand out to customers and colleagues—hats, pens, notepads, and the like
- In classified advertisements in your local newspaper
- In small display ads in your local newspaper
- In classified or display ads in hobbyist and trade magazines and periodicals
- On the packing slips you send out with the items you sell
- If you have a bricks-and-mortar location, on your store invoices and shopping bags

The more people who see the URL, the more people who go online to check out your eBay Store. And, as you know, the more Store visitors you have, the more sales you'll make!

tip

Don't forget non-eBay online advertising. You can include your eBay Store URL in all your personal and business email messages (as part of your signature), in newsgroup and forum postings, in blog postings, and so forth.

Promoting Your Half.com Listings

As you can see, there are lots of ways to promote both your eBay fixed-price listings and your eBay Store. But what about the listings you've placed on the Half.com site?

Unfortunately, there's not a lot you can do to promote your Half.com listings. That's because, if you recall, you really don't create listings per se; instead, you enter your inventory into the Half.com database, where it can be displayed when a buyer is shopping for a particular product. This display is your "promotion"; it's the only visibility you have on the site, and it's primarily product visibility, not seller visibility.

So when it comes to Half.com, promotion isn't the thing—price is. You'll get noticed when your price is lower than those of your competitors for a given product. Buyers shop by price on Half.com; seller reputation is much less important there than it is on the eBay site.

Disappearing Visibility

If you're an established eBay seller, you're probably used to not doing much promotion. After all, that's what eBay is supposed to do—provide visibility for you and the products you sell. Listing on the eBay site *is* your promotion, and you pay for that promotion with your eBay fees.

It's certainly true that many big eBay sellers got big without spending a penny in additional promotion. They listed their items and got those items noticed within eBay's search results. They didn't have to advertise elsewhere to draw attention to what they were selling.

That was then, however, and this is now. Most eBay product categories have become so crowded that it's unlikely that you'll ever show up on the first page of search results. (That's especially true with eBay's new search weightings in favor of larger sellers.) And, if you go the eBay Stores or Half.com route, your listings won't show up in eBay's search results period.

It's an unhappy fact that you can no longer rely on eBay to put your products in front of potential buyers. This means, of course, that you have to promote your products yourself. The salt in the wound is that that even though eBay now provides less visibility for most sellers, it hasn't reduced its fees. So you're still paying for eBay's "promotion" even though you're getting much less of it. This is why so many sellers are moving off eBay and starting to sell on other online marketplaces—as you'll learn in the following chapters of this book. ■

Selling via craigslist Online Classifieds

7

Online Classifieds: Are They Right for Your Business?

Many experts believe that eBay and other online auction sites (most of which are now defunct, victim to the eBay juggernaut) helped to kill traditional newspaper classified ads. Instead of buying and selling via paid classified advertisements in their local newspapers, consumers migrated to buying and selling via the eBay marketplace. Goodbye, newspaper classifieds.

Except that the classified ad concept didn't die. In fact, newspaper classifieds remained a viable way to sell larger items that were difficult to ship long distances (such as cars), as well as local services. But old technology always gives way to newer ways of doing things, and print-based classified ads are now in the process of moving online, thanks to craigslist and similar online classifieds sites.

Many eBay sellers are finding that they can sell their products via online classified ads. Is online classified selling for you? Read on to learn more.

Understanding Online Classifieds

First, a little background on this whole online classifieds thing.

Online classifieds are the web-based evolution of traditional print-based classified advertisements. Virtually every local newspaper and magazine has a classifieds section, in which short, text-based ads are posted by individuals and businesses selling products and services. (And by individuals running personal ads, as well.) Traditional classified ads are typically sold on a per-word or per-line basis and include no graphics or other images.

---

note

Classified advertising got its name because the ads are typically grouped under headings that classify the product or service being offered, in a separate section of the publication. (Display ads, on the other hand, are larger ads full of images that are placed throughout the publication.)

For many decades, classified ads were *the* way to sell items locally. If you had an old piece of furniture to sell, you placed a classified ad. If you had a used car to sell, you placed a classified ad. If you had a garage sale to announce, you placed a classified ad. Businesses also used classified ads to solicit new employees, in the classic "help wanted" format.

As popular and useful as classified ads have been, the popularity of print media has been declining over the past decade or two. Part of this is due to a shift of readers from print to online media; it's also no doubt partly due to America's declining literacy in recent years. Fewer and fewer people are reading newspapers and magazines, thus decreasing the audience for classified advertising.

---

note

Classified advertising revenue dropped 20% in 2007 at the large newspaper chains, while online classified advertising increased 23% during the same time period.

Of course, eBay has also been a factor in the decline of print-based classified advertising. Instead of advertising used clothing or vintage toys or whatever in a local classified ad, sellers now have the option of selling these items worldwide via eBay—and, thanks to the online auction format and much larger base of potential buyers, realizing higher prices. If you're selling something with limited appeal, why limit yourself to your local market when there may be dozens if not hundreds of interested buyers you can reach via the Internet?

But eBay isn't the best way to sell all types of merchandise. Not all sellers want to offer their goods worldwide; some items are better suited for local sale. This is particularly true of large or heavy items that might be difficult or expensive to ship across the country via the U.S. Postal Service, FedEx, or UPS. These goods—including appliances, televisions, large power tools, furniture, and vehicles—are best delivered or picked up locally.

In addition, some sellers simply prefer selling locally—as some buyers prefer buying from local sellers. Not everything has to be offered everywhere, and eBay doesn't do a good job of handling local sales.

Hence the continued resilience of traditional print-based classified ads—and the rise of online classifieds sites. These websites function much like the print-based classifieds of old, but on the web. These sites accept ads from local sellers and serve them up to local buyers. Interested buyers contact sellers directly; sales are arranged privately between buyers and sellers.

Unlike print-based classifieds, most online classifieds sites offer more than just text-based ads; sellers can add pictures to their ads, which then more resemble eBay listings. Most sites don't charge listing fees, nor do they take a commission on the final sales price, which makes them attractive to cost-conscious sellers. It's zero-cost selling.

The typical classified ad lists an item at a fixed cost; there is no bidding process. As with traditional classified ads, some sellers might accept lower prices or may list an item at a fixed price "or best offer." All negotiations are between the seller and the buyer.

Unfortunately, most online classifieds sites also don't offer the range of tools and services that buyers and sellers get from eBay. craigslist and other online classifieds sites offer no listing creation or management tools, nor do they offer online payment services such as eBay's PayPal. It's up to each individual seller to create listings, manage those listings, and arrange payment. And, of course, it's up to the buyer to pick up the item from the seller—or arrange for the seller to ship it to him or her, at additional cost.

Online classifieds sites also don't offer the buyer and seller protection plans that you find on eBay. If a buyer pays with a bad check, there's not much the seller can do about it; if a seller gets an item home and finds out it doesn't work as promised, *caveat emptor.* Unlike eBay, which has gone to great lengths to safeguard its marketplace (sometimes to the annoyance of smaller sellers), the world of online classifieds is more like the Wild West of America's past.

The key thing to know about online classifieds sites is that they're local sites. Even if a site itself has national exposure, buyers and sellers log into (or browse) to local listing pages. This makes online classifieds ideal for sellers who want to keep it local, for whatever reason.

Examining Major Online Classifieds Sites

If you're interested in offering a product via an online classified ad, where do you turn? Today there are a handful of viable online classifieds sites, led by the big dog known as craigslist.

craigslist

craigslist (www.craigslist.org) is the dominant online classified advertising site in the United States today. As you can see in Figure 7.1, craigslist offers a minimalist text-based interface to its network of local sites. It has local sites for all major U.S. states and cities, as well as select international countries and cities—450 cities in all.

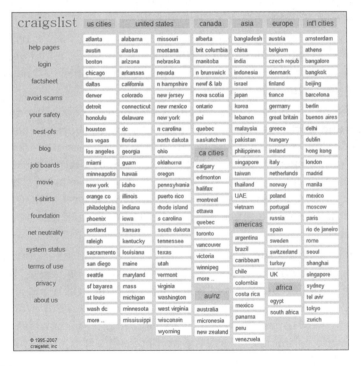

FIGURE 7.1

The leading online classifieds site, craigslist.

The site works like most other online classifieds sites. Click a city or state on the home page, and you see all the product and service classifications offered for that location on the next page. Click a category, and you see all the listings for that category, with the most recent listings displayed first. Alternatively, users can search for specific items offered for sale on the site.

Posting a classified ad on craigslist is completely free; there are no listing fees or sales commissions involved. And, in many categories and in many locations, craigslist is a major force, equal to eBay in terms of number of listings and sales.

note

While most craigslist ads are free, not all are. In particular, craigslist charges for job listings in some major cities, as well as brokered apartment listings in New York City.

Overall, craigslist boasts more than 30 million unique visitors each month, which puts it in the top 50 of all sites on the web. That far out-shines any competing online classifieds site and compares favorably to eBay's 49 million unique visitors per month.

But here's the thing about craigslist—and other online classifieds sites, for that matter. Whether its viable or not depends on the number of users in a given location. So if you're in a big city such as San Francisco or New York, craigslist is a vibrant marketplace. If you're in a smaller city, how-ever (such as my old hometown of Indianapolis), you'll find far fewer list-ings and far fewer potential buyers. Whether craigslist makes sense for you is a matter of whether your city has reached critical mass.

note

Learn more about craigslist in Chapter 8,"Doing Business on craigslist."

Oodle

The second-biggest online classifieds site is one you might not have heard of. That's because being second-biggest, compared to craigslist, really isn't that big at all.

This number-two site is Oodle (www.oodle.com), shown in Figure 7.2. Unlike craigslist, which hosts all its own listings, Oodle is a classifieds list-ing consolidator—it pulls together classified ads from more than 80,000 different sources. In addition, you can post your own ads to the Oodle site, which then publishes those listing on hundreds of other sites that belong to its network. It's an interesting business model.

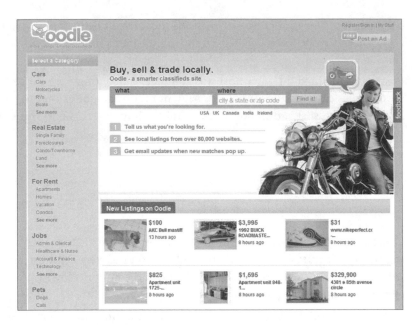

FIGURE 7.2

Oodle, an online classifieds consolidator.

note

Oodle was launched in 2005 by former executives from eBay and Excite.

Oodle claims to host 40 million listings, though I find that claim somewhat suspect; craigslist itself claims only 30 million listings. Still, Oodle powers the online classifieds listings for hundreds of leading web brands, including Cox Interactive, Lycos, Media General, *San Diego Union Tribune*, and *The Washington Post*. In addition, Oodle recently signed a deal with Wal-Mart to put its auto, real estate, job, and tickets listings on the retailer's site, thus gaining more visibility for listings in those categories.

Before the Wal-Mart deal, Oodle was attracting more than 3.5 million monthly visitors, which makes it a top 500 site. Its demographics skew slightly more female than does craigslist, for some reason.

Listing is free on Oodle, and there are no commission or final value fees, either. Finding products is a little easier with Oodle than with craigslist, thanks to a more visible and effective search function. Buyers can also sign up for email notifications when merchandise they're looking for becomes available.

Kijiji

The number-three online classifieds site is owned by eBay. Kijiji (www.kijiji.com), shown in Figure 7.3, is eBay's attempt to compete directly with craigslist. It draws about 2.5 million visitors each month, although the majority of these visitors are outside the United States. While it's not a huge factor here in the States, Kijiji is a big deal in Germany, France, Italy, and Turkey; it also has a significant presence in Canada, China, England, India, Japan, and Taiwan.

FIGURE 7.3

A local Kijiji site; it's bigger overseas.

note

Kijiji is Swahili for "village."

eBay launched Kijiji outside the U.S. in 2005; the U.S. site launched in June 2007. Kijiji grew out of eBay's 2004 acquisition of Netherlands classifieds site Marktplaat.nl, which also operated Inktoko-branded sites throughout Europe and in Canada. Those sites were merged into the Kijiji brand, alongside eBay's other classifieds acquisitions (Gumtree in the

United Kingdom, Australia, and New Zealand; Loquo in Spain; and OpusForum in Germany).

Like most other online classifieds sites (and unlike its parent, eBay), Kijiji charges no listing or selling fees. While its presence is relatively small in the United States, selected cities are starting to achieve a critical mass. Check to see if it's big enough in your area to consider.

backpage.com

Have you ever perused the classified ads in the back of your local alternative newspaper? Then you'll be familiar with backpage.com, which displays online the classified ads printed in various local alternative newspapers, such as the *City Pages* (Minneapolis), *LA Weekly* (Los Angeles), *Seattle Weekly* (Seattle), *SF Weekly* (San Francisco), and *Village Voice* (New York). As you can see in Figure 7.4, you just click through to your city to see your local paper's ads.

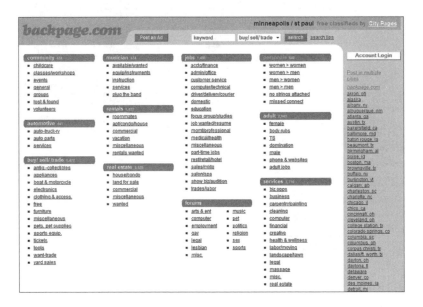

FIGURE 7.4

Local backpage.com listings from the Twin Cities' City Pages newspaper.

note

backpage.com is owned and operated by the Village Voice Media and partners with local newspapers and media outlets across the United States.

The backpage.com site claims 1.8 million monthly visitors overall; obviously, the number of visitors for any local site is a subset of this figure. Normal classified ad listings are free, although you can pay for sponsored ads (with preferred display) and to also put your ad in the associated print publication. Pricing for these enhanced ads varies by market.

LiveDeal

LiveDeal (www.livedeal.com), shown in Figure 7.5, combines online classifieds ads with Yellow Pages directory listings. That's not a surprise when you consider that LiveDeal, founded in 2003, was acquired by YP Corporation (which runs the yp.com Yellow Pages website) in 2007.

FIGURE 7.5

Online classifieds mix with Yellow Pages listings at LiveDeal.

Unlike competing sites, LiveDeal isn't always free. Sellers with a free Personal Account can post 10 listings each month in general merchandise categories, 10 listings in the pets category, and 2 listings in the vehicles and real estate categories. If you sign up for a Basic Store account ($9.95 per month), you get unlimited listings in general merchandise categories, 20 listings in the pets category, and 5 listings in the vehicles and real estate categories. More expensive categories are also available.

Even with the Yellow Pages connection, LiveDeal manages just 1 million visitors per month. That doesn't make it a viable alternative for sellers in many locales.

Google Base

The final online classifieds site we'll discuss is one that showed a lot of promise but has yet to live up to that promise. Google Base (base.google.com), shown in Figure 7.6, is Google's answer to the online classifieds phenomenon. It blends features from both craigslist and eBay, with a lot of Google technology thrown in for good measure.

FIGURE 7.6

Google's online classifieds service, Google Base.

In essence, Google Base is a big database of product listings. Google uses its proprietary search technology to let buyers search through the database for matching items for sale in their area. (In fact, users don't have to search the Google Base page; they can also use the main Google search page or Google Product Search.) Items purchased via Google Base can be paid for via Google Checkout, which is Google's payment service that competes directly with PayPal.

Like craigslist and similar sites, Google Base is completely free to use, with no listing or sales fees. However, with just 743,000 unique visitors each month, it's a distant competitor in the online classifieds category.

---

note

These aren't the only online classifieds sites on the web, just the largest. Other sites include OnlineClassifieds.com and Stumblehere (www.stumblehere.com), each of which has under 100,000 monthly visitors.

The Pros and Cons of Selling via Online Classifieds

So there are a half-dozen or so viable online classifieds sites on the web today, with craigslist being the most viable by far. Is online classifieds selling a good thing—or something you should avoid?

Pros of Online Classifieds Selling

There are several plusses to selling via online classifieds. Here are what I consider to be the major benefits:

- **It's free.** For many eBay sellers, this is the point that grabs their attention. Unlike eBay, which can take 20% or more in fees of various types, most online classifieds sites are completely free for sellers. There are no listing fees, no commission or final value fees, and no credit card processing fees. You sell something for $20, you keep the full $20. That can definitely cut back on your costs—and increase your profits.

- **It's local.** With eBay, you're dealing with customers all across the nation and possibly around the world. Some sellers might like that, but others might prefer running a more local business—which is what you get from classifieds selling. Online classifieds are targeted at local buyers and sellers, so you're selling to your neighbors. If what you really want to be is a local retailer, online classifieds are for you.

- **No shipping involved.** Because you're selling locally, you don't have to ship the items you sell across the country. Instead, your local buyers will, more often than not, pick up the goods at your place.

No shipping, no packing, and no buying expensive boxes and packing material.

- **It's good for items—and services—that aren't a good fit on eBay.** Some things are difficult to sell on eBay. In particular, big and heavy items aren't eBay friendly, simply because they cost too much to ship. Well, that's not a problem when you're selling locally. Online classifieds sites are perfect for selling furniture, automobiles, and other bulky items that are best targeted at local buyers. In addition, online classifieds sites are ideal for selling services, such as housecleaning or lawn care or whatever it is you offer to your local market. You can't sell services you can't personally deliver!

Bottom line: Online classifieds selling is *local* selling, with all the benefits that accrue from that. If, for whatever reason, you want or need to target your sales to local customers, online classifieds are the way to do it.

Cons of Online Classifieds Selling

Of course, there are also several good reasons *not* to sell via online classifieds. It's not all milk and honey—and, in fact, online classifieds selling is considerably more difficult than what you're used to with the eBay marketplace. Here are the things that aren't so good about online classifieds selling:

- **It's not national.** Maybe you don't want to limit your sales to where you live. Maybe you can reach more customers (and make more sales) by selling anywhere in the country, or in the world. If you don't want to limit your sales to your local area, then online classifieds are not for you.

- **You have to provide your own payment services.** This is a big one. eBay lets you collect payment by credit card via its PayPal online payment service. Online classifieds sites (with the notable exception of Google Base) offer no such payment services. Most online classifieds sellers accept payment via cash—and sometimes via cashier's check, money order, or (if careful about it) personal check. Most online classifieds sellers are too small to sign up for commercial credit card services and thus can't accept payment via credit card. This can limit your customer base to those who have cash on hand.

- **There are no listing management tools available.** If you're used to all the tools and support that eBay offers its sellers, you're not going to like online classifieds selling. These sites, craigslist included, offer few (if any) tools to sellers. You get a form to fill in when you list your item, but that's it. Managing your listings is totally up to you.

- **There's no protection from shady buyers.** eBay is very protective of both its buyers and sellers. If you have a buyer who tries to take you for a purchase, you have recourse from the eBay site. Not so from online classifieds sites. If a buyer decides not to pay, or writes you a rubber check, you're on your own.

- **You have to deal with a lot of flakes and frauds.** I hate to generalize, but chances are you're going to run into a lot more flakes and frauds on an online classifieds site than you did on eBay. craigslist in particular is home to interested buyers who don't show up as scheduled and to human and automated scamsters who try to defraud you out of money and merchandise. In my personal experience, somewhere between 10% and 25% of potential buyers back out without so much as a phone call or email; that's a lot of wasted effort for most sellers.

- **It's a local pickup business.** Okay, it's nice not having to pack up and ship everything you sell, but it can be a pain to arrange to be home for potential buyers to look at your merchandise in person or pick up items they want to buy. And do you really want a lot of strangers traipsing around your home or office? That's one of the "joys" of local selling—effectively establishing a retail presence.

caution

Beware especially of potential buyers who email you saying they'll send a cashier's check for the purchase and have a "local agent" pick it up for them. This is almost always a fraud that leaves you out the merchandise with a phony cashier's check in your hand—and perhaps out some cash, if you were asked to refund the difference for a cashier's check that was written in excess of the purchase price.

- **It's not geared to businesses.** This may be the biggest drawback to selling via online classifieds. Most of these sites are targeted at individuals selling onesies and twosies from their basements and garages; they're not targeted at ongoing businesses. In fact, craigslist explicitly warns against businesses selling on its site—although it can't really bar them from doing so. Know that your professional presence on craigslist and other sites might not be welcomed by all in the community, and act accordingly.

The bad thing about the world of online classifieds is that it's where eBay was a decade ago. There's very little available in the form of tools, support, and protection, and buyers are less obligated and less professional than what you find on the established online auction site. It's an unregulated, somewhat chaotic marketplace—more like garage sale selling than retail selling. If you're comfortable with that, great; if not, move on.

Do Online Classifieds Make Sense for Your Business?

Knowing what's good and what's bad about online classifieds, you need to decide: Is online classifieds selling right for you? It all depends on the type of business you run and what type of merchandise you sell.

The Best Businesses for Migrating to Online Classifieds

In a nutshell, online classifieds are best for selling larger items or goods and services targeted at a local audience. This includes (but is not limited to) the following types of merchandise:

- Autos and other motor vehicles
- Bicycles and motorcycles
- Exercise equipment
- Furniture
- Large antiques
- Computers
- TVs and audio equipment
- Large appliances
- Musical instruments
- Aquariums and other large pet supplies
- Home and garden items

craigslist can also be good for selling used clothing, tickets to local sports events and concerts, and digital still and video cameras. It's also effective for selling real estate, announcing garage and estate sales, soliciting employment opportunities, offering local services, and advertising small businesses. Finally, the more unique the item you're selling, the more viable it may be for online classifieds selling.

> **tip**
>
> Because of their fixed-price nature, online classifieds may be less than ideal for selling unique items of indeterminate value. If you think you can get a higher price by having interested parties bid on an item, stick to selling via eBay.

Remember, you're selling to a local audience that is expected to pick up the merchandise from your location and pay you at that time. Most buyers are comfortable paying cash, although you may close more sales if you can offer some form of credit card payment.

You're also less likely to sell large volumes of merchandise in this fashion. It's easy enough to ramp up an eBay or Amazon business moving hundreds of low-priced items each week. It's much more difficult to move those kinds of quantities when you're selling locally—and when you depend on your customers to travel to your location to pick up those items. For this reason, craigslist and similar sites are best for moving onesies and twosies of larger items.

The Worst Businesses for Migrating to Online Classifieds

As you can sense from the previous section, lots of different types of items are not really suited for local classifieds sales. In general, online classifieds are not ideal for selling smaller and commodity items, such as the following:

- Office supplies (including printer ribbons, computer paper, and cables)
- CDs, DVDs, and videotapes
- Videogames
- Books
- Small antiques and collectibles
- Small consumer electronics items (DVD players, iPods, etc.)

Remember, if you're competing with a local or national retailer who's selling a similar new product, you're probably not going to attract individual buyers. This is especially true if you're not price competitive—that is, if they can find it cheaper online, they're not going to drive to your house to pay you more.

In addition, rare items with a small potential base of buyers may not be ideally suited for selling locally in this fashion. If there are more collectors in California than in Iowa—and you live in Iowa—you may be limiting your potential by selling on a local online classifieds site.

So if your current eBay business involves moving large quantities of low-priced items, online classifieds definitely are not for you. Nor are online classifieds recommended if you've established a nationwide (or world-wide) base of customers. You can't migrate customers from another coast to a local classifieds-based business!

Migrating from Print to Online

The real opportunity represented by online classifieds is for sellers who currently sell locally via print-based classified ads. The migration is from print to online, not necessarily from eBay to craigslist.

That's because online classifieds are inherently different from either online auctions or online retailing. Online classifieds sites are, at heart, local media, where online auctions and retailing know no such geographical boundaries. While it's possible for an Ohio seller to sell to San Francisco buyers on the craigslist site, online classifieds buyers tend to shy away from distant sellers; they want to purchase locally because that's what they're used to doing from print classifieds listings.

Print classifieds appear in local newspapers; they let local sellers offer goods and services to local buyers. You don't find too many New York buyers reading the classifieds section of a Los Angeles newspaper; you read the classifieds to find local bargains.

This same mentality carries over to online classifieds. You don't search all of craigslist for something to buy; you click to the craigslist site for your city and then browse the items offered for sale locally. And if someone from another city is listing on your local site, you tend to skip over that item.

Local newspapers are worried about craigslist a lot more than eBay is. (Not that eBay isn't worried; I'm just saying.) The revenues they used to generate from classified listings are evaporating, and more and more buyers and sellers are moving online. While this isn't a new phenomenon (major newspaper chains first identified the problem back in the late 1990s, when they formed Classified Ventures, a joint venture designed to migrate their classifieds listings online), it's a problem that is accelerating in magnitude. While newspapers can't blame all their current financial problems on craigslist and similar sites, these online sites are certainly a contributing factor.

So the majority of people using craigslist and other online classifieds sites are those who used to use print classifieds. That's why the majority of online listings are for things like cars, boats, furniture, appliances, real estate, and jobs. If that's the kind of thing you want to sell, online classifieds are for you. If, however, your current business is more about smaller stuff sold in greater quantities, then another type of online selling may be a better bet. ∎

8

Doing Business on craigslist

As noted in Chapter 7, "Online Classifieds: Are They Right for Your Business?" far and away the largest online classifieds site on the Web today is craigslist. If you're serious about selling locally, craigslist is the place to do it—assuming that the site has reached critical mass for your city. (Not all locales are equally big on the craigslist thing.)

How do you sell items on craigslist? What's involved in creating a listing, making a sale, and collecting payment? This chapter covers the mechanics of doing business on craigslist, so read on to learn how to sell your products via craigslist online classifieds.

Understanding craigslist

craigslist (www.craigslist.org) is an online classifieds site. Actually, it's hundreds of different mini-sites, each one containing listings for a specific city or state.

The site was launched in 1995 by Craig Newmark, who provided the idea and the name. The original craigslist site was a classifieds site for the San Francisco Bay area only; it took five years for Newmark to expand the site to other locations. Nine U.S. cities were added to the site in 2000, 4 more in both 2001 and 2002, and another 14 in 2003. It's now operating in more than 450 cities in 50 countries around the world.

craigslist is one of the top 10 websites in the United States, and it's among the top 50 worldwide. It boasts more than 30 million unique visitors each month—although, obviously, that number is much lower for any specific local mini-site. In reality, craigslist isn't completely viable in all cities in which it operates; some cities have a thriving craigslist business, and others have far fewer listings (and sales).

The company behind craigslist is a private one and thus isn't obligated to release its financials—and, in fact, it does not. That said, the company is estimated to have in the neighborhood of $150 million in revenues, generated from those few categories in which craigslist charges listing fees. This includes job listings in Atlanta, Austin, Boston, Chicago, Dallas, Denver, Houston, Los Angeles, New York, Orange County (California), Philadelphia, Phoenix, Portland, Sacramento, San Diego, Seattle, south Florida, and Washington, DC ($25 per listing); job listings in the San Francisco Bay area ($75 per listing); brokered apartment listings in New York City ($10 per listing); and listings in the erotic services category ($5 per listing). All other listings are completely free.

note

While craigslist is a big site for people looking to buy and sell goods and services, it's also a major factor in the jobs market. craigslist is one of the top employment sites on the web, with more than 2 million new job listings each month.

Items are offered for sale by individuals and businesses that create item listings. Each listing includes a contact email address for the seller; interested buyers email the seller directly to arrange to view or purchase the items for sale. The buyer pays the seller directly, and craigslist collects no commission on these sales. In fact, craigslist doesn't even know when a sale has been made; the seller has to manually delete the listing after a sale has been made.

craigslist offers no listing creation or management tools to its sellers, nor does it provide access to any payment service, as eBay does with its PayPal service. Most craigslist sales are local, paid for with cash, and picked up by the buyer from the seller's location. It truly is an online version of traditional print-based classified ads, and it operates in much the same fashion—except over the web.

Navigating craigslist Listings

To use the craigslist site, users first have to navigate to their specific local site, which they do by clicking their city or state on the main page. Users then see links to all the product and service categories offered by craigslist, as shown in Figure 8.1.

FIGURE 8.1
craigslist's listing categories.

Let's leave aside all the services listings, personal ads, help wanted listings, and discussion forums. What we're interested in are the For Sale listings. craigslist offers the following categories for sellers:

- Arts + Crafts
- Auto parts
- Baby + Kids
- Barter
- Bikes
- Boats
- Books
- Business
- Cars + Trucks
- CDs/DVD/VHS
- Clothes + Acc(essories)

- Collectibles
- Computer
- Electronics
- Farm + Garden
- Free
- Furniture
- Games + Toys
- Garage Sale
- General
- Household
- Jewelry

- Material
- Motorcycles
- Music(al) Inst(ruments)
- Photo + Video
- RVs

- Sporting
- Tickets
- Tools
- Wanted

When a buyer clicks through a category, he sees all the listings in that category, as shown in Figure 8.2. The newest listings are first on the page; even though there are 100 listings per page, if a category is heavily trafficked, a single listing can slide off the first page relatively quickly. For that reason, some buyers use craigslist's search feature to find items in which they're interested in, instead of browsing.

FIGURE 8.2

Listings within a For Sale category.

The listing page displays the title for each item, as well as the item's location and whether there's a picture available. Most sellers put the item's price in the title, to help buyers decide whether to check out the listing.

When you click a listing title, you see the listing itself, as in Figure 8.3. Most listings are relatively short and sweet, although savvy sellers include as much text as necessary. craigslist lets you include up to four photos of your item within the listing.

FIGURE 8.3
A typical craigslist listing, complete with pictures.

While some sellers include a phone number or website address in their listings, it's safer to handle all communication through craigslist's anonymous email system. When you create a listing, you must supply your email address. This address is never shown in the listing; instead, craigslist creates a "blind" address that potential buyers can email. Messages sent to this address are forwarded to your email address. You can then respond to these emails as you wish.

Listings stay on the craigslist site for anywhere from 7 to 45 days, depending on your city. (As a rule of thumb, bigger and busier cities turn over their listings faster.) If you sell your item before the expiration date, you can manually delete the listing. Likewise, you can repost a listing if it's fallen off the site. Remember, all For Sale listings are free.

Before You List...

Before you list on craigslist, you need to do a little prep work. The first thing to do is make sure you actually have in hand the item you're selling. You should also make sure that it's cleaned up and ready to sell, as much as you can.

Second, take a few pictures of what you're selling. As with eBay listings, the better the pictures, the more potential buyers you'll attract. Grab your digital camera, make sure the item is well lit and positioned against a neutral background, and start snapping. You can use up to four pictures in a craigslist listing, so take as many shots as you want and pick the four best. Make sure to shoot the item from multiple angles—and to shoot close-ups of any distinguishing details or damage.

Third, write your item description. While many craigslist descriptions are one-line affairs, I recommend that you pay as much attention to your craigslist descriptions as you do the ones on eBay. Write in complete sentences and paragraphs, use illustrative text, and include all necessary brand, model, and other descriptive information.

Next, search craigslist to see what price others are asking for similar items. This type of pricing research is helpful when determining what price to ask for the item. If other sellers are asking $100 for a particular item, you can't charge $200 for the same thing. Conversely, you probably don't want to give that same item away for just $50, either. You need to price your merchandise at the going rate—which you can determine by searching the craigslist listings.

Finally, before you create your first listing, you want to establish a craigslist account. Doing so is completely free, and having an account makes it easier to manage multiple listings on the site. You sign up for an account by clicking the My Account link on the left side of the home page; when the next page appears, click the Click Here to Sign Up link. You're now prompted to enter your email address and type the verification word. Do so and then click the Create Account button. craigslist now sends you an email with instructions for completing the sign-up process.

note

Before you create subsequent listings, make sure you first sign into your account by clicking the My Account link on the craigslist home page.

Listing an Item for Sale

Listing an item for sale on craigslist is similar to creating a fixed-price listing on eBay. The differences are more in what you *don't* have to do with craigslist; there are fewer "blanks" to fill in, and you don't have to pay for the listing, of course.

Start by going to the home page for your local craigslist community and then click the Post to Classifieds link on the left side of the page. When the next page appears, as shown in Figure 8.4, click the category in which you want to list—probably the For Sale category. You're now prompted to select an appropriate subcategory; do so.

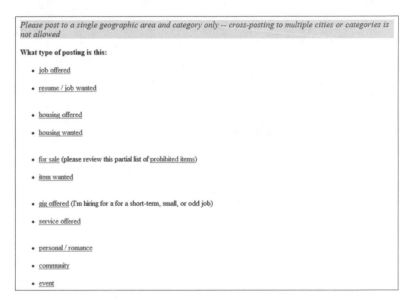

FIGURE 8.4

Choosing the category for your listing.

You now see the listing creation page, shown in Figure 8.5. Here you enter specific information into the appropriate fields, as follows:

- **Price.** This is the asking price (fixed price) for your item.

- **Specific Location.** If you're in a large metropolitan area, enter a more precise neighborhood location. For example, if you list on the San Diego site but live in La Jolla, enter La Jolla in the Specific Location box.

- **Posting Title.** This is your listing title. Keep it relatively short but include as many keywords as you can that potential buyers are likely to search for.

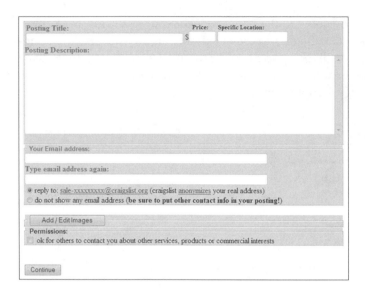

FIGURE 8.5

Filling in the blanks to create an item listing.

- **Posting Description.** This is where you can go into some detail, describing your item. Unlike with eBay, you can't do fancy formatting in a craigslist description; it's basically a paragraph or two of plain text. You can, however, include some rudimentary HTML formatting, which I'll explain in the "Using HTML Formatting" section, later in this chapter. For the time being, remember that you need to include a detailed description of what you're selling—something more than just "antique table." Make sure you include dimensions, sizes, colors, model numbers, and anything else the customer needs to make a smart buying decision.

- **Your Email Address.** craigslist forwards replies to your listing to your email address. Your address is *not* displayed in the listing itself.

- **Reply To.** Select the Reply To option to have craigslist "anonymize" your email address—that is, to insert a "blind" email address into your listing. Email sent to this address is forwarded to your real email address; your email address does not appear in the listing. If you'd rather display *no* email address in your listing, select the Do Not Show Any Email Address option—but make sure you include some contact information in your listing's description!

- **Add/Edit Images.** Click this button to include up to four photos in your listing description. See the "Inserting Images into Your Listings" section, later in this chapter, for more details.

- **Permissions.** If you want to receive all sorts of spam email, check this option. Otherwise, don't.

After you've entered all the necessary information, click the Continue button. craigslist displays a preview of your listing; if you like what you see, click Continue. (If you don't like what you see, click the Edit button and make the necessary changes.) Your listing appears on the craigslist site within 15 minutes or so.

---

note

Unfortunately, craigslist offers no bulk listing tools of its own and, in fact, outlaws auto-posting on its site. That means you have to do all your posting manually—one listing at a time.

Formatting Your Item Description

Most craigslist item listings are bare-bones affairs, but they don't have to be. You can use the techniques you learned on eBay to create more visually interesting item listings, complete with text formatting and product photos.

Using HTML Formatting

The first step in creating a visually compelling item listing is to learn a little HTML. That's because craigslist lets you include some basic HTML codes in your description. All you have to do is insert the appropriate codes into your text description; craigslist interprets the codes and applies the formatting.

Which HTML codes can you include? Table 8.1 details the HTML codes that craigslist allows.

Table 8.1   craigslist HTML Codes

HTML Code	Formatting
`<b>`	Applies bold
`<i>`	Applies italic
`<u>`	Applies underline
`<s>`	Applies strikethrough
`<big>`	Increases text size
`<small>`	Decreases text size
`<center>`	Centers text
`<font>`	Formats text by using the `size` and `color` attributes
`<p>`	Indicates a new paragraph; can be used with the `align` attribute
` `	Inserts a line break within a paragraph
`<hr>`	Inserts a horizontal line (rule); can be used with the `align`, `size`, and `width` attributes
`<blockquote>`	Formats text as an indented quote
`<h1>`, `<h2>`, `<h3>`, `<h4>`, `<h5>`, and `<h6>`	Formats text as a heading, in one of six heading sizes (with `h1` the largest)
`<ul>` and `<li>`	Creates a bulleted (unordered) list
`<ol>` and `<li>`	Creates a numbered (ordered) list
`<dl>`, `<dd>`, and `<dt>`	Creates a definition (unbulleted, unnumbered) list
`<a href="`*URL*`">`	Inserts a hyperlink to another web page; also supports the `target="_blank"` attribute to open the URL in a new window
`<img src="`*URL*`">`	Inserts an image
`<pre>`	Formats text as preformatted—with all spaces and line breaks as you typed them
`<table>`, `<th>`, `<td>`, and `<tr>`	Creates a table

tip

You can use the `<img>` tag to include more than the normally allowed four photos in your item listing.

Inserting Images into Your Listings

As the old saying goes, a picture is worth a thousand words. That's certainly the case when you're selling products online. You need to show potential buyers just what it is you're selling, and the best way to do that is with pictures.

craigslist lets you include up to four pictures in an item listing. All you have to do is upload the pictures from your computer; craigslist hosts the pictures, for free.

You upload your pictures when you're creating the item listing. Go to the bottom of the listing page and click the Add/Edit Images button. This expands the page to show four image boxes, as shown in Figure 8.6. The images you upload are displayed two wide, two tall. When you've uploaded an image into a slot, a green circle appears; a slot waiting to be filled contains a red X.

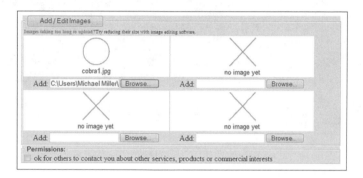

FIGURE 8.6

Adding photos to your item listing.

Managing Your Listings

Once you've posted your listing, some rudimentary listing management is possible. craigslist lets you edit and delete existing listings.

Editing a Listing

Sometimes you make a mistake when you're creating a listing. Sometimes you need or want to change a listing description or price to reflect changing market conditions. Whatever the reason, it's relatively easy to edit a listing that you've previously created.

Start by clicking the My Account link on the craigslist home page. After you've logged in, craigslist displays a list of your recent item listings, as shown in Figure 8.7. Click the listing you want to edit, and craigslist displays the listing; click the Edit This Posting button, and you see the original listing creation page. Make any changes you want and then click the

Make Changes button. Your listing is now revised with the changes you specified.

26 most recent postings
of **150** maximum returned [change]

[active pending removed by me expired flagged/deleted]

regardless of status (active, expired, deleted), all posts will appear on this list. we are not able to offer a removal option at this time.

ID	Date	Site	Category	Title	Fee
956791204	Dec 13 08	min	baby & kid stuff	Baby Crib	
956789072	Dec 13 08	min	collectibles	1974 Fibes Drum Set	
718453045	Jun 13 08	min		Dining Room Chairs -- 4 Great Condition, Oak w/Green Fabric REDUCED	
718449142	Jun 13 08	min		Computer Desk Hutch on Wheels	
714717930	Jun 10 08	min		Computer Hutch on Wheels	
714276445	Jun 09 08	min		Oak Wood L-Shaped Bar	
714270554	Jun 09 08	min		Queen Sized Futon Sofa/Bed Excellent Condition	
714257316	Jun 09 08	min		Couch and Matching Loveseat Great Condition!	
714256129	Jun 09 08	min		Four dining room chairs -- Wood frame, green fabric, on castors	
613751256	Mar 21 08	min	household	Refrigerator Jenn-Air Side by Side 23.5 Cu. Ft.	

FIGURE 8.7

Managing your craigslist listings.

Deleting a Listing

Because craigslist doesn't know when an item has been sold, you need to manually delete your listing once a sale has been made. To do this, click the My Account link on the craigslist home page. When the listing list appears, click the listing you want to delete. When the listing appears, click the Delete This Posting button. Confirm the deletion, and the listing is removed from the craigslist site.

Making a Sale

When someone replies to your listing, craigslist forwards you that message via email. You can then reply to the potential buyer directly; in most instances, this means arranging a time for the potential buyer to come to your house to either view or purchase the item of interest.

That's right: Most craigslist sales are made in person. Unlike with eBay, where you have to ship the item to the buyer, craigslist buyers more often than not pick up the items they purchase. That means you have to be at home for the buyer to visit, and you have to be comfortable with strangers visiting. You also have to be prepared to help the buyer load up whatever it is you're selling into his or her vehicle for the trip home—which can be a major issue if you're selling big stuff and you're a small person.

---

caution

When selling on craigslist, be prepared for a lot of no-shows. For some reason, a large percentage of interested craigslist buyers don't show up as promised, which is a major annoyance—and a big waste of your time.

As to payment, the vast majority of craigslist purchases are made with cash. While eBay discourages cash payments, because of the inherent dangers of sending cash via the mail, taking cash in person is a good deal. It certainly spends easily enough.

---

tip

Depending on the price of your item, you may have to keep some spare cash on hand to make change if the buyer pays with larger bills.

For higher-priced items, you might want to accept payment via cashier's check or money order. Just be sure that the check or money order is made out for the exact amount of the purchase; you don't want to give back cash as change for a money order purchase.

What you don't want to do is take payment via personal check. It's far too easy for a shady buyer to write you a check and take off with the merchandise, only for you to discover a few days later that the check bounced. If you *must* accept a personal check, hold onto the merchandise for a full 10 working days to make sure the check clears; it's probably easier for all involved for the buyer to just get the cash.

You can, if you wish, arrange to accept credit cards, either with a merchant account or by enlisting a payment service such as PayPal or Google Checkout. Know, however, that most craigslist buyers will be very nervous about paying in this fashion and prefer to pay via cash. That's okay; you don't have to pay any service fees when you accept a cash payment. That said, it's possible that you may be able to accommodate more buyers by accepting credit cards. That's certainly an option you might want to consider but not one that's necessary to sell in the craigslist marketplace.

---

note

Learn more about PayPal and Google Checkout in Chapter 19, "Choosing an Online Payment System."

What *Not* to Do on craigslist

While craigslist doesn't have nearly as many formal rules and regulations as does eBay, there is a sort of unofficial code of conduct that you violate at your own risk.

Most of the policing on the site is done by the craigslist community. Individual users are very touchy about what is and isn't "proper" and are quick to take action against suspected offenders. This action typically consists of "flagging" inappropriate listings; flagging brings the listings in question to the site's attention for further scrutiny. craigslist staffers review flagged listings and, more often than not, delete them—and there's nothing you can do about it.

So what do craigslist users find inappropriate? They're particularly sensitive about spam and commercial listings—particularly in categories thought to be the province of individuals. This is particularly tricky when we're talking about the For Sale categories, which is probably where you want to list your items for sale. Some users insist that the For Sale categories are for individuals only, not for businesses, and may aggressively flag these listings for possible deletion.

For this reason, some experts recommend that if you're a professional seller, you should place all your listings in the Sm Biz Ads (Small Business Ads) subcategory within the Services category. I'm not sure I endorse this strategy; that category more often than not contains just what you'd expect—services targeted at small businesses. A better approach, because these sort of unofficial standards vary from community to community, is to test the waters first. Try listing in the appropriate For Sale category and then switch to the Sm Biz Ads category only if your listings are constantly flagged.

You also have to be careful about posting on more than one local site. That's because craigslist removes listings that are cross-posted in multiple communities; cross-posting is viewed as a sign of spamming, not of offering legitimate local merchandise. Remember, craigslist is for *local* transactions—so post on your local craigslist site only.

You also run a risk by posting too many listings in too short a time. While you may be used to posting dozens or even hundreds of listings on eBay nearly simultaneously, this sort of thing can get flagged as potential spamming on craigslist. Better to spread your listings out over a day or two rather than post everything on the same day and at the same time each week.

Finally, because craigslist is a site primarily for cash transactions, be careful about offering other payment options in your listings. While it's okay to offer buyers the option of paying via credit card, saying so upfront in your listing could get it deleted.

Moral of the story? Don't offend or annoy or otherwise get on the wrong side of the craigslist community, or you'll find all your listings being systematically flagged and deleted. ∎

9

Migrating from Online Auctions to Online Classifieds

After reading the previous few chapters, you may be wondering just how to go about shifting your current eBay sales to craigslist or other online classifieds sites. While *how* is a good question, you should probably first ask yourself *whether* you should migrate your business. After all, online classifieds are quite a bit different from online auctions—at least those offered in the established eBay marketplace.

We'll tackle both the *whether* and the *how* questions in this chapter. And if you do decide to make the move, get ready for some major changes in the way you do business.

What Items Should You Move to craigslist?

Just what types of products are best suited for online classifieds sales? We covered this issue briefly in Chapter 7, "Online Classifieds: Are They Right for Your Business?" but it bears further evaluation here.

Here's what we know sells well on craigslist:

- **Used items, not new.** craigslist is not the ideal site to sell new merchandise. Online classifieds shoppers are looking for used items at a bargain price. craigslist is not the place to sell new books and DVDs, new electronics equipment, new cars, new anything.

- **Big items, not small ones.** People aren't going to drive clear across town to buy a 99-cent CD. Maybe they'll drive that far to buy a lot of CDs for $20, and most certainly they'll make the drive for a good deal on a used refrigerator or sofa or electric guitar, but whatever it is has to be worth the trip and hassle. That means you want to sell relatively large items, not small, low-priced merchandise.

- **Unique items, not commodities.** Buyers aren't going to buy something from an individual if they can get an identical product for the same or lower price from a named retailer conveniently located just down the street. They will, however, travel relatively long distances for a unique item or deal. Don't even think about offering printer ribbons or USB cables or plain white yarn on craigslist; buyers can get all that stuff elsewhere.

note

Remember that craigslist, while a national website, is a local marketplace. When you sell on craigslist, you're selling locally; you can't offer your goods in other cities, states, or countries.

So here's the deal: If you're selling big, unique items—such as antiques, furniture, appliances, musical instruments, exercise equipment, certain types of sporting goods, and the like—craigslist may be a better marketplace for your business than eBay. But if you're selling smaller, lower-priced, commodity items, craigslist is bound to disappoint; you should probably stick with fixed-price sales on eBay.

I look at it this way: If you're a budding online retailer with a constant stock of easily shipped items that are also sold by other online and brick-and-mortar retailers, you don't belong on craigslist; that's not what online classifieds buyers are looking for. If, on the other hand, you acquire a variety of unique items from garage sales, estate sales, and the like and find them hard to sell (and ship!) on eBay, then craigslist may be a perfect match for your business.

craigslist may represent some new opportunities for some sellers. Think about what craigslist does well and consider whether there are new items you can add to your selling mix. If you're selling small collectibles, maybe you can expand to larger antiques that you can sell locally. If you're selling musical accessories, maybe it's time to start trading musical instruments—guitars, drums, electronic keyboards, and the like.

Some sellers might take a look at the online classifieds marketplace and decide to go into completely different product categories. Furniture is big on craigslist; maybe you can find a supply of merchandise at live auction sales, estate sales, and the like and start selling individual pieces via craigslist. Or maybe you can hook up with a local appliance retailer to resell its trade-ins on craigslist. You get the idea.

If you also run a traditional brick-and-mortar store, you may find using craigslist a viable way to move excess merchandise. If you run a pet store, for example, you may be able to move aquariums and other larger items on craigslist. Guitars and amps and such are always good craigslist fodder, so if you run a music store, craigslist might work well for you.

And here's another thing: Sometimes simply repacking several smaller items into a larger lot may be what it takes to make the shift to the craigslist marketplace. If you sell used clothing, for example, maybe you package a dozen or so jeans or shirts or dresses or whatever into a package that craigslist shoppers will be interested in. Same thing with used books or CDs or DVDs or video games; a large lot (at an attractive price) will attract more shoppers than a single item.

Don't expect, however, to seamlessly migrate all your existing eBay sales to the craigslist marketplace. They're different marketplaces with different shoppers; you need to adapt your sales accordingly.

Changing Your Business Model

Selling on craigslist is different from selling on eBay—in many ways. Let's count them.

Going Local

With craigslist, you're selling locally, not nationally or worldwide. Get used to that, for both the good and the bad it represents.

On the plus side, you won't get anymore emails in fractured English, wanting to know if you'll ship to Outer Mongolia, or if you'll accept payment in togrogs. It also means fewer attempted scams from eastern Europe, Africa, and the Far East. You'll be dealing with neighbors—or at least people who live in your same city or state.

On the minus side, you won't have any sales outside your city or state. For many sellers, this geographic limitation is a real revenue killer. Look at your eBay sales for the past six months; what percentage of sales were made outside your local area? Well, kiss all those sales goodbye. If you sell items with limited appeal that need far-away bidders to reach their true value, you'll make a lot fewer sales—at much lower prices—when you're limited to craigslist's local markets. That's just the way it is.

For most sellers, this means substantially revising the types of items you sell. As we've discussed, some items are better suited to the local market than others; these are the things you should be selling. If you don't want to sell these types of items, you shouldn't be selling on craigslist.

Pickups, No Shipping

Here's another side effect of selling locally: Instead of packing the items you sell for shipment across the country and around the world, you'll wait for your buyers to come to you to pick up their purchases. Again, this can be both good and bad.

The upside of local pickups is that you don't have to deal with packing and shipping, which is a major thorn in the side of many eBay sellers. No more spending money on boxes and peanuts and wrapping tape; no more trying to fit this sized item into that sized package; no more long waits in line at the post office; no more spending more on shipping than you collected in shipping/handling fees. These are all good things.

On the other hand, you now have to open your home to all sorts of strange people—including a lot of folks who look but don't buy. Customers will travel to you to view and hopefully purchase your merchandise, which means you have to arrange to be home when these folks say they'll show up. (If, in fact, they show up at all—another issue with this model.) If you're not comfortable opening your home to strangers, you're not going to like doing business this way.

---

caution

There may be some danger in letting strangers into your home. If you live alone, consider having a friend standing by when you have customers scheduled to visit. Alternatively, you may want to arrange to meet customers in a neutral location, such as a local coffeehouse—although it may not be feasible to carry your merchandise with you for this type of offsite rendezvous.

And here's another minus to having customers pick up their purchases: You may have to help load them. This isn't a big deal if you sell used clothing and guitars, but if you sell a big side-by-side refrigerator or wooden hutch, lifting that beast into the back of a pickup truck (or, even worse, squeezing it into the backseat of a VW Bug) can be a major pain in the back—literally. Many buyers will come equipped to do the heavy lifting themselves, but some will either be unprepared or expect you to lend a hand. Depending on what types of items you sell, you may want to start working out now.

Cash Is King

Before a customer leaves with her purchase, she has to hand over payment. The vast majority of the time, that means dealing with cash—which isn't necessarily a bad thing.

Cash is good. When someone pays in cash, you don't have to pay any handling or processing fees; you get to keep the entire payment. And you know that because it's cash, it's good. Cash doesn't bounce.

On the other hand, you may not want to handle large bundles of cash. It's a good idea to make frequent bank deposits, so that you don't have a lot of cash sitting around your house. And hope that your bank doesn't question you about all those bills you're filtering through their system.

You'll also need to have some change around the house. Few buyers will bring payment in the exact amount of the purchase price; if your item sells for $14.95, be prepared to make change from a $20 bill—or maybe even a $50 or a $100. It's the closest you'll come to working a cash register at retail.

But what about PayPal or Google Checkout or other payment services that let you take credit card payments? While you *can* offer payment via credit card, most buyers won't take advantage of it—and many potential buyers might get spooked by the idea. They're used to buying from individuals and paying by cash; anything fancier than that might sound like a scam. So get comfortable with cash. You'll be seeing a lot of it.

We Don't Need No Stinking Tools

By now you know that craigslist doesn't offer any payment services. The site also doesn't offer any serious listing creation or management tools. If you have 100 listings running at one time, you have to keep track of them all yourself. And that can be a pain.

This takes us back to the very early days of the eBay marketplace. You old-timers in the audience can remember before eBay offered tools such as Turbo Lister and Sales Manager. You had to create each of your listings by hand (including hard-coding HTML) and manage your listings in an Excel spreadsheet or something similar. Well, eBay got better over time, but craigslist isn't there yet. The more items you list on craigslist, the more manual work you'll have to do. Maybe it's time to dust off all those old HTML templates and Excel spreadsheets?

In any case, manual listing management is the rule of the day. Do whatever you need to do to make your life easier, but don't expect much in the way of help from craigslist.

It's the Wild West

Don't expect much help from craigslist if you find yourself the victim of a scam. There's no seller protection plan on the craigslist site; if a customer slips you a bad check or makes off with something he shouldn't, you're on your own. Yes, you can contact your local authorities, but you'll still be out whatever it is you're out.

Let's face it: eBay has become quite civilized. While some old-school users might regret this development, it's made buying and selling a lot easier for all involved. craigslist, for better or for worse, is about where eBay was 10 years ago in terms of user safety and convenience. It'll get better, I'm sure, but it isn't there yet. For both buyers and sellers, craigslist is the Wild West of online marketplaces. Yee-haw!

Businesses Aren't Always Accepted

One last thing. If you're a seller who's spent years cultivating a professional business identity on eBay, you might as well throw all that in the trash if you move to craigslist. Online classifieds are for individuals selling individual items, not for businesses selling large inventories. Not only is the craigslist marketplace simply not set up for retail sales, the community is not receptive to businesses posting on the site. An overly commercial posting is apt to get flagged and deleted, just because it is what it is. The community does not like commercial postings.

That doesn't mean that businesses can't list on craigslist, just that you have to be subtle about it. There's no need to hide that you're a business, but you shouldn't advertise that fact. In fact, a listing shouldn't advertise your business, period; it should push the particular item that you're selling and maybe mention your business in passing.

The takeaway here is that you should focus on the particular items you're selling, not on your business as a whole—at least in your listings. In most instances, a customer is interested in one thing (the thing you're selling), not in the fact that you have other things for sale. So list one item per listing and post that listing to one local craigslist site (and in one category) only. Maybe, just maybe, you can show other items to the customer when she comes to purchase the first item, but don't push too hard. It's the difference between individual sales and retail sales, and craigslist is the former.

Making the Move

So what does it take to migrate your eBay sales to craigslist? Here's a general to-do list:

- Evaluate what you sell and ensure that it makes sense in the local craigslist marketplace.

- Use the same types of listing titles and descriptions as you do on eBay—there's not much to change here, other than the fact that you may want to manually code some text formatting with HTML.

- Use the same digital camera as you do for eBay to take product photos; photos are just as important on craigslist as they are on eBay.

---

tip

If you currently subscribe to a photo hosting service for your eBay listings, you can cancel your subscription; craigslist hosts up to four photos per listing for free.

- There's no best time to post a craigslist listing because there's no set end time, as with eBay auctions. That said, you probably want to schedule a time each day to post new listings—and avoid posting more than a half-dozen or so listings at a time so you don't look like a spammer.

- Develop some sort of mechanism to track your craigslist listings. An Excel spreadsheet works for many sellers.

- As part of your listing tracking process, plan on manually deleting listings for sold items; craigslist doesn't do this automatically.

- Plan on answering lots of emails about the items you're selling. Potential customers will ask a lot of questions, as well as need to schedule time to see and hopefully purchase what they're interested in.

- Don't bother with a subscription to PayPal or Google Checkout; craigslist purchases are almost exclusively in cash.

- Make sure you have some spare cash on hand, to make change for the cash sales you make.

- Throw out all the boxes and packing material you used for eBay sales; your craigslist customers will most likely pick up their purchases themselves.

- Schedule regular hours when you'll be home to show merchandise and make sales—or be flexible and arrange showings at the customers' request.

- For safety's sake, arrange for a friend or family member to be present when customers visit.

- Plan for frequent and immediate visits to the bank; you want to deposit the cash you collect quickly so that you don't have large sums sitting around the house.

As you can see, selling on craigslist is both less work and more work than selling on eBay. You don't have to bother with packing and shipping, but you do have to show your items in person and manually manage your listings. The compensation for doing any extra work is that you make more money on each item you sell because craigslist doesn't charge any fees. And you won't have to pay any PayPal fees, either, because your customers will be paying in cash. For many sellers, this is a good deal all the way around.

Blending craigslist with eBay

There's nothing that says you have to move 100% of your eBay business to craigslist. Many sellers have found that online classifieds can coexist quite nicely with online auctions—and, in fact, complement each other in many ways.

For some sellers, this means bifurcating their product mix and selling channels. Sell the smaller, more commodity products on eBay and sell the larger, local-pickup products on craigslist. It's often a pretty clean split, without a lot of spillover. Think of it this way: If you can ship it, sell it on eBay. If it has to be picked up, sell it on craigslist.

Some items can be sold on both marketplaces, although maybe with a slightly different spin. The small things you sell on eBay may be able to be bundled together into larger lots you can sell on craigslist. You may even be able to sell some larger items on eBay, as long as the shipping and handling doesn't become prohibitive.

In any instance, don't assume that moving to craigslist means you have to abandon eBay. It may be that you can actually increase your sales by selling on both marketplaces! ∎

10

Promoting Your craigslist Business

I'll tell you up front: There's not a lot you can do to drive viewers to
your craigslist listings. craigslist, like eBay to some degree, is
designed to let customers search for what they want—not to have
merchandise pushed at them. Potential buyers have to find your listings, which they do by using craigslist's search function.

The good part of this is that posting on craigslist is itself a form of
promotion; the craigslist site provides tremendous visibility for what
you're selling. The downside, of course, is that you're on a level
playing field with other craigslist sellers; there's not much you can
do to gain more visibility than your competitors.

Choosing the Right Community and Category

The first step in gaining visibility for your craigslist listings is to
make sure they're placed in the right place—both geographically
and categorically. Because most users search a particular locale and
category, if your listing is misplaced, it simply won't be found.

Remember, the craigslist site is actually a collection of local sites. So
if you're marketing to a particular city or location, make sure your
listing is placed on the site for that location. Because you can't post
the same listing in multiple locations, you have to choose carefully.

Equally important, know that most craigslist buyers browse the listings within a specific category rather than search for an item. If
your listing isn't in the category that potential customers are browsing, they won't see it. Choose your category carefully and then post
in that category.

Optimizing Your Listings for Search

Even though most customers browse craigslist, some do use the site's search feature to find items to purchase. That means you need to optimize your listings for search, just as you do on eBay.

---

tip

Optimizing your listings for search doesn't obviate the need to place your listings in the correct category because one of the offered search options is to search within a given category only. Likewise, a user's search query is directed at the contents of that user's local site only—not across the entire craigslist network of local sites.

---

craigslist's search function searches both the item's title and description, which means you can place keywords in either or both locations. It really doesn't matter whether the keyword is in the title or the description, or how the keyword is used because the site's search isn't that sophisticated. Basically, if someone includes a keyword in a query, any listing that includes that keyword will appear in the search results.

And those search results are not ranked by relevancy. Instead, craigslist groups search results by date, with the most recently posted listings displayed first. So, for example, if you're searching for an "aquarium" on December 15th, all listings posted on December 15th that include the word "aquarium" will be displayed first, then all listings posted on December 14th, then those posted on December 13th, and so on.

As I said, it's not a very sophisticated search algorithm, which means you don't have to get too sophisticated in your SEO. Just make sure your listing includes all the right keywords *somewhere*, and you're good to go.

Keeping Your Ad at the Top of the List

Your ultimate goal is to keep your listing near the top of the category in which you're posting. When someone browses this category, you want your listing to be among the first they see; you definitely don't want your listing to show up on the second or third or fourth page of listings.

Because craigslist always displays the newest listings first, both for browsers and searchers, the way to stay at the top of the results is to frequently delete and then repost older listings. Reposting a listing creates a new listing, and new listings always display at the top of the list. It's that simple—even if it is a bit of work on your part.

caution

Don't try to post a copy of a listing while the original is still live on the craigslist site. craigslist blocks listings that are identical to other current listings, thus effectively banning multiple copies of the same listing.

How often should you repost your listings? It depends on the volume of listings in that particular category. If your listing can stay on the first category page for a week, then delete and repost in a week (if the item hasn't sold). If your listing bounces off the first page in a day or less, than delete and repost daily. Your listing has to be fresh to stay on top.

craigslist Listings in Google Search Results?

In the early days of craigslist, you could get a double boost in visibility by having your craigslist listings show up in Google search results. A user searching Google for the item advertised in your craigslist listing would see that listing in Google's search results. That was a very good deal.

However, sometime in 2006, craigslist blocked Google and other search engines from spidering its network of websites. As a result, Google no longer sees the individual pages that comprise craigslist's large database of listings. That is not a good deal.

Why did craigslist block Google and its ilk—especially when the added exposure clearly helped drive more business to the site's sellers? It may be that Google's index included many old ads, and craigslist wanted to avoid widespread exposure for these expired listings. It may also be that craigslist wanted to be the sole destination site. Whatever the reason, don't expect your craigslist listings to show up in Google's search results; it's just not going to happen. ■

Selling on the Amazon Marketplace

11

The Amazon Marketplace: Is It Right for Your Business?

Now that you've read Part III, "Selling via craigslist Online Classifieds," you may be questioning whether craigslist is a viable alternative for established eBay sellers. And I'm with you; personally, I don't think craigslist is a good option for most businesses selling on eBay today (although the site does represent some opportunities for sellers of larger items and those wanting to establish a local presence).

If craigslist isn't for you, where can you move your eBay business? For many sellers, the most logical alternative is Amazon—the website, not the rain forest. Amazon has several well-thought-out merchant programs for sellers of all types and sizes, and it certainly offers up a large customer base. It may not be ideal for all sellers, but it's a marketplace worth considering.

Understanding the Amazon Marketplace

I don't have to introduce you to Amazon (www.amazon.com). Originally founded as an online bookseller (originally billed as the "Earth's biggest bookstore"), Amazon has since diversified into just about every type of merchandise imaginable. Today, Amazon is the world's largest online retailer, a major player in virtually every major product category. The site boasts 47 million unique visitors each month—just a tad shy of eBay's 49 million visitors. (Figure 11.1 shows Amazon's home page—a gateway to all kinds of shopping delights.)

FIGURE 11.1

Amazon.com, the world's largest online retailer.

What you might not know is that Amazon is also a marketplace for third-party sellers. If Amazon doesn't have a product in stock, it directs customers to other sellers offering that product. In fact, Amazon offers this shopping alternative on all its products; it lets third-party sellers compete with itself on its own product pages.

Emphasizing third-party competition might seem like a crazy thing for a retailer to do, but Amazon is crazy like a fox. You see, Amazon takes a cut of all third-party sales made from its site, and because it doesn't have to stock or ship any of the third-party merchandise itself, it makes just as big a profit from third-party sales as it does from sales of its own merchandise. Bottom line: Amazon is indifferent as to whether customers buy a product from Amazon itself or from its third-party sellers—so why not encourage those third-party sellers?

This is exactly what Amazon does, through its various merchant sales programs. Whether you have one item to sell or a thousand, Amazon has a program tailored to your needs. While you'll be competing with dozens if not hundreds of other sellers (as well as Amazon itself), it's a compelling opportunity for many sellers.

What the Buyers See

Third-party sellers first appear on Amazon's product pages, in the More Buying Choices box, as shown in Figure 11.2. When a customer clicks the link in this box, Amazon displays a list of sellers offering this product, like the one shown in Figure 11.3. Customers can filter this list to display either new or used items and can sort the list by either price or price plus shipping. Ordering takes place directly from this list, when the customer clicks the Add to Cart button next to a seller listing.

FIGURE 11.2

Amazon offers more buying choices from third-party sellers.

FIGURE 11.3

A typical list of third-party sellers offering a product for sale on the Amazon site.

For customers, ordering from a third-party seller is as seamless as buying directly from Amazon. Third-party purchases are added to your Amazon shopping cart, and you pay for the purchases through Amazon's normal checkout system. The only thing that's different is that the item ships from the third-party seller rather than from an Amazon warehouse; everything else (including buyer protection and returns) is integrated into the Amazon system.

The Many Ways to Sell on Amazon

How do you get your products listed on the Amazon marketplace? Amazon offers several different selling plans for different types of merchants.

The most basic plan, called the Amazon Marketplace, is targeted at individual low-volume sellers. This plan doesn't require any investment; there's no subscription fee to pay. Instead, you list items one at a time and pay a series of fees if and when the items sell. These fees include a commission (final value fee) of 6% to 20% of the selling price, depending on the type of item sold; a closing fee of $0.45 to $1.35 per item, again depending on the type of item sold; and a per-transaction fee of $0.99.

> **note**
>
> For non-media items, the closing fee is based on the weight of the item—for standard domestic shipping, a flat $0.45 plus $0.05 per pound. So, for example, if you sell an item that weighs 10 pounds, you pay a closing fee of $0.95.

If you're a higher-volume seller of books, CDs, DVDs, or videotapes, it's probably worth the expense to become an Amazon Pro Merchant. Pro Merchants pay a monthly subscription fee of $39.99, but in return get use of bulk posting and management tools and don't have to pay the $0.99 per-transaction fee. (Do the math; if you plan on selling more than 40 items a month, your costs are lower if you have a Pro Merchant subscription.)

If you sell something other than the media products just described, the Pro Merchant account is called a Selling on Amazon account and comes with the same pricing, fees, and services. The difference is that you can't sell media items with a Selling on Amazon account, while you can sell all types of items, media or non-media, with a Pro Merchant account. For that reason, I recommend that most sellers go the Pro Merchant route, as it works with all product categories.

Finally, for even larger sellers, Amazon lets you create your own e-commerce storefront. The Amazon WebStore program makes it easy to create your own online store, complete with credit card processing, shopping card, checkout system, and the like. You pay $59.99/month for an unlimited number of WebStores and pay Amazon a 7% commission for each item sold, with no other fees charged. Note, however, that items listed in your WebStore do not appear in Amazon's third-party product listings; this is solely a program to provide your own freestanding website.

All these programs may sound a little confusing; Table 11.1 should point you in the right direction.

Table 11.1 Amazon Selling Options

Monthly Sales Volume	Products Sold	Recommended Program	Monthly Subscription Fee	Commission	Closing Fee	Per-Transaction Fee
<40 items	Any	Amazon Marketplace	None	6%–20%	$0.45–$1.35	$0.99
40+ items	Books, CDs, DVDs, and non-media items	Pro Merchant	None	6%–20%	$0.45–$1.35 or weight based	None
40+ items	Non-media items only	Selling on Amazon	None	6%–20%	$0.45–$1.35 or weight based	None
Any	Any—on your own e-commerce website	Amazon WebStore	$59.99	7%	None	None
Any	Any—on your own e-commerce website plus on Amazon.com	Amazon WebStore plus Amazon.com	$99.98	7% for WebStore, 6% to 20% for Amazon Marketplace sales	None on WebStore, none on all Amazon Marketplace sales *except* software and video games ($1.35)	None

For most larger sellers who offer a diverse selection of merchandise, the Pro Merchant program is the best way to go. You may, however, want to get your toes wet by signing up as an individual seller first and see how it goes; if you like the results, you can upgrade to a Pro Merchant account.

Selling Individual Items on the Amazon Marketplace

Let's start with the easiest type of third-party selling—selling individual items via the Amazon Marketplace plan. It's so easy anyone can do it, with no upfront expense.

> **note**
>
> Learn more about selling individual items using Amazon Marketplace at
> www.amazon.com/gp/help/customer/display.html?ie=UTF8&nodeId=1161232.

Understanding the Amazon Marketplace

Amazon lets anyone sell anything—as long as Amazon offers that item for sale, of course. What you do is tag along with Amazon's normal product listing; you're listed among the third-party sellers also offering this product for sale.

You list an item by finding the product page for your item on the Amazon site and then clicking the Sell Yours Here button in the More Buying Choices box. You're then prompted to enter the condition of the item (New, Used, Refurbished, or Collectible) as well as your selling price and the quantity you have for sale. Amazon dictates the shipping terms and fees, although you can choose which of several available shipping methods to offer.

> **note**
>
> Learn more about listing your items on Amazon in Chapter 12, "Doing Business
> in the Amazon Marketplace."

The selling price you ask is totally up to you, although you need to be competitive with both other sellers and Amazon itself. For most items, you'll do best by listing a price below that of Amazon's, especially if it's a used item. The exception to that rule is if you're offering a collectible item; in fact, collectible items have to be priced *above* the manufacturer's suggested retail price (MSRP) or $10, whichever is higher.

The other stipulation that Amazon has is that the total price of your item (selling price plus shipping/handling) must be the same or below the price you offer in any other online sales channel. So if you're selling an item for $10 plus $4 shipping/handling ($14 total) in your eBay Store, you can't list it for $12 plus $2.98 shipping ($14.98 total) on Amazon.

As part of this process, Amazon automatically tacks the appropriate shipping/handling fee onto the customer's order. You, the seller, don't receive this fee; it goes straight to Amazon. Amazon does, however, reimburse you a shipping credit on each sale, per the schedule listed in Table 11.2.

Table 11.2 Amazon Shipping Credits

Product Category	Domestic Standard Shipping	Domestic Expedited Shipping	International Standard Shipping
CDs	$2.98	$5.19	$6.89
DVDs and videotapes	$2.98	$5.29	$12.29
Books	$3.99	$6.99	$12.49
Video games, computer software	$3.99	$6.99	N/A
Non-media items	$4.49 + $0.50/lb.	$6.49 + $0.99/lb.	N/A

When someone purchases your item, Amazon notifies you via email, and you're then expected to ship the item within 2 business days of the purchase. The buyer pays via Amazon's normal checkout system; funds are electronically deposited in your checking account every 14 days.

If your item doesn't sell within 60 days, Amazon closes the listing, and you pay nothing. You can, however, relist the item at that time.

Understanding Amazon's Fees

As noted previously, you pay nothing to list an item on the Amazon marketplace. You do pay, however, when the item sells. For individual items, you're assessed three different fees:

- Per-transaction fee of $0.99
- Commission, a percentage of the total price (selling price plus shipping/handling fee)
- Closing fee, a flat fee based on the type of item you're selling

First, the $0.99 per-transaction fee. Think of this as a handling fee of sorts—and know that this fee is waived if you upgrade to a Pro Merchant or Selling on Amazon subscription.

The second fee is the sales commission, Amazon's version of eBay's final value fee. The commission is calculated on the total price (selling price plus shipping/handling fee) and varies by product category, as noted in Table 11.3.

Table 11.3 Amazon Commission Rates

Product Category	Commission
Personal computers	6%
Camera and photo	8%
Consumer electronics	8%
Automotive parts and accessories	12%
Musical instruments	12%
Watches	13%
Apparel	15%
Books	15%
CDs/music	15%
Cell phones	15%
Computer software and games	15%
DVDs and videos (VHS)	15%
Amazon Kindle	15%
Baby products	15%
Health and personal care	15%
Home and garden	15%
Kitchen	15%
Office products	15%
Shoes and accessories	15%
Sporting goods	15%
Tools and hardware	15%
Toys and games	15%
Video games	15%
Beauty	20%
Grocery and gourmet food	20%
Jewelry	20%

The last fee is the closing fee, which I have trouble explaining—in part because it feels kind of arbitrary. I'm not really sure what it compares to, but you have to pay it nonetheless. As with the commission, the closing fee varies by category—but also by shipping method, for some reason. Unlike the commission, the closing fee is a flat fee, independent of the final selling price. (But for non-media items, that flat fee is actually based on the shipping weight.) Table 11.4 provides the details.

Table 11.4 Amazon Closing Fees

Product Category	Domestic Standard Shipping	Domestic Expedited Shipping	International Standard Shipping
CDs and music	$0.80	$0.80	$0.80
DVDs and videos (VHS)	$0.80	$0.80	$0.80
Books	$1.35	$1.35	$1.35
Video games	$1.35	$1.35	N/A
Computer software and games	$1.35	$1.35	N/A
All other products	$0.45 + $0.05/lb.	$0.65 + $0.10/lb.	N/A

All these fees are deducted from the funds collected from the buyer before the funds are deposited in your checking account.

By the way, there's one type of fee that is missing from this list. With Amazon, you don't have to pay any credit card processing or online payment fees. This is because all payments are handled through Amazon's built-in payment system; you don't have to use a third-party system, such as PayPal. So consider it a plus that you don't have to pay the 2.9% plus $0.30 per-transaction fee you pay to PayPal on most eBay sales; that's a big cost savings you get when you move to Amazon.

Selling as a Pro Merchant

If you move more than 40 items in an average month, you should subscribe to Amazon's Pro Merchant program. You pay $39.99 for this privilege but don't have to pay the standard $0.99 per-transaction fee. If you sell fewer than 40 items in a given month, you're better off paying the $0.99 per-item fee and not the $39.99 monthly fee; when you reach the 40-item level, the $39.99 fee is the cheaper way to go.

note

Learn more about Amazon's Pro Merchant program at www.amazon.com/gp/help/customer/display.html?ie=UTF8&nodeId=1161306.

The following are some of the other benefits of joining the Pro Merchant program:

- You can use Amazon's Inventory Loader program for bulk uploading of multiple listings
- You get access to reports that detail your current inventory, orders, and sales data

- You can maintain an unlimited number of listings in the Amazon marketplace.
- You can create an Amazon storefront that displays all your listings in a single place.

Commissions and closing fees for a Pro Merchant are identical to those for individual item sales, as detailed in Tables 11.3 and 11.4. The post-sale process is also identical.

---

tip

While the Pro Merchant program is tailored for sellers of selected media products—books, CDs, DVDs, and VHS videotapes—you can also sell non-media items under the program. For this reason, it's the program of choice for most high-volume sellers.

Selling on Amazon via Selling on Amazon

If you don't sell books, CDs, or DVDs and still move more than 40 items per month, Amazon recommends that you skip the Pro Merchant program and subscribe to the Selling on Amazon program instead. I'm not sure why; the two programs have the same cost, fee structure, and features. The only difference is that you *can't* sell media items through the Selling on Amazon program, while you can sell all types of items through the Pro Merchant program. In other words, Selling on Amazon is for non-media items only, while the Pro Merchant program lets you sell all types of items.

---

note

Learn more about the Selling on Amazon program at www.amazonservices.com.

Table 11.5 details what you can and can't sell via the Selling on Amazon program.

Note that to sell in some categories, you need prior approval. To request approval, go to www.amazonservices.com/content/sellers-contact-amazon.htm and provide the requested info.

Table 11.5 Selling on Amazon Program Categories

Categories Allowed	Categories Allowed with Prior Approval	Categories Not Allowed
Baby	Apparel	Books
Camera and Photo	Automotive	CDs and Music
Computer Software	Beauty	DVDs and Videos (VHS)
Electronics	Cell Phones and Accessories	Adult Toys
Grocery	Gourmet	Gift Cards and Gift Certificates
Health and Personal Care	Jewelry and Watches	
Home and Garden	Personal Computers	Guns and Ammunition
Musical Instruments	Shoes and Accessories	Magazines and Newspapers
Office Products	Toys and Games	Photo Processing
Sports and Outdoors		Prescription Medication
Tools and Hardware		Tobacco and Alcohol
Video Games		

Selling in an Amazon WebStore

If you want to establish your own online store, Amazon can help you out there, too. The Amazon WebStore program costs $59.99 a month and provides a complete e-commerce solution; it's actually a pretty good deal.

Know however, that items offered in your WebStore are *not* listed in Amazon's third-party seller listings, as with Amazon's other seller programs. You can, however, sign up to sell both in your WebStore and on the regular Amazon site for $99.98/month; your items are listed alongside those of other third-party sellers, and you pay standard Selling on Amazon fees for those sales.

> **note**
>
> Learn more about Amazon WebStore in Chapter 17, "Setting Up an E-Commerce Website."

Using Amazon to Fulfill Your Orders

Here's something else you can use Amazon for: to warehouse and ship your merchandise. And let's face it, after shipping millions of orders each year, Amazon is pretty good at the fulfillment thing.

The Fulfillment by Amazon program will distribute your inventory for sales you make on the Amazon site or for sales you make on other sites—including your own website. You send your inventory to Amazon, retain ownership of that inventory, but let Amazon handle all the warehousing and fulfillment. For a fee, of course.

---

note

Learn more about the Fulfillment by Amazon program at www.amazonservices.com/content/fulfillment-by-amazon.htm.

How It Works

The program is actually very simple. You start by sending your products—new or used, it doesn't matter—to any one of Amazon's twenty specified fulfillment centers. These are big climate-controlled warehouses that can store any type of product. You determine how much product you send and pay only for the storage you use.

If a customer buys one of your products from the Amazon marketplace, Amazon automatically picks, packs, and ships that product to the customer from your inventory. If you need to ship to a customer on another marketplace, you need only supply that information to Amazon and the order will be thusly shipped.

---

note

You use Amazon's Basic Fulfillment service to notify Amazon of sales from other channels. You can submit fulfillment requests using a simple web form, a flat file upload (for bulk requests), or, for larger merchants, direct website-to-website XML integration.

Understanding Fulfillment Pricing

To use Fulfillment by Amazon, you must first be a subscriber to the Selling on Amazon service. You are then charged an inventory storage fee for the items that Amazon is warehousing, as well as various fulfillment fees to pack and ship sold items.

Let's start with the inventory storage fee. This fee is based on the cubic feet of space taken up by your products. You're charged $0.45 per cubic foot per month for items stored from January through September; the rate goes up during the holiday season, to $0.60 per cubic foot per month.

Fulfillment fees for items sold through Amazon are calculated by adding together fees for order handling, picking and packing, and weight handling. Table 11.6 details these fees.

Table 11.6   Fulfillment Fees for Amazon Orders

Type of Fee	Media Items	Non-Media Items	Oversized Items
Order handling	$0	$1.00	$0
Pick & pack: Items priced under $25	$0.50	$0.75	$3.00
Pick & pack: Items priced over $25	$1.00	$1.00	$3.00
Weight handling	$0.40/lb.	$0.40/lb.	$0.40/lb.

note

For Amazon's purposes, media items include books, CDs, DVDs, videotapes, computer software, and video games. Any item (media or non-media) that is larger than 18" long x 14" wide x 8" high or that weighs 20 pounds or more is classified as an oversized item.

Items sold outside of Amazon are fulfilled via the Basic Fulfillment program. For these items, the total fee is calculated by adding together separate fees for picking and packing, shipping method, and shipping weight. Table 11.7 details these Basic Fulfillment fees.

Table 11.7   Basic Fulfillment Fees for Non-Amazon Orders

Type of Fee	Media Items	Non-Media Items	Oversized Items
Pick & pack	$0.60	$0.75	$3.00
Shipping method: Standard	$1.90	$4.75	$7.00
Shipping method: Expedited	$7.40	$7.75	$10.00
Shipping method: Priority	$14.40	$14.75	$17.00
Weight handling: 1-15 pounds	$0.45/lb.	$0.55/lb.	$1.50/lb.
Weight handling: each additional pound up to 70 pounds	$0.45/lb.	$0.70/lb.	$1.75/lb.
Weight handling: each additional pound up to 150 pounds	$0.45/lb.	$0.85/lb.	$2.00/lb.

note

Amazon also offers an online payment service that you can integrate into your own e-commerce website. Learn more in Chapter 19, "Choosing an Online Payment System."

The Pros and Cons of Selling on Amazon

Now that you know the different ways you can sell on Amazon, let's examine whether Amazon makes sense for your business. As with any other online marketplace, Amazon has plusses and minuses.

Selling on Amazon: Pros

First, the good things about selling on Amazon. These include the following:

- **Easy listing process.** Because you're uploading only product name/number and price, you don't have to create a detailed product listing—no description to write, no photos to shoot and upload, and so forth. It's a quick and easy process.

- **Exposure to large customer base.** When you sell items on the Amazon site, you get exposure to Amazon's 45 million or so monthly visitors. That's huge exposure, pretty much equal to what you get on the eBay site.

- **Relatively low fee structure.** We'll do the comparisons in a minute (in Chapter 13, "Migrating Your eBay Business to Amazon"), but for many types of products you pay less in fees than you do when selling on eBay. The lack of a PayPal-type fee is particularly appealing.

- **Ease of payment for customers.** For buyers, purchasing an item from an Amazon marketplace merchant is no different from purchasing from Amazon itself. They go through the same checkout process, which is as easy as pie—easier even than the eBay/PayPal checkout.

- **Optional use of fulfillment services.** If you need to, you can have Amazon warehouse, pack, and ship your items for you. That's a service that eBay doesn't offer.

- **Instant credibility via Amazon association.** If you're an unknown or little-known seller, you get instant credibility by selling on Amazon. In fact, many customers see you as part of Amazon. That's a great way to become a trusted seller virtually overnight.

Selling on Amazon is easy and relatively inexpensive, and it offers exposure to a large customer base. What's not to like about that?

Selling on Amazon: Cons

Well, it turns out there are several things not to like about selling on Amazon. These drawbacks include the following:

- **No individual seller identity.** When you sell on Amazon, it's tough to establish your own identity as a seller. Amazon customers tend to view you as just another purchasing option; they never see you separately, and you don't even have your own storefront. It's anonymous selling, which makes it difficult to establish a base of loyal customers.

- **Listings are displayed alongside those of competitors— which results in intense price competition.** So why do Amazon customers purchase from one merchant over another? Ninety-nine times out of a hundred, it's price and price alone. Because you have little or no seller identity, the only thing you have to offer is price— and if your price is higher than those of competing sellers, you won't get the sale.

- **Competing with Amazon itself.** Perhaps the biggest drawback to selling on Amazon is the fact that you're selling on Amazon—which means you're competing with Amazon. You're unlikely to grab sales away from Amazon unless (1) you have a significantly lower price or (2) Amazon happens to be out of stock on that particular item.

In other words, when you sell on the Amazon marketplace, all you get are the crumbs of the Amazon cake. You're essentially a parasite living off the Amazon host.

That said, many parasitic organisms survive—and thrive—in nature, and the same may be true for an Amazon-based business. Amazon presents a large and profitable marketplace, and in many categories, there's enough business to go around for both Amazon and its third-party sellers. Just recognize your place in the food chain and be sure you can live with that.

Other Online Marketplaces?

Amazon isn't the only online marketplace alternative to eBay. While Amazon is the major competitor, there are other online marketplaces—such as Etsy (www.etsy.com) and Wigix (www.wigix.com)—that are striving for a cut of your business.

These rival marketplaces typically trumpet lower seller fees but also deliver smaller customer bases. While it may be tempting to switch to one of these marketplaces, keep in mind the lower customer numbers. Do you want to sell to the 45 to 50 million people a month who frequent Amazon or eBay, or the 3 million who visit Etsy? For most sellers, it's an easy choice.

Bottom line: Amazon and eBay are the big dogs of online marketplaces, with craigslist joining the pack with its own unique way of doing things. While it's always possible that a new marketplace will rise in prominence to challenge the big dogs, today you probably want to go where the customers are—and that means Amazon or eBay. ■

12

Doing Business in the Amazon Marketplace

If you're convinced that selling on Amazon is in your future, just how do you do it? As you might suspect, Amazon makes it quite easy to start selling in the Amazon marketplace—at any level of sales.

This chapter starts by showing you how to list individual items for sale, which is a good place to start—it gets your feet wet and gives you a feel for how things work on Amazon. After you've achieved some level of success with individual item selling, you can move up to the Pro Merchant program and learn how to manage your sales with Amazon's Seller Central. It's all here!

Listing Individual Items in the Amazon Marketplace

Amazon encourages not only professional sellers but also casual sellers to offer their goods in the Amazon marketplace. So if you have only a thing or two to sell, it's relatively easy to post your listings and see what happens.

Listing Your First Item

Amazon Marketplace is Amazon's program for small sellers listing one item at a time. You can, of course, sell multiple items simultaneously; it's just that listing them is a series of singular activities.

Here's how it works: You start by finding Amazon's product page for the item you want to sell. That's right, you're piggybacking on Amazon's own product offerings—and can sell only items that Amazon itself is already selling. Such is the nature of this type of selling.

Once you've found the appropriate product page, click the Sell Yours Here button in the More Buying Choices box, as shown in Figure 12.1. When the next page appears, as shown in Figure 12.2, confirm that this is the item you want to sell and then pull down the Condition list and select the condition of the item you're selling: New, Used—Like New, Used—Very Good, Used—Good, Used—Acceptable, Collectible—Like New, Collectible—Very Good, Collectible—Good, or Collectible—Acceptable. If you want, you can add comments about the item's condition, which isn't a bad idea if you're selling a used or collectible item. When you're done, click the Continue button.

FIGURE 12.1

Getting started selling an individual item on Amazon.

FIGURE 12.2

Entering the condition of the item you're selling.

The next page, shown in Figure 12.3, is where you enter price and shipping information. Enter the price you're charging in the Enter Your Price box and the quantity you have for sale into the Quantity On-Hand box.

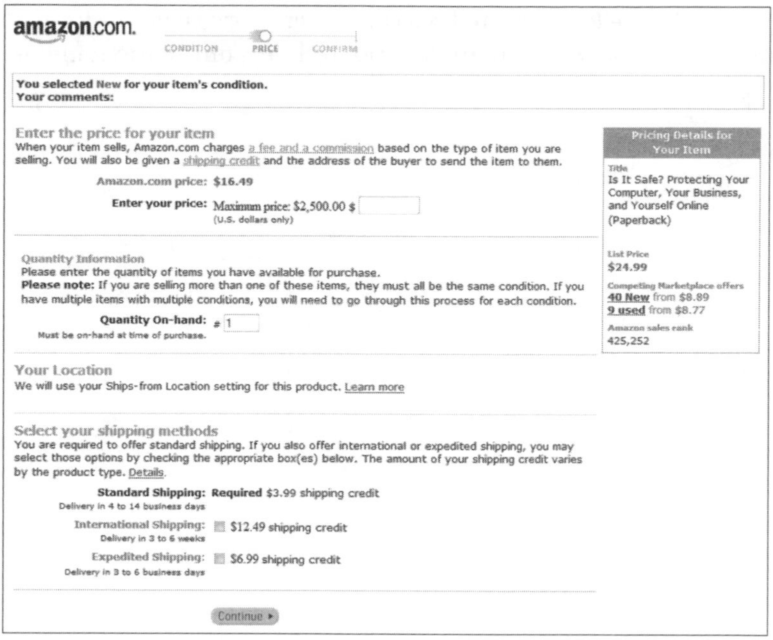

FIGURE 12.3

Entering price and shipping information.

> ## tip
>
> If you're selling a new item, you want to price it below Amazon's price, or you won't get any sales. Some sellers recommend checking out the lowest price offered by competing sellers (shown in the Pricing Details for Your Item box on the right) and then pricing your item a penny below the lowest price.

You then select how you want to ship the item. Amazon will require that you offer standard shipping; if you want to offer international or expedited shipping (for the shipping credits that Amazon dictates), check either or both of these options. Click the Continue button when you're done.

If you've not yet signed into your Amazon account, you're prompted to do so now. (Amazon requires that you have an account—a regular buyer's account—before you can start selling.) If you've never purchased anything from Amazon before in your entire life, you can use this opportunity to create a (free) account.

If this is your first time selling on Amazon, you're prompted to sign up to sell with Amazon. When you see the page shown in Figure 12.4, enter your desired seller name and select or enter a new credit card, which is used for authentication purposes and to charge any outstanding fees.

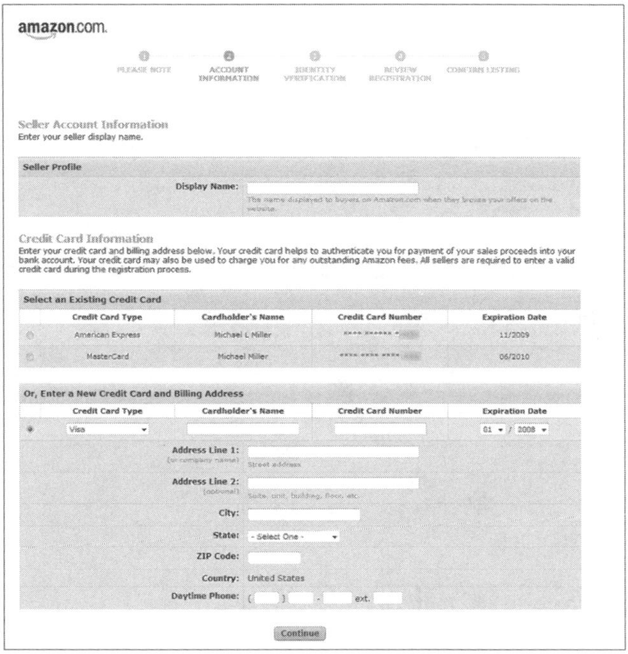

FIGURE 12.4

Signing up to sell on Amazon.

You're now asked to provide a phone number, again for verification purposes. Do so, and Amazon displays a one-time PIN. In a few minutes, you'll get an automated call from Amazon; enter the PIN when prompted. When you return to the Amazon website, check to confirm that you've read and accepted the terms of service and then click the Confirm button.

note

When listing subsequent items, you skip the account signup pages and go directly from the Enter the Price for Your Item page to the Review and Sell Your Product page.

Now you're shifted to the Review and Sell Your Product page, shown in Figure 12.5. If you like what you see, click the Submit Your Listing button, and your item is added to Amazon's database and made available for sale.

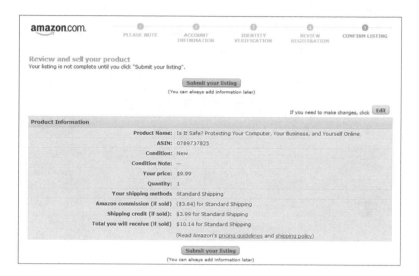

FIGURE 12.5

Submitting your item information.

Managing Your Account and Inventory

You manage your Amazon seller's account via the Seller Central tool, shown in Figure 12.6. You access this page at sellercentral.amazon.com. There's a lot here, so let's look at what you can do.

First, you can get a quick view of activity in your seller's account by observing the panels along the right side of the page. From top to bottom, you see the number of recent orders, your feedback ratings from buyers, and any claims made against your account by dissatisfied customers.

To perform other important operations, do the following:

- Add more items for sale by clicking the List Single Items link and working through the process previously described.

- View the items you currently have for sale by clicking the View Your Current Inventory link.

- View all the orders you've received by clicking the View Your Orders link.

- Search for a specific order by clicking the Search Orders link.

- View your payment status by clicking the View Your Payments Account link.

- View various sales and performance reports by clicking the links in the Reports section.

- Edit various settings for your Amazon seller's account by clicking the links in the Settings section.

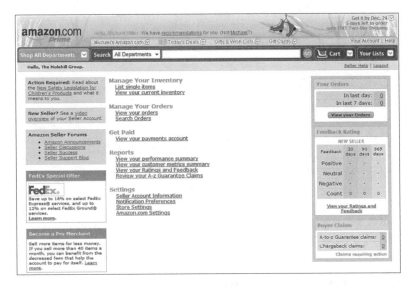

FIGURE 12.6

Managing your account with Seller Central.

I want to elaborate on one particular item: If you need to change any aspect of a current listing, start by clicking the View Your Current Inventory link. This displays the Your Marketplace Open Listings page, shown in Figure 12.7. This page displays all pertinent information about the items you currently have listed for sale. If you need to change the quantity available or an item's price, just enter new numbers into the appropriate boxes. To edit more about an item, click the Edit link; to delete a listing, check the Close Listing box. Click the Save Changes button when you're done.

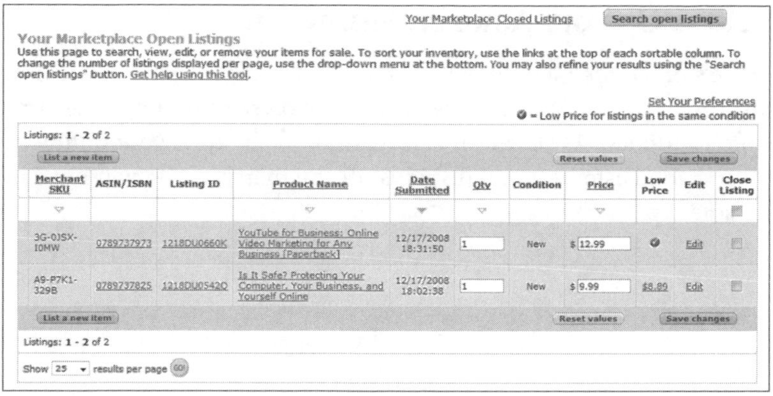

FIGURE 12.7

Editing item information.

Selling an Item

The next part of the selling process is one with which you're no doubt intimately familiar: You wait for someone to buy something.

If and when someone decides to purchase an item, Amazon notifies you via email. At this point, the order appears on your Manage Your Orders page (click the View Your Orders link on the Seller Central page).

tip

If this is your first order, follow the instructions in the notification email to submit your checking account number so you can be paid (electronically) for the sale.

Amazon expects you to ship the item within two business days of receiving this email. The best way to do this is to open the order on your Manage Your Orders page and follow the instructions to print a shipping label. Attach the label to your package and ship it out, using the shipping method you agreed upon when creating the listing.

Amazon automatically credits your account for the payment due but holds onto the funds for 14 days. At that point, the funds are deposited into your checking account via electronic transfer, and you can consider the transaction complete.

caution

Amazon is supposed to send you an email when a product sells but that doesn't always happen. I suggest you check your Seller Central page on a regular basis to make sure no orders fall between the cracks.

Setting Up Your Amazon Storefront

There's one more piece of business you want to take care of, even if you're just an occasional Amazon seller. This involves setting up your Amazon storefront page. As shown in Figure 12.8, this page is your online presence to Amazon customers and displays all the merchandise you have listed for sale.

FIGURE 12.8

A typical Amazon seller storefront page.

You configure your Amazon presence from the Seller Central page. Click the Store Settings link, and you see the Store Settings page, shown in Figure 12.9. From here you can do the following:

- View your public storefront page by clicking the View My Storefront link.

- Upload a logo for your storefront page by clicking the Add button in the Branding section.

- Enter or edit descriptive information and your customer service and returns policy by clicking the Edit button in the Info & Policies section.

- Change your home country or international shipping preferences by clicking the Edit button in the Shipping Settings section.

- Put your listings on temporary hold when you go on vacation by clicking the Edit button in the Vacation Settings section.

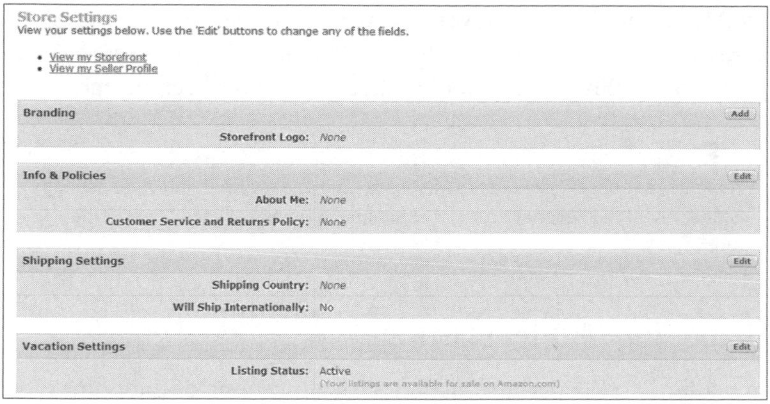

Store Settings
View your settings below. Use the 'Edit' buttons to change any of the fields.

- View my Storefront
- View my Seller Profile

Branding		Add
	Storefront Logo: *None*	

Info & Policies		Edit
	About Me: *None*	
	Customer Service and Returns Policy: *None*	

Shipping Settings		Edit
	Shipping Country: *None*	
	Will Ship Internationally: No	

Vacation Settings		Edit
	Listing Status: Active	
	(Your listings are available for sale on Amazon.com)	

FIGURE 12.9

Changing your storefront settings.

Moving to the Pro Merchant Program

Once you've gotten familiar with the process and are selling more than 40 items per month, you probably want to upgrade to either the Pro Merchant program or Selling on Amazon program. Both programs cost $39.99 per month, and both waive the $0.99 per-transaction fee you pay for individual item sales. Remember that the Selling on Amazon program is for non-media items only, so if you sell media items or a mix of media and non-media items, the Pro Merchant program is the better way to go. (Other than the merchandise restrictions, both programs have the same cost, fees, and features.)

---

note

Learn more about the Pro Merchant and Selling on Amazon programs in Chapter 11, "The Amazon Marketplace: Is It Right for Your Business?"

Upgrading to Pro Merchant Status

To upgrade to the Pro Merchant program, go to your Seller Central page and click the Seller Account Information link. When the next page appears, scroll down to the Selling Plan section. This should say that your current selling status is Individual; to move to the Pro Merchant plan, click the Upgrade button. When the next page appears, read all about the

Pro Merchant plan, and if you like what you see, click the Proceed to Upgrade button. When you return to the Seller Account Information page, your selling status should reflect your Pro Merchant membership.

---

tip

To remove yourself from the Pro Merchant plan and return to Individual selling status, revisit the Seller Account Information page and click the Downgrade button.

Uploading Multiple Listings

In addition to the per-transaction fee savings, one of the primary benefits of Pro Merchant status is the ability to upload multiple listings in bulk. You do this from your Seller Central page by clicking the Upload Multiple Items link. When you click this link, you see the Upload Multiple Items page, shown in Figure 12.10. From here, click the Download Template button, and you're presented with a list of available templates to download; click the Inventory Loader link. When prompted, opt to save the template file to your hard drive.

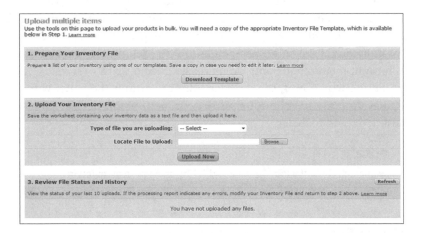

FIGURE 12.10

Amazon's Upload Multiple Items page.

This template is actually an Excel spreadsheet file named MyAmazonInventory.xls. As you can see in Figure 12.11, you enter each item you want to sell into a new row in the spreadsheet, filling in specific information about that item in each column, as specified. Table 12.1 details the information you need to provide.

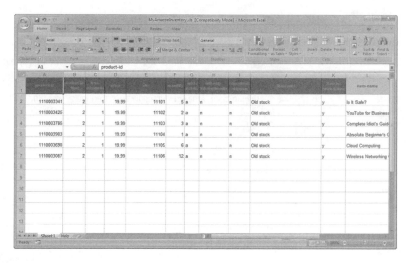

FIGURE 12.11

Entering multiple items into the Inventory Loader template.

Table 12.1 Required Information for the Inventory Loader Template

Column	Description
product-id	Enter the standard industry identifier for the product—UPC, ISBN, EAN, or Amazon's ASIN code
product-id-type	Enter the type of product identifier used in the previous column: 1=ASIN, 2=ISBN, 3=UPC, 4=EAN
item-condition	Enter the condition of the item, using a numeric code: 1=Used, Like New; 2=Used, Very Good; 3=Used, Good; 4=Used, Acceptable; 5=Collectible, Like New; 6=Collectible, Very Good; 7=Collectible, Good; 8=Collectible, Acceptable; 9=Used, Refurbished; 10=Refurbished (for specific categories); 11=New
Price	Enter your selling price for the item.
Sku	Enter your own identifying model number for the item.
Quantity	Enter the number of items you're listing for sale.
add-delete	To add this item to your Amazon inventory, enter a; to delete this item from your inventory, enter d.
will-ship-internationally	To ship internationally, enter 2 or y; to ship to the United States only, enter 1 or n.
expedited-shipping	To offer expedited shipping, enter y; to not offer expedited shipping, enter n.
item-note	Enter any text notes you want appearing beside your item in the Amazon listings.
item-is-marketplace	If you want your item to appear in Amazon marketplace listings, enter y; to not have your item appear in Amazon marketplace listings, enter n.
item-name	Leave this column blank; Amazon will supply information when the list is uploaded.

(continued)

Table 12.1   Continued

Column	Description
item-description	Leave this column blank; Amazon will supply information when the list is uploaded.
category1	Leave this column blank; Amazon will supply information when the list is uploaded.
image-url	Leave this column blank; Amazon will supply the correct image when the list is uploaded.
shipping-fee	No longer used; leave blank.
browse-path	No longer used; leave blank.
storefront-feature	No longer used; leave blank.
boldface	No longer used; leave blank.
asin1	No longer used; leave blank.
asin2	No longer used; leave blank.
asin3	No longer used; leave blank.

note

This template was originally designed in the era of Amazon's zShops merchant program, which has been discontinued for several years. Several of the columns were used in the zShops days but aren't used under Amazon's current seller programs.

When you're done adding data to your spreadsheet, select File, Save As. When the Save As dialog box appears, pull down the Save As Type list and select Text (Tab-delimited) (*.txt). Select a location for the file and then click Save.

Now you're ready to upload the saved file. Return to the Upload Multiple Items page and move to the Upload Your Inventory File section. Pull down the Type of File You're Uploading list and select Inventory Loader. A new Purge option now appears; check this option if you want this data to replace all your current listings, or leave the option unchecked if you want to add these items to your current listings.

Click the Browse button and locate the file you want to upload. Select the file and click the Upload Now button, and the new listings are added to the Amazon system.

Creating a Product Detail Page

There's one more notable benefit to having a Pro Merchant subscription: While individual sellers in the Amazon marketplace are limited to selling only items that Amazon itself sells, Pro Merchants can also sell items that only they offer—for which Amazon doesn't have product pages.

To sell a new product not currently found on the Amazon site, you create a new Product Detail Page, just like the ones Amazon displays for all the other products it sells. To create a Product Detail Page, go to your Seller Central page and click the Create a Product Detail Page link. When the next page appears, search or browse for the correct product category.

note

When you create a Product Detail Page, it becomes part of the Amazon catalog, and other sellers—including Amazon itself, at some future point—can sell their versions of the product from that page.

When the category is selected, you see the Product Identification page, shown in Figure 12.12. Here is where you enter details about what you're selling. This information is different for different product categories; enter the information you need to enter and then click the Continue button.

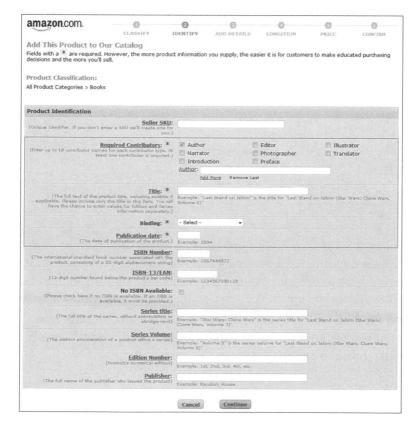

FIGURE 12.12

Entering product information for a new item in the Books category.

The next page prompts you to provide more product details, in particular a text description and product image. Do so and then click the Save & Continue button.

On the next page, shown in Figure 12.13, you confirm the information you just supplied and select the condition of the product. You can also supply a short note regarding the item's condition. Click the Continue button to proceed.

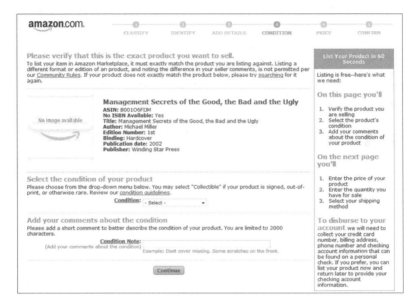

FIGURE 12.13

Describing the condition of the item.

The next page, shown in Figure 12.14, is where you enter the item's price and the quantity you have available. You also need to choose your shipping methods; Amazon requires that you offer Standard Shipping; all other options are optional. Click Continue when you're done.

On the final page, you confirm all the details for the listing. If you like what you see, click the Submit Your Listing button, and the item is added to the Amazon product database.

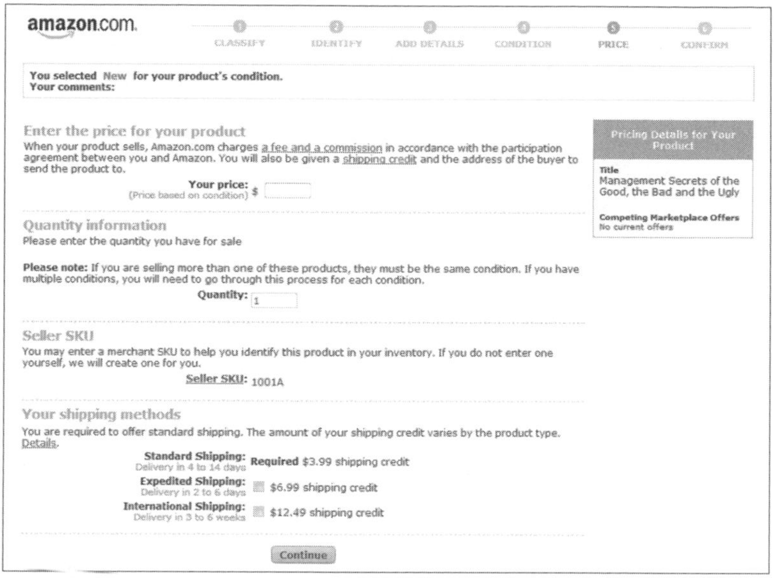

FIGURE 12.14
Entering the item's price and the quantity you have available.

Amazon's Other Programs and Promotions

As a seller in the Amazon marketplace, you get to take advantage of the various programs and promotions that customers love about Amazon.

For example, customers can use their Amazon gift certificates when ordering from you. The gift certificate is applied during the checkout process, and because you use Amazon's checkout, your customers can use their gift certificates to pay for your order. (You still get paid in real money, of course; Amazon handles the whole gift certificate transaction.)

If you use the Fulfillment by Amazon service, you can also have Amazon provide gift wrapping and gift messages to your customers. Because Amazon ships your merchandise from its warehouse, it treats your products just as it does its own when it comes to gift services. This is definitely an advantage to having Amazon do your fulfillment.

Bottom line: There are numerous advantages to selling on Amazon. Just about anything Amazon offers to its customers, you can also offer to yours. And that's a good thing! ■

13

Migrating Your eBay Business to Amazon

Selling on Amazon represents a real opportunity for many current eBay sellers. The Amazon marketplace is big and relatively easy to use; you may even find that you make a higher profit per sale by selling on Amazon than you do by selling on eBay.

If you think that the Amazon marketplace provides a viable channel for the products you sell, how do you make the move from eBay to Amazon? For most types of products, it's an easy transition, as you'll learn in this chapter.

Does Migrating to Amazon Make Sense?

Before we talk about migrating your business to Amazon, let's take a few moments to examine whether that migration makes sense for your business. Amazon can be a good place to sell products, but it isn't for every seller.

Comparing Fees

For many types of items, selling on Amazon is more profitable than selling on eBay—especially when you consider the lack of payment service fees. (You pay PayPal for accepting credit card payments on eBay; you don't pay Amazon for accepting credit card payments.)

Because many fees vary by product category, comparing fees between the two sites pretty much has to be on a product-by-product basis. That said, Table 13.1 compares a few different items selling on

Amazon and on eBay (for a fixed price). The comparison assumes membership in the Selling on Amazon program—which carries a $39.99/month fee that should be factored into your total numbers.

Table 13.1 Comparing Amazon and eBay Fees

Item	Listing Fee	Commission (Final Value Fee)	Closing Fee	PayPal Fee	Total Fees
$5 book (Amazon)	$0	$0.75	$1.35	$0	**$2.10**
$5 book (eBay)	$0.15	$0.75	$0	$0.45	**$1.25**
$10 DVD (Amazon)	$0	$1.50	$0.80	$0	**$2.30**
$10 DVD (eBay)	$0.15	$1.50	$0	$0.59	**$2.24**
$20 vintage toy (Amazon)	$0	$3.00	$0.55	$0	**$3.55**
$20 vintage toy (eBay)	$0.35	$2.40	$0	$0.88	**$3.63**
$25 jacket (Amazon)	$0	$3.75	$0.60	$0	**$4.35**
$25 jacket (eBay)	$0.35	$3.00	$0	$1.03	**$4.38**
$30 video game (Amazon)	$0	$4.50	$1.35	$0	**$5.85**
$30 video game (eBay)	$0.15	$4.50	$0	$1.17	**$5.82**
$50 DVD player (Amazon)	$0	$4.00	$0.80	$0	**$4.80**
$50 DVD player (eBay)	$0.35	$4.00	$0	$1.75	**$6.10**
$100 digital camera (Amazon)	$0	$8.00	$0.55	$0	**$8.55**
$100 digital camera (eBay)	$0.35	$6.25	$0	$3.20	**$9.80**
$200 necklace (Amazon)	$0	$40.00	$0.50	$0	**$40.50**
$200 necklace (eBay)	$0.35	$15.00	$0	$6.10	**$21.45**
$500 notebook computer (Amazon)	$0	$30.00	$1.20	$0	**$31.20**
$500 notebook computer (eBay)	$0.35	$19.88	$0	$14.80	**$35.03**

Here's the interesting conclusion: For most media items, your costs are a little higher on Amazon than on eBay—although, given Amazon's emphasis on books, CDs, and DVDs, you may get better sell-through on these items on Amazon compared to eBay. For many—but not all—non-media items, though, your costs are lower with Amazon.

So if you sell media items, you have an interesting choice. Your costs will be a little higher on Amazon, meaning you'll make less profit per item, but you may have greater sell-through on your inventory—and, as we'll discuss in a moment, you may even see a higher average sales price.

If you sell non-media items, you'll probably make more profit per item on Amazon than you do on eBay—although not necessarily. However, Amazon may not be as good a marketplace for some types of items, collectibles especially. Again, there may be a bit of a trade-off.

All of which points out the value of doing your own comparison, based on the actual costs for the products you sell. You may find that Amazon is a better deal—or you may not. It really depends on the items you sell and your average sales price per item.

tip

Don't forget to factor Amazon's $39.99 monthly subscription fee into your costs—even though that fee quickly gets absorbed if you're selling a lot of high-priced items.

Comparing Sales and Effort

Now for some real-world comparisons that go beyond the basic fees.

First, a fact I've already alluded to: Amazon is definitely a better place than eBay to sell media items these days. That's partly due to Amazon's traditional emphasis on books, CDs, and DVDs, I suspect; there simply are more people shopping for these items on Amazon than on eBay, which means you'll get a higher sell-through rate in these categories in the Amazon marketplace.

Many sellers also find that they actually get higher prices for items sold on Amazon versus the same items sold on eBay. I'm not sure why that is; perhaps eBay buyers are more bargain conscious, or maybe Amazon shoppers are more affluent. In any case, you may find that your average selling price increases when you move from eBay to Amazon.

tip

Getting a higher selling price on Amazon may not be true for all items. While Amazon is a great place to move commodity items, eBay remains the superior marketplace for most types of collectibles. You'll probably have to test your particular items to see what moves best where.

Along with higher prices come higher customer expectations. Amazon customers expect faster shipping and overall better performance than do eBay buyers. That's probably because eBayers are used to dealing with individual sellers, while Amazoners are used to dealing with Amazon—and with Amazon's top-notch customer service. That means you'll need to offer a decent returns policy and be prepared for some returns. While eBay buyers might be willing to talk with you and work something out, Amazon buyers are more likely to just return an item they don't like.

Of course, when comparing the two marketplaces, you also have to examine the effort it takes to get up and running and to manage your listings and sales. Here is where Amazon wins, hands down: No picture taking, no description writing, not much of anything else. Just list your inventory and wait for sales—that's all you have to do.

tip

Selling on Amazon is more like selling on Half.com than it is like selling on eBay proper. And here Amazon is a hands-down winner; it gets significantly more traffic than the low-visibility Half.com site. So if you like the way Half.com works but don't like your current results, moving to Amazon could be the solution.

Which Items Should You Migrate?

Knowing what we think we know about fees and sales rates and everything else, which items benefit most from exposure in the Amazon marketplace? Or, to put it another way, where can you get a better bang for your buck on Amazon than you can on eBay?

In my mind, the no-brainer merchandise includes those media items we've been talking about—books, CDs, and DVDs. eBay has lost a lot of traction in these categories, and many sellers have found their sales tanking. That's not the case on Amazon, where most third-party sellers see good sales on these items. And, not only are sell-through rates higher, but you often get a higher average sales price. This makes Amazon a good marketplace for items in these categories.

Categories for larger and more expensive items, however, are not as vibrant on Amazon. This may simply be due to the fact that Amazon itself is less competitive with these kinds of items; in any case, it's less evident that you'll do better, sales-wise, by switching from eBay to Amazon for products in these categories. Some small-scale testing may be in order before you make a wholesale switch.

There are other types of products that are just better suited for eBay—and, in particular, eBay's online auction format—than for fixed-price selling in the Amazon marketplace. This is certainly the case with collectibles and antiques, where their real value comes out when multiple collectors are able to bid up the price. And, let's face it, few customers come to Amazon looking for vintage items; that's what eBay is known for.

For the same reason, you may have some difficulty selling some types of used merchandise. While some Amazon customers appreciate the option of purchasing a used item at a discounted price, Amazon may not be the first choice for shoppers looking for used items. This is one that varies by category, so again, testing may be in order.

Bottom line: Don't expect Amazon to outperform eBay in every category. It pays to test the waters with a few items at a time and see what happens. And when you evaluate your results, make sure you look at the total profit generated, not just sell-through rates; you could end up making more money by selling fewer items, if the fee structure is right.

Evolving Your Business Model

Moving even part of your eBay business to Amazon requires changing the way you do things, to some degree. Let's look at what's different when selling on Amazon.

First, you have to get used to not creating item listings. Unless you're selling a product that is not currently in the Amazon database (such as rare or handcrafted items), you'll be tagging along on Amazon's existing product pages. That means that you don't have to write a product description, shoot and upload product photos, and the like. That's a lot of time savings, especially if you have a large inventory.

Correspondingly, you also have to get used to not having a true retail presence on the Amazon site. It's difficult if not impossible to establish a brand identity for your business; most sales are made because of price, not because of retailer identification. While it's true that you need to provide exemplary service and keep up your customer feedback rating, this is just part of the price of admission; it doesn't provide you with a competitive advantage at all.

So what you're doing on Amazon is a bit different from what you're used to doing on eBay. Instead of actively selling each individual item, you're letting Amazon do the selling; you're just providing Amazon with inventory listings. You have to make sure your pricing is competitive, of course, but it's a different ballgame than the eBay model.

Obviously, the Amazon ballgame is a little less labor intensive than listing on eBay—at least on the front end. After a sale has been made, it's pretty much the same game; you print an invoice and a packing slip, pack the item, and ship it out. You do have to learn how to work with Amazon's fixed shipping costs and shipping rebates and the like, which is a little more complicated than the eBay model, but once you get the hang of it, it's not so bad. In fact, it may even be balanced out by the fact that you don't have to do all that PayPal work that you have to do with eBay. Amazon's checkout and payment process is smooth as silk and almost labor free for most sellers.

The final difference between eBay and Amazon has to do with how fast you can collect your funds. Most sellers get their eBay/PayPal funds within 3 to 5 days of closing a transaction, while you're looking at 14 days before being paid from Amazon. If you're continually cash strapped, this may be a big issue. For most of us, though, it's simply a matter of budgeting the longer time period.

For most sellers, then, there are some changes you have to make in the way you do things—but none are too drastic. In fact, you might find that selling on Amazon is less time intensive than selling on eBay, which is a good thing.

Making the Move

When it's time to make the move to Amazon, my advice is to start slowly until you get the hang of things. Don't invest in the Pro Merchant account just yet; list a few items on the site for sale and see what happens. Make a few sales and see how you handle the end-of-sale process. See if you can ship items as fast as Amazon requires and make sure you can live with the 14-day payment period. In other words, take your time getting used to the Amazon way of doing things.

Once you're convinced that you can make a go of it on Amazon, you should upgrade to a Pro Merchant account. Learn to use Amazon's Inventory Loader tool so that you can list multiple items in bulk. And always, always do your research to make sure you're price competitive with other sellers—and with Amazon itself.

As noted, Amazon is a great place to sell inventory that has a lot of individual SKUs, such as books, CDs, and DVDs. If you have a 1,000-item inventory, plug it all into that Inventory Loader spreadsheet and get your items out there for Amazon customers to see. You can't sell until your inventory—all of it—is listed.

Then make sure you stay on top of your sales. Monitor your email for item sold notices and visit your Seller Central page at least daily. Amazon is quite serious about its sellers satisfying its customers with prompt shipping; you can't pile up your items to ship just one day a week, as some eBay sellers are known to do. You're going to have to ship every day of the week, which may mean more trips to the post office. But it's what Amazon requires and thus becomes part of your new business model.

Finally, take advantage of Amazon's various reports and data feeds. You need to analyze your Amazon performance—not just unit sales but also the net profit you generate. You may find that Amazon is less rosy than it appears at first, but you'll discover this only if you keep on top of your sales and profits. If your Amazon profits disappoint, you'll need to come up with an alternative strategy. But that's just good business—and Amazon rewards good business. After all, Amazon got to be the number-one online retailer by doing everything by the book. It expects the same from its third-party sellers.

Blending Amazon with eBay

Many sellers find that it's possible to build a business that incorporates the best of both the eBay and Amazon marketplaces. You're not, after all, limited to selling on only one site. You can move some items on eBay and other items on Amazon, and neither site is going to complain.

This works best when the merchandise you sell on one site is distinct from those items you sell on the other. Sell small media items on Amazon, for example, and move your larger, more expensive items on eBay. Or sell only new items on Amazon and vintage and collectible items on eBay. You get the idea.

Where you run into potential problems is when you choose to sell the same items on both sites. And by the same items, I mean literally the same items—not just the same SKUs, but rather the same physical items. You have one *Best of Kenny Loggins* CD, for example, and you list it on both Amazon and eBay. That can be problematic.

We'll discuss the challenges of selling in multiple marketplaces in Chapter 22, "Selling in Multiple Channels." For now, recognize that you face a significant inventory management challenge if you try to sell one item in two places. It behooves you to keep up with your inventory listings; if you have an item listed both on Amazon and on eBay, and you make an eBay sale, you better delete that item from your Amazon inventory ASAP. Otherwise, you might have an Amazon customer purchasing an item that no longer exists—which is not good business. ■

14

Promoting Your Amazon Business

Selling on the Amazon marketplace is a lot like selling on eBay's Half.com. Your business identity takes a backseat to the items you sell and the price you sell them for.

The good thing about selling on Amazon is that you don't have to do a thing to drive customers to your listings; Amazon does all that work for you. If a customer is looking for a particular product, Amazon makes sure she finds it. It's what happens next that you can affect—whether a customer clicks through and purchases the item from you, from a competing third-party seller, or from Amazon itself.

Therefore, you don't have to do much of anything to promote your listings on Amazon. It's not like eBay, where you have full listings to work with; on Amazon, your listing consists only of the condition of the item, your price, and your business name and feedback. And of those items, the most important one is probably the price.

Keeping Your Listings Competitive

You don't drive customers to your Amazon item listings; Amazon does that. Or rather, Amazon drives customers to its own product pages. Most customers purchase directly from the product page, from Amazon. But some click through the More Buying Options link to see that product offered by other sellers. It's here that you make your first contact with the customer.

By default, the More Buying Choices page lists sellers offering an item by price, with the lowest-priced items first. If you have the lowest price on an item, your listing appears at the top of the page; if you don't have the lowest price, your listing appears lower on the page or perhaps on a second or third page of results.

As you can see, the emphasis here is on price—and the reason most customers buy from third-party sellers instead of Amazon is also price. A customer is unlikely to purchase from a relatively unknown seller if Amazon is selling the same item for a lower price. And when choosing between third-party sellers, the one with the lowest price almost always wins.

The lesson here is simple: If you want to sell your items on Amazon, your price has to be competitive. Competitive might mean having the lowest price, or perhaps the second- or third-lowest price. But you have to be close, and it's best if you're the cheapest on the list. In the Amazon marketplace, price-competitive sellers win; higher-priced sellers don't sell their products.

Competing on Feedback

The lowest-priced seller doesn't always get the sale. Sometimes customers choose a competitive seller who has a better feedback rating.

Just as eBay lets buyers rank sellers via a feedback system, so does Amazon. Amazon ranks sellers using a five-star system—the higher the number of stars, the better. The stars are also expressed as a percentage, where, again, the higher percentage, the better.

Customers give a seller anywhere from zero to five stars. They can also opt to leave detailed comments about the seller. These comments are often useful to other customers who want to know more about what a seller does right or wrong.

To view a seller's detailed feedback rating, a customer need only click the XX% Positive link next to the seller name on any More Buying Choices page. The page shown in Figure 14.1 appears. The box on the upper left details the feedback rating as a percentage, for transactions made in the past 30 days, 90 days, 365 days, and lifetime of the seller. The most recent feedback comments are listed below this table; additional comments can be read by selecting the Feedback tab. The rest of the page contains information about the seller's return policy, shipping rates, and the like.

FIGURE 14.1

A typical feedback page for a typical Amazon merchant.

Here's where maintaining a high feedback rating is important: When a customer faces a choice between two merchants with similar prices on a product, the one with the higher feedback rating often gets the sale. For example, Figure 14.2 shows a Bob Dylan CD boxed set priced at $20.58 from one merchant and at $20.60 from another. That's not much of a price difference, and the customer may be tempted to simply buy from the lowest-price seller. But the seller with the lower price has a feedback rating of 89% positive, while the other seller has a 98% positive rating. Many customers will pay the extra $0.02 to buy from the merchant with the significantly better feedback rating.

FIGURE 14.2

Two sellers with significantly different feedback ratings.

So that's why it's important to keep your feedback rating up—which you do by providing superior customer service. Make sure you pack safely and ship promptly, and answer any customer questions or complaints quickly and effectively. Happy customers will leave you higher feedback, and higher feedback ensures more sales.

Placing Product Ads on the Amazon Site

There is really little point in advertising your Amazon product listings. That's because Amazon does all the necessary work to get customers to the appropriate product page; you're just along for the ride. And even if you did bring more traffic to a product page, you'd also be bringing more traffic to your competitors, as all sellers share the same More Buying Choices page.

That said, Amazon does offer a pay-per-click (PPC) advertising program that you can use to drive traffic to your own e-commerce website. Amazon's PPC advertising program, called Product Ads, lets you place clickable text ads, like the one in Figure 14.3, on Amazon's product pages and product search pages.

FIGURE 14.3

A typical product ad on an Amazon product page.

> **note**
>
> Learn more about creating your own online store in Chapter 15, "Establishing Your Own Website: Is It Right for Your Business?"

Product Ads works like Google's AdWords and other PPC programs. In essence, you "purchase" a keyword, and your ad appears on pages that feature that keyword. In Amazon's case, the keyword is actually a product, and your ad appears on that product page. You pay nothing for this placement; instead, you pay if and when a customer clicks the ad to visit your website.

note

Amazon's PPC and display ads (see the next section) are for sellers with their own e-commerce websites, not for sellers with listings in the regular Amazon marketplace.

How much you pay for a keyword is totally up to you. You select the maximum amount you want to pay for a click, as well as your daily advertising budget. Amazon will never charge more than your maximum cost-per-click (CPC) rate and will never exceed your daily budget. That said, the average CPC varies by category. For example, keywords in the Apparel and Accessories category typically run from $0.30–$0.50, while keywords in the Computers and Peripherals category run from $0.55–$1.00. Check with Amazon for keyword ranges before you make your bids.

When you sign up for the program, you upload the catalog of items you're selling and set your desired CPC bid for each item. Amazon then creates a product ad for each item in your catalog. When an interested customer clicks the Visit This Site button in your ad, they're taken to your own website, where you can (hopefully) make the sale. At the same time, Amazon charges you for that click at the rate you previously specified.

note

To learn more or to sign up for Product Ads on Amazon, go to www.amazonservices.com/content/product-ads-on-amazon.htm.

Advertising Your Business with a Display Ad

In addition to offering the Product Ads program, Amazon accepts display advertising on its site. Display advertising, as you might suspect, is significantly more expensive than PPC advertising, and as such it is typically done by larger companies.

Display ads can be purchased in a variety of sizes, called *ad units*. Ad units range from a 300 × 250 pixel "medium rectangle" to a 300 × 600 "half page" to a 900 × 45 "site stripe" that displays down the side of a page. (Figure 14.4 shows a medium rectangle ad.)

FIGURE 14.4

A display ad on the Amazon site.

note

You can learn more about Amazon's display ad program at www.amazon.com/advertising/, or you contact an account executive at adtraffice@amazon.com.

Promotion on Amazon: No Worries

Amazon is much different from eBay in many ways, but here's one similarity: You don't need to spend much time or money promoting your products on either site. That's because the sites themselves are the promotion.

Here's what I mean: If you have your own e-commerce website, nobody knows about it. (At least at first…) To sell anything, you have to find some way to drive traffic to the site, which is where promotion comes in. If you don't promote your site, nobody visits, and nobody buys anything.

When you list on Amazon or eBay, however, you get to take advantage of each site's built-in traffic—those 40-some-million people who visit every month. These people visit Amazon or eBay with the express intent of shopping; they're prequalified. Once they're on the site, they search for what they're looking for, and hopefully your listing comes up in the search results. On eBay, the most you have to do is optimize your listing for search, in order to display near the top of those search results.

There's even less to do on Amazon because you're not creating your own item listings. A customer searches for a particular product, and that brings up Amazon's product page, already populated with item details and pictures and such. There's no competing for search result placement because there are no separate listings by seller.

Where you compete is when a customer clicks to see what other Amazon marketplace sellers offer the item. At this point, you're competing primarily on price—and, in some instances, on feedback rating. There's nothing you have to do (or can do) to drive customers to this page or to your listing; they get there on their own and then make their choices.

This gets us back to the fact that listing on Amazon itself is your promotion. This promotion isn't free; it's part of why you pay commissions and other fees to Amazon. Those fees are part of your advertising and promotion cost. You're paying Amazon for all the traffic it brings to the table. For most sellers, that's money well spent. ■

V

Selling on Your Own Website

15

Establishing Your Own Website: Is It Right for Your Business?

When it comes to moving beyond eBay, the holy grail for many sellers is running their own e-commerce website. For small sellers, this is what Selling Online 2.0 is all about—controlling your own online sales from start to finish, with no reliance at all on eBay, craigslist, Amazon, or any other online marketplace.

The grass, however, is not always greener. Creating and maintaining your own online store takes a lot of time and money. While you may be able to generate more profit per sale (by not paying any marketplace fees), you also have expenses that you don't have on eBay—and you also need to promote your site to attract potential customers.

The big question then, is whether establishing your own website is right for *your* business. Read on and then make up your mind.

Building an Online Store—What's Involved?

Selling on eBay or Amazon is one thing. Selling on your own website is quite another. Just what is involved with building your own e-commerce site—and how much does it cost?

The Components of an E-Commerce Website

When you sell on eBay or Amazon, you're taking advantage of everything these sites offer—the existing infrastructure, the built-in customer traffic, the fully functioning checkout and payment services, you name it. When you launch your own e-commerce website, you have to build all this from scratch. It isn't easy, but the end result is *your* online store, one that looks and functions just the way you want it.

What constitutes an online store? To successfully sell merchandise to customers online, every web storefront needs the following components:

- **Site hosting.** First things first: Your website needs a home. That means contracting with a website hosting service, to provide storage space and bandwidth. Note that some website hosting services provide services specific to online retailers, offering various selling-related features, such as checkout and payment services—for a price, of course.

- **Domain name registration.** Your website also needs a name. You'll want to register a unique domain name for your site, one that reflects the name and nature of your business. You'll then want to provide that domain name to your site hosting service, so that your site and your name are connected.

---

tip

Most website hosting services also provide domain name registration, so you can do all this front-end work in a single stop.

- **Home page/gateway page.** Every website needs a home page, but the home page for a retailer's site is especially important. Your home page must not only promote your business but also profile key products. The page can't be static, either; you need to refresh the featured products on a fairly constant basis so that returning customers always see new deals when they visit. It's easiest if you use some sort of template for the home page design, into which you can easily place the products you're currently promoting. This argues for some sort of home page automation, as opposed to you manually recoding the page each time you change featured products.

- **Navigation and search.** While you may sell some of the products you feature on your site's home page, it's more likely that customers are going to either browse or search for the precise products that they're looking for. That means you need to organize your site in a logical fashion (by product categories, most likely) and then establish an easy-to-use navigation system that can be accessed from all pages. You'll probably do this via a sidebar or drop-down menu. You'll also need to integrate a search function across your entire site, with a search box at the top of each page that visitors can use to search for specific items.

- **Product pages.** Every product you have for sale should have its own page on your site. That page should be kind of like an eBay product listing, except more professional looking. You need to include one or more product photos, a detailed description, all relevant dimensions and sizes and colors and such, as well as any other information that a customer might need to place an informed order.

- **Customer reviews.** Many sites let their customers rate and review the products they sell. This provides another key information point for shoppers, and it provides unique feedback to the seller. While customer reviews aren't a necessity, many customers are coming to expect this feature.

- **Inventory/listing management.** You don't want to manually update your site's product pages whenever you sell an item. Instead, you want some sort of automatic inventory and listing management system, so that when a product sale occurs, both your inventory database and your product pages update automatically.

- **Shopping cart and checkout system.** When a customer purchases a product, that product needs to go into the customer's shopping cart—the online equivalent of a physical shopping cart. The cart holds multiple purchases and then feeds into your site's checkout system, which then interfaces with your online payment service.

- **Payment service.** If you sell something, you need to get paid. That means, for all practical purposes, accepting credit card payments. While you can try to establish a merchant credit card processing account, more likely you'll sign up with one of the major online payment services—PayPal, Google Checkout, or Checkout by Amazon. The payment service you choose should integrate with your own checkout system so that customers have a seamless purchasing experience.

- **Customer management.** Your customers will want to contact you with questions or issues. You'll want to contact your customers with purchase confirmation and shipping information. It's best if you can automate all these customer communications.

In addition to all these necessary components, you'll also need to promote your website; unlike with eBay and Amazon, you won't automatically have 40-plus-million potential customers stopping by your first month in business. That means an investment—in both time and money—in various promotional activities, from pay-per-click advertising to email marketing to whatever works for you.

Bottom line: You need to do a lot of work to get an online store up and running—and even more work to keep it running on a daily basis. You're used to eBay or Amazon providing most of these pieces and parts and doing most of the heavy lifting for you. When you launch your own web store, however, you're on your own; you have to do everything eBay and Amazon do, and then some.

Different Ways to Build a Store

How do you go about building your own online store? There are a few different approaches.

First, you can literally build your site from scratch. You start with a blank page and go from there, designing your home page and product pages, plugging in navigation and search modules, integrating a shopping cart and checkout, and signing up for an online payment service. If you're an HTML master with a lot of time on your hands, you can do this yourself; otherwise, you'll probably hire a website design firm to do most of the work for you.

Hiring a contractor to design your website can save you time but cost you more money. Let's face it, hiring out website design is an expensive proposition. Although you get a site that is as custom-designed as possible, you (and your designer) end up reinventing a lot of wheels along the way.

For many sellers, a better approach is to go with a prepackaged storefront. When you contract with one of these services, you essentially plug your logo and product inventory into a predesigned store template. Everything you need is provided—automatically generated product pages, inventory and customer management, shopping cart and checkout system, and online payment service. With this kind of service, you can get your site up and running quite quickly, with a minimum amount of effort. The downside of this approach is that you pay for it—and keep on paying for it. Most of these services not only charge you an upfront cost (typically quite low) but also an ongoing commission on everything you sell. In other words, you pay for the convenience of this type of prepackaged storefront.

Between these extremes is a sort of middle ground. Many third-party services provide the needed features for a quality online storefront, so you don't have to do the coding from scratch—and you don't have to cede a portion of your ongoing profits to a service. You simply pick and choose the modules and services you need and plug them into your site. You can find inventory management modules, shopping cart and checkout modules, and the like. (And, of course, it's relatively easy to connect any checkout module with an online payment service.) Depending on the provider(s) you use, you may pay a larger upfront cost with no ongoing fees, or you may "rent" the services via a monthly or yearly subscription.

---

note

Learn more about the various ways to build an online store in Chapter 17, "Setting Up an E-Commerce Website."

How Much Does It Cost?

How much you have to invest in an online store depends on the size and nature of the store, as well as the approach you take to constructing the site. That said, I can provide some general cost guidelines.

If you build your site yourself, you don't have any upfront costs except for your domain registration, which can be as little as $10 or so for the first year. You do, of course, have monthly site-hosting fees; while some free site-hosting services exist, you'll probably spend anywhere from $10 to $50 a month for professional hosting.

More likely, you'll contract out the site design, which costs real money. Depending on the size of the job and the firm you choose, expect to spend several thousand dollars at a minimum, perhaps $10,000 or more. Most design firms charge by the hour, so you'll want to work through an estimate beforehand. Here is where it pays to shop your needs to several design firms and go with the one that not only offers the best price but also is best attuned to your needs.

The prepackaged storefront route offers perhaps the lowest initial investment—often with *zero* upfront costs. For example, an Amazon WebStore can be had for no money upfront. Instead, you pay $59.99 per month, plus a 7% commission on all sales you make. That's a low-cost way to get into the market, although you have to share your future profits with the storefront host.

If you decide to forgo the prepackaged storefront and instead purchase or subscribe to seller services from third-party providers, your costs are dependent on the services you need, the size of your business, and the provider itself. Some online shopping modules go for as little as $50 per month, while larger retailers may end up spending $1,000 per month or more.

Then, of course, there are services that charge a fee per transaction. Most notable are the online payment services you need to process credit card transactions. Whether you go with PayPal or one of its competitors, expect to pay anywhere from 2% to 3% of each transaction paid for via credit card, perhaps with a $0.30 or so flat fee per transaction as well.

So, how much does it cost to create your online storefront? As little as nothing or as much as five figures upfront, plus (perhaps) monthly fees and transaction fees and commissions. So if you think that establishing your own storefront frees you from all those niggling fees that eBay charges, think again; nothing is free.

Pros and Cons of Running Your Own Website

When you're slave to the eBay marketplace, running your own online store certainly looks attractive. But is the grass really greener on the other side of the fence? Not always, as you'll see.

Pros of Running Your Own Online Store

There are many benefits to being your own boss, which is essentially what you get when you run your own online store. Here are some of the good points:

- **You create your own business identity.** This is a big one. When you sell on the eBay marketplace, you're often viewed as just another eBay seller, no matter how hard you try to establish your own identity. It's even worse on Amazon, where you're just an anonymous face behind a simple product listing. But when you create your own website, you're not part of any marketplace—you're not an eBay seller or an Amazon seller, you are your own business. You can establish your brand however you like, and you can build your own business on your own name.

- **You pay fewer transaction fees.** Well, at least you might, depending on how you do things. eBay sellers complain about being nickel-and-dimed to death with eBay's various listing and final value fees—not to mention the ever-present PayPal fees. So it's a quarter here and a few percent there, but it adds up fast. It's tempting to think that running your own website means escaping all those annoying and costly fees, and that's mostly true. While you can't fully escape all fees (you'll still have to pay a fee for credit card transactions), it's likely you can at least reduce the per-transaction fees you pay.

- **You're not beholden to a marketplace's rules.** Many sellers chafe under eBay's various rules and regulations. You can't do this, you have to do that; you're not really in charge of your business— eBay is. Well, when you're running your own website, you're not beholden to anyone but yourself. You make up the rules, you run your business as you please. You're finally free!

- **You're not held hostage by a marketplace's feedback policy.** Here's something else that many eBay sellers find particularly annoying: A few cranky customers can completely ruin your feed-back rating and perhaps force eBay to drop you from the market-place. (And you can't even retaliate with negative feedback of your own!) Well, moving to your own website means that you deal with dissatisfied customers on your own terms, not on theirs. (Or on eBay's, for that matter.)

In general, moving from eBay to your own online store means freedom— freedom from rules and regulations, freedom from control, freedom from fees. There is a price to pay for this freedom, however—which is one of the cons we discuss next.

Cons of Running Your Own Online Store

If running your own e-commerce website was so great, everybody would be doing it—but everybody isn't. All the benefits of running your own online store are counterbalanced by a few negatives, including the following:

- **It's a lot of effort—both upfront and on an ongoing basis.** When you run your own online store, you have to do everything that eBay does—and that's a lot. In fact, you don't really start to appreciate eBay until you have to do it all yourself. You may find that it's worth paying a few eBay fees to receive all the benefits you get from the eBay marketplace. In any case, get ready to start put-ting in longer hours when you're running your own shop; a lot of time and effort is required.

- **There may be substantial upfront costs.** Depending on the route you go, you may have to invest a substantial amount of money upfront to get your site up and running. If you go completely from scratch (that is, eschew the prepackaged storefront approach), you could spend $10,000 or more to create a unique and fully func-tioning website. That's not small change, folks.

- **There may be ongoing fees.** Let's say you don't have all that money to invest upfront. Instead, you go with a prepackaged storefront or contract out for various prepackaged e-commerce services. This lets you get into the game without a big upfront investment, but instead you have to pay ongoing monthly fees to use those services. Sometimes the fees are a flat monthly subscription, sometimes the fees are a commission on what you sell; in any instance, make sure you don't pay more in fees for your own site than you did in the eBay marketplace.

- **You still have to pay for credit card sales.** Here's one expense you can't get away from. Some of the most disliked fees on eBay are PayPal fees; some sellers just don't get that you have to pay for the privilege of accepting credit card orders. To that end, PayPal's 2.9% fee isn't that out of line. It's likely you'll pay at least 2% for third-party credit card processing. You may also be stuck (or prefer to go) with PayPal on your site—which means you still pay that dreaded 2.9% fee per transaction. Get used to it.

- **You won't have any customers on day one.** One of the primary advantages of selling on eBay or Amazon is that you get to tap into their huge established customer bases. Millions of potential customers come to those sites every day, looking to buy something; they're great places for a seller to be. Unfortunately, when you create your own online store, you don't have those millions of visitors. In fact, you don't have *any* visitors on day one. How do you get customers to your site? That leads us to our next disadvantage…

- **You have to promote your own business.** Smart sellers know that the exorbitant fees they pay to eBay are primarily not service fees but rather advertising fees. That is, they pay to have eBay drive business to their product listings. Well, on your own website, you have to do all the promotion yourself. That means paying for pay-per-click or display ads, organizing your own email mailing lists, doing all your own online public relations, you name it. If you have a marketing degree, this is probably second nature to you; if not, you may be in over your head. And whether you know what you're doing or not, it costs time and money to conduct a full-fledged online marketing campaign. How much money do you have in your marketing and advertising budget?

- **You're not completely your own boss.** So you got yourself out from under the yoke of eBay to be your own boss. Good for you! Except that you're never totally your own boss. You're still at the mercy of your customers, of course; if you can't make them happy, they'll find a way to get back at you. (And you won't get any new ones, either.) Plus there are various restrictions you may have to follow if you subscribe to a storefront service; there may even be rules that your web hosting service enforces. And, of course, your online payment service will tell you various things that you can and can't do when accepting payments. It's not quite like being a slave to eBay, but it's not that different, either. Meet the new boss, same as the old boss.

Put simply, running your own website takes a lot more time, effort, and money than you probably expect—and you may not have the specific expertise required. Are you really ready to run everything yourself? Some sellers are, some sellers aren't. That's a judgment you need to make.

Does an Online Store Make Sense for Your Business?

Pros and cons weighed, it's time for the tough question: Does it make sense for you to abandon eBay and build your own online store? As with all other questions of this nature, it depends.

When you move from eBay to another online marketplace, such as Amazon, one of the key considerations is what type of products you sell. It's a fact: Some items sell better on eBay, some sell better on Amazon.

But that's less an issue when you're creating a stand-alone web presence. You can sell virtually anything from your own website; it doesn't matter whether you're selling $2 cables or $2,000 industrial supplies: If you can draw customers to your site, you can sell it. No one type of merchandise is any better or any worse in this regard.

To my mind, then, the key consideration isn't the products you sell but rather your own experience and skill set. eBay makes selling easy; selling on your own website is a lot harder. This is what a lot of eBay complainers fail to consider. Yes, you pay a lot of fees to eBay, and sometimes rankle under eBay's many rules and regulations. But this is all in service to what is truly an easy selling environment. You don't have to do a lot more than put together an item listing in order to sell on eBay; practically anyone can do it, to some degree of success.

In fact, eBay makes selling so easy that it's a relatively level playing field—which constrains some truly skilled sellers. But it also makes it easy for the little guys to compete with the big guys, even if they're not particularly skilled or experienced. Just follow the rules, and you'll do okay.

The same cannot be said for selling on your own website. If you're not an experienced seller or trained businessperson, you'll quickly find yourself over your head with your own website. There's a lot involved; it's running a real business, complete with all the issues and headaches that entails. If you're not prepared for that, you can fail spectacularly.

To run a successful online store, you need to treat it like a real business— because it *is* a real business. That means creating a business plan, arranging proper financing, researching site design and product sales, closely managing the day-to-day operations, devising compelling marketing campaigns and promotional activities, and providing exemplary customer service. You don't have to worry about many or any of these things when you're selling on eBay, but it's all there every day when you're running your own site.

So my advice is simple: If you have formal business training or previous business experience, by all means consider creating your own e-commerce website. But if your business experience consists only of selling via eBay auctions, think twice before you go this route. It's a big jump from eBay to your own website, and it may be better to take an intermediate step (such as moving to the Amazon marketplace) before you put all your chips on your own online business. It's a big risk and a big effort; make sure you know what you're getting into before you're in too deep.

Are You Ready to Go It Alone?

Many successful sellers got their start by putting a few old items up for auction on eBay. Those auctions went well, so they found more stuff to sell. And then even more stuff. And then they started purchasing items specifically to sell on eBay, and before they knew it, they were "professional" sellers.

But the thing is, making it big like this is more a matter of luck than of skill. Not that anyone can be successful on eBay (there are lots of folks who aren't), but eBay does provide a marketplace that is incredibly kind to inexperienced sellers. Yes, you've learned a lot over the years, but chances are you got started selling on eBay before you really knew what you were doing. I call it "stumble-on success," and eBay is home to lots of it.

When you move away from eBay, out onto your own website, you have to be more prepared. All that hand-holding and support you get from eBay? It's not there anymore. Inexperienced, unskilled sellers are most likely to fail when they launch their own online stores; there is little or no stumble-on success to be had.

Are you ready to go it alone? Some sellers are. Some sellers think they are. Some sellers most definitely are not. Yes, I provide a lot of advice in the following chapters on how best to make a go of it, but if you're not sufficiently skilled or experienced in the ways of running a business, all the books in the world won't help you.

Running a website is a great way for some sellers to expand their online presence. It's also a way for many sellers to go belly-up. It all boils down to whether you know what you're doing. Do you? ■

16

Planning Your Online Presence

If you want to launch your own e-commerce website, you need to have a plan. Without a plan, you'll end up spinning your wheels and spending more time and money than you need to. Planning is essential to success.

So what do you need to do—and when? That's what we discuss in this chapter.

Step One: Create Your Plan and Define Your Goals

Call this blatantly obvious, but the first step in planning for an e-commerce website is to create a plan. That's right, you need to work up a somewhat detailed business plan before you do anything else.

> **note**
>
> Learn more about creating a business plan in Chapter 2, "Planning for Selling Success."

A business plan is essential, as it both provides a roadmap for what you need to do and sets out goals for what you want to achieve. That said, I don't think you need to overthink your plan; it doesn't have to be 100 pages long and professionally designed. A few pages with key bullet points is good enough, assuming that you cover the tasks you need to do and the sales numbers you hope to hit.

As noted previously, a business plan needs to detail your mission, opportunity, strategy, organization and operations, and strengths and weaknesses. It also needs to include your financial goals and projections. Concentrate on the meat of what you want to do, and don't worry too much about the fine details.

Again, it's not important how professional your plan is, only that it describes what you want and need to accomplish. You then need to follow the steps in your plan—and, at regular intervals, compare your performance with the projections you put in the plan.

Step Two: Determine What You're Selling

With your business plan in hand, you need to outline the basics of your business—and your business is defined by the products you sell. Now, this might seem like a simple step: You sell on your website what you currently sell on eBay, right? This might end up being the case, but if you haven't already, now is as good a time as any to reevaluate your product mix and fine-tune it for your own online store.

Think about what you're currently selling and what's selling best and what isn't—and why. Then consider how those same products might sell on your own website. Consider that you won't have the built-in customer base that you have on eBay, that you'll have to somehow drive customers to your site from across the web—and, if you're lucky, from eBay. Consider whether there are other sites selling similar merchandise and consider how you'll compete with them.

Consider all these points and then reconsider your merchandise mix. Maybe your current mix is still appealing; maybe you have some doubts. Maybe you think there are other types of items you can do better with on your own site.

Whatever you decide, your choice of merchandise will influence the look and feel of your new website. It may even influence the type of site you build—your own custom site or a prebuilt site on an existing marketplace. In any case, it's important to know what you're selling before you start building your site.

Step Three: Choose a Hosting Service

Aside from essential business decisions, one of the most important things you need to decide is what kind of website you want to build—that is, how you want your site designed and hosted. As you learned in

Chapter 15, "Establishing Your Own Website: Is It Right for Your Business?" you have several options. To recap, you can choose to do any of the following:

- **Build your site yourself.** This means doing all the HTML coding by hand and then finding a hosting service to host the site. This requires lots of work but involves little cost—if you know what you're doing.

- **Hire a design firm to build your site.** This is probably the approach with the largest upfront costs—although you won't have much in the way of ongoing fees or commissions, which means it could be quite profitable in the long run.

- **Build a site using available e-commerce services and modules.** This is a popular approach, as you don't have to reinvent a lot of wheels from scratch. You do, however, have to pay to use these services—either upfront as a purchase or via ongoing monthly fees.

- **Create a prebuilt site at an existing e-commerce marketplace.** This approach gets you a good-looking store with a minimum amount of startup cost and effort—although you typically have to pay ongoing fees and commissions to the e-commerce host.

You'll probably want to investigate several of these approaches to see which best fits your skill set and budget. You can then shop around for the best services for the approach you pick; prices vary considerably even for similar services.

tip

It's important to balance upfront costs and ongoing costs—which will vary depending on the amount of business your site does. Run your sales projections through the fee structure of any service you consider to get an idea of what you'll be charged each month.

Step Four: Build Your Website

Once you've chosen an e-commerce host or service provider, it's time to build your website. Obviously, what you need to do depends on the hosting approach you're taking.

If you've decided to design your own site from scratch (or have a designer do it for you), you need to do virtually everything—from coding each page to purchasing a domain name to contracting with a website hosting service. If you decided to use one of the variety of third-party e-commerce services, you'll still need to put together each page and then plug in the appropriate modules, as necessary. If you choose to go the prebuilt site route, your job is a lot easier; creating a site typically involves choosing a template, signing up for necessary services, and then uploading your inventory listings.

However you proceed, you'll need to establish your brand via site design, logo placement, and the like. Unlike with an eBay Store, which pretty much looks like a regular eBay page with your logo on the top, you can design your entire site, top to bottom, to reflect the look and feel of your business. And if you haven't yet developed a business image, now's the time to do so. It's Marketing 101, folks, and your e-commerce website is the online equivalent of a retail storefront.

You'll also need to create an appropriate navigational structure so that customers can quickly and easily find the products they're looking for. At the very least, this means organizing your products into logical categories and letting users click on a link or menu item to view all products in that category. You may even want to provide drill-down navigation within a category so that customers can more easily fine-tune their buying choices. For example, if you sell big-screen TVs, you might want to provide drill-down links so that customers can view TVs by size, by type (plasma, LCD, CRT, etc.), by brand, by price, and so forth.

The key thing is to think through how your customers will use your site before you start building it. It's tough to go back and redesign or reorganize a site after it's up and running; it's much easier to take your time and think it through thoroughly beforehand.

note

Delve into the details of building an online store in Chapter 17, "Setting Up an E-Commerce Website."

Step Five: Choose an Online Payment Service

An online store isn't just a listing of products that you have for sale. You also need to provide a mechanism for ordering those products—and collecting customer payments.

The ordering process is made possible by a shopping cart and checkout system. If you go with a prebuilt online store, this will be provided to you by your hosting service. If you're designing your own site, I recommend that you sign up for a shopping cart/checkout service, which you typically subscribe to for a monthly fee. There are several such cart/checkout services available, and there's no point in reinventing the wheel; it's just too hard a process to code from scratch when there are viable preexisting solutions available.

It's the same story with the payment function: The best approach for most sellers is to sign up with an existing online payment service, such as PayPal, Google Checkout, or Checkout by Amazon. If you go with a prebuilt online store, chances are the hosting service will offer some sort of online payment service, even if it's just a connection to PayPal or a similar service. Alternatively, you can sign up for your own merchant charge card account, although that's probably more hassle (and possibly a higher cost) than most beginning sellers are willing to deal with. In any instance, do your research upfront and make sure the online payment service you select seamlessly interfaces with your shopping cart/checkout service.

note

Learn more about online payment systems in Chapter 19,"Choosing an Online Payment System."

Step Six: Plan Your Promotion

Building a website is the easy part of going it alone online. It's much, much harder to find customers for your site—not at all what you're used to on eBay.

Promotion is an essential function for all online businesses. You have to do *something* to drive customers to your site, and that something is variously called *promotion* or *marketing*.

Online promotion can take many forms; there are many different ways to find customers. You may elect to purchase pay-per-click advertising, such as Google AdWords. You may opt to purchase larger, more expensive display ads on select sites. You may choose to promote your site via friendly bloggers or on social networks such as Facebook. You most definitely want to optimize your site so that it ranks high on Google and other search sites, and you probably want to submit your site listings to Shopping.com and other comparison shopping sites. And once you get a few customers, you'll want to coax additional sales out of them via a targeted email mailing list.

We're talking about promotion as part of your upfront plan because marketing costs money. You need to develop a promotion or advertising budget so that you know upfront how much money you need to spend to build your customer base. Having a marketing plan also provides a roadmap for what you need to do, promotion-wise, in the weeks and months following your site's launch.

It's tempting to leave the promotion until after your site is launched, but that's tempting fate. Launching an online store without having a marketing plan in place is like running a marathon without doing a day's worth of training—yes, you'll be off and running when it's starting time, but you won't be around at the finish. Knowing how you'll be promoting your site is every bit as important as deciding what products to sell, how your site will look and feel, and what checkout and online payment services you'll use. An un- or underpromoted site is a site with few, if any, customers. And that's a sure ticket to business failure.

note

Learn more about online marketing in Chapter 20, "Promoting Your E-Commerce Website."

Step Seven: Launch Your Site

Only after you've done the proper preparation is it time to launch your website. If you launch before you're ready, you may not be able to properly fulfill any orders you receive. And that's if you get any orders; if you haven't put together a marketing plan, your newly launched site is likely to be a very lonely place, indeed.

You have to have everything in place before you open your site to the general public. But don't expect customers to be knocking down your virtual door on day one. It takes time for a business to build, for customers to hear about you and visit you and decide that your business is a viable place to spend their money.

So when you're putting together your sales projections, don't plan for big business in your first month—or even your first few months. It's more likely that your expenditures will outpace your sales for several months, until you build a customer base. This isn't like eBay, where there are millions of potential customers already on the site, looking for stuff to buy. When you launch your site, you have *zero* customers, and you have to build from that.

This means, of course, that you need to have enough money in the bank to make it through the lean times. Alternatively, you can continue your existing eBay sales while you grow your own online sales. In any case, don't believe that you'll be an exception to the rule that it takes time to build a business—even an online business.

Step Eight: Evaluate Your Performance

After your site has been up and running for several months, you're starting to build a customer base. How do you know if your business is successful?

Amateurs judge success by how much money they have in the bank at the end of each month. (Or each day!) Professional businesspeople know that there are better yardsticks to use—and that it's important to evaluate your performance on an ongoing basis.

How do you evaluate your success? First, you want to look at your business's revenue—how many sales you're booking. This is your top-line number, the actual dollars that flow in from your customers before you subtract product costs and other expenses. Revenue is how you judge the size of your business, and the more revenue the better.

More important, however, is your business's profit or loss. Not cash flow, although that's important on a day-to-day basis, but actual profit or loss—how much money you have left over when you subtract all your costs and expenses from the revenues you generate. If your profit is negative, you're not doing too well. If it's positive—well, that's a start.

Generating a profit, however, isn't the ultimate measurement. How *much* profit you generate is much more important. That is, you need to have a profit goal, in terms of both percentage and dollars, and judge your actual performance against that goal. If you said in your business plan that you'd generate a 20% profit margin on $100,000 worth of sales, it won't do to discover that your actual profit margin is only 15%—or that your actual revenues are only $75,000, for that matter.

In other words, you need to know how you're performing compared to plan. If you're behind plan in any metric, you need to know why—and figure out what to do to get back on track.

Equally important is how often you evaluate your business. I suggest generating monthly profit and loss statements and comparing these results to the monthly projections you did as part of the planning process. It's a waste of time to worry about daily or weekly numbers, but you also don't want to wait six months or a year before you find out that something's going wrong. Evaluate your business monthly and be prepared to make any corrections necessary for business success.

And here's the thing: Your business might *not* be successful—or at least not as successful as you'd like. That happens; we don't always plan perfectly, and sometimes we get hit by marketplace changes or fading economic conditions that we just couldn't predict. What's important is how you react to the business realities you face. You can't just sit back and hope for things to get better. Instead, you need to read the numbers and figure out how to adjust in response. It's okay to change what you're doing midstream; in fact, business is all about making necessary changes. Keep aware of developments and keep on your toes. It's the only way to succeed.

How Long Does It Take?

How long does it take to launch an e-commerce website? Depending on how you do it, you could be up and running in a day or two—although that's probably not the best way to go.

The fastest way to get up and running is to go with a prebuilt e-commerce hosting service, such as Amazon WebStore or eBay's ProStores. If you have a list of inventory handy (and in the correct format), launching a store with one of these services is as simple as filling in a few online forms and uploading your inventory data.

Obviously, building a site from scratch is going to take longer—much longer. This sort of project isn't measured in days but rather in weeks or months. It goes faster if you use existing services or modules for some of your site features, but it's still a painstaking and sometimes painful process. Be warned.

All this said, launching quickly isn't necessarily a good thing. You need to devote adequate time to the planning process; that's not something you should hurry. Take your time, do all the research and thinking and number crunching you need to do. There's nothing to be gained by rushing the planning process. Do it right, and you stand a better chance of success; do it fast, and you're more likely to fail—and fail more quickly. ■

17

Setting Up an E-Commerce Website

As you've learned, there are many ways to build an e-commerce website. While some sellers choose to build a site from scratch (either by coding it themselves or by hiring a web design firm), a better alternative for most sellers is to use a hosting service that offers pre-designed storefronts. With this approach, your upfront costs are surprisingly low, and creating your site is often as easy as filling in a few forms and uploading your product inventory.

Which e-commerce hosting service should you use? Just how easy is it to design your own site with one of these services? What can you expect once you get your site up and running? These are the questions we answer in this chapter—so read on to learn more!

Choosing a Hosting Service

Lots of companies out there would love to host your online store. Most of these companies offer similar features—the hosting itself, of course, as well as catalog/product listing pages, shopping cart and checkout services, even connections to online payment services. Some firms go above and beyond the call of duty by also providing their own online marketplace for the sites they host, as well as additional marketing and promotional services.

You can pay anywhere from $5 to $150 per month for e-commerce hosting; some sites also charge a commission on each transaction you make. In some instances, the monthly fee depends on how many items you have for sale. In other instances, the monthly fee depends on what e-commerce services you use. It's a big smorgasbord.

Features to Look For

As you might suspect, the online store you build is going to be different from the one your competitor builds. You may need some services but not others; some features offered may be totally unimportant to you, while others may be essential.

Let's look, then, at what you're likely to find when you go shopping for e-commerce hosting services. Here are some of the most popular features:

- **Site design tools.** Of course, an e-commerce hosting firm is going to offer various tools to help you design your online store. If the site is simple and template driven, this might take the shape of a series of online forms that let you pick and choose from various design options. Other providers offer software or web-based HTML editing tools for more customized sites. Make sure the hosting firm provides the tools you need to create the type of site you want.

- **Product listing/creation.** If you're selling items online, you have to create selling pages for those items. Find out exactly how a hosting provider lists the items you have for sale—what the product pages look like and what you have to do to create those pages. This is especially important if you have a business with a large number of SKUs; the ability to quickly create hundreds of product pages is more important to you than it would be to a business that has only a few dozen items for sale. In fact, you may want to be able to generate product pages on the fly as you upload your inventory lists, thus creating dynamically generated web pages for your customers.

tip

While you're at it, see how many items the hosting service lets you list. Some lower-priced plans let you list only a few dozen or at most a hundred items; if you have more SKUs, look for a plan that offers unlimited inventory listings.

- **Inventory management.** If you have a large number of SKUs, you want to be able to manage that inventory quickly and easily. Find out how you upload new inventory listings, how the inventory gets adjusted when a sale is made, and how difficult it is to change pricing or other parameters on an item after it's been listed. The best hosting plans provide robust inventory management modules; the least among them require you to do all the inventory management and simply create product pages from the information you provide.

- **Shopping cart and checkout system.** You can't run an online store without a shopping cart or a checkout system, and every e-commerce hosting service provides these items. Make sure you try out the system before you sign up, though; you want to make sure that it's a painless process for your customers and that it's easy for them to add more items to their orders.

---

tip

Make sure that the checkout system includes secure ordering for your customers.

- **Online payment services.** Getting paid is a good thing. With an online store, that means accepting credit card payments. Many e-commerce hosting services tie their checkout systems into PayPal, Google Checkout, or similar online payment services. Other providers offer their own merchant credit card payment services. Some providers offer various alternatives and let you choose the one that best fits your business needs. Make sure you like the options offered—and factor the per-transaction and possible monthly fees into your expense plan.

---

note

Don't assume that a merchant account costs less on a per-transaction basis than PayPal; it isn't necessarily so. Learn more in Chapter 19, "Choosing an Online Payment System."

- **Order processing and management.** After a customer purchases a product, what happens next? Ideally, you get notified of the sale and how and when it should be shipped. You may even get some shipping assistance, in the form of printing shipping labels with pre-paid postage. Check to see just what sort of order processing the e-commerce hosting firm offers.
- **Automated customer service.** How do you interact with your customers? Many e-commerce hosting firms offer pre-designed forms that your customers can use to contact you or leave feedback. You may also want to investigate features such as customer message boards, customer product reviews, and the like that you can integrate into your site.
- **Online marketplace placement.** Some e-commerce hosting firms simply set you up with a website at the domain of your choice. Others link together all their clients into their own online directories

or marketplaces. Still others link you to other online marketplaces, such as eBay and Amazon. See what's available; it may be worth paying a little more to a provider that gives you increased visibility in this fashion.

- **Marketing services.** With some e-commerce hosting firms, you're on your own in terms of promoting your site. Other providers, however, offer a variety of promotional services, including email marketing, search engine optimization, submittal to online shopping sites, and so forth. Check to see what's available—and what you need.

- **Reporting.** The final thing to look at is one of the most important. You need robust reporting capabilities to track the success of your business—and to help manage sales and inventory. Take a good look at the reports and analyses offered and make sure they're all that you need. (It helps if the reports can be customized—and downloaded to your computer in Excel format for further analysis.)

---

tip

If you use QuickBooks for your business's accounting, make sure your e-commerce hosting service offers QuickBooks integration so you can easily port your data into your accounting software.

In addition to picking and choosing the features you need, you also need to evaluate how easy a firm is to work with. That includes not only the ease of creating a website but also the technical support and customer service offered to you. If you run into any problems along the way (not just building the site, but also after you're up and running—like if your site goes down in the middle of the holiday shopping season), you want to be able to talk to a live human being and get the problem resolved lickety-split.

Comparing Prices

Even though most providers offer similar services, comparing prices between them is a little like comparing apples and penguins; it's often difficult to do a head-to-head pricing comparison because of the ways they approach their fees. For example, some firms charge a setup fee, while some don't; some have a lower monthly subscription fee but a higher sales commission, while others have a higher monthly subscription fee but no sales commission; and there's even one company (Amazon) that doesn't charge any payment processing fees—but makes up for it with much higher transaction fees. It's all a bit confusing.

So which firms offer the best deals? It depends, to some degree, on the number of individual products you stock and the volume of monthly sales you hope to conduct. In addition, the features and services offered by the different companies differ to some degree, and you may have to pay extra to get exactly what you want. Finally, some companies (such as Amazon and eBay) offer some visibility on their main online marketplaces, whereas with most firms, you're pretty much on your own in terms of attracting customers. Again, you pay for this service.

All that said, some hosting services are more attractive and subsequently more popular than others. We'll look at three of the top providers separately—eBay's ProStores, WebStore by Amazon, and Yahoo! Merchant Solutions. These services are all relatively easy to use and offer their own distinct pros and cons for budding online retailers.

Using eBay ProStores

Because you're already familiar with eBay's auction marketplace, let's start by examining eBay's e-commerce solution. eBay's ProStores (www.prostores.com) was designed to lure back some of the sellers who were leaving the auction marketplace, by offering easy-to-use web store-fronts with a subtle but significant connection to the eBay that everybody used to know and love. (Even if they now know and hate it.)

Whatever your current opinion of eBay, ProStores is actually a pretty good deal. Monthly fees are reasonable, and transaction fees are low—just 0.5% for the most popular plans. ProStores uses PayPal for payment processing, which makes for a smooth transition from your current eBay sales. Shipping integration with the U.S. Postal Service, UPS, FedEx, and Canada Post is built in, as is the ability to print shipping labels and packing slips.

Beyond these essential features, ProStores's higher-end plans provide a plethora of site promotion services. The highest-level subscription also offers various supplier management features.

ProStores for eBay Sellers

If you're a current eBay seller, know that ProStores integrates well with the main eBay site. You can easily port your ProStores product listings to listings on the eBay marketplace and then have eBay buyers check out through your ProStores store. This is made easier by the fact that you can also keep a joint inventory between your eBay Store and your ProStores store; if you sell an item in one, it is subtracted from the inventory of the other. No other e-commerce hosting service offers this level of eBay integration, which makes ProStores ideal for sellers who want to market both on and off eBay.

---

tip

ProStores offers a QuickStart feature for eBay sellers, automatically importing all your current eBay listings into your ProStores inventory.

In addition, ProStores offers a 30% discount on monthly subscription fees to eBay Stores sellers. That amounts to savings of a whole $3 per month for the lowest subscription level but up to a $75 savings per month for the more advanced levels.

Subscription Levels

ProStores offers four subscription levels, each with its own feature set and maximum number of SKUs allowed:

- **Starter Store** ($9.95 per month), good for part-time sellers or those with fewer than 20 SKUs.
- **Business Store** ($29.95 per month), good for smaller full-time sellers.
- **Advanced Store** ($74.95 per month), for sellers who want more advanced promotional tools.
- **Enterprise Store** ($249.95 per month), for sellers who need advanced supplier management tools.

Starter Store subscribers pay a 1.5% transaction fee (commission) on each sale; this fee is reduced to 0.5% for all other subscription levels. Table 17.1 details the fees and basic services for each subscription level.

Table 17.1   eBay ProStores Subscription Levels

	Starter Store	Business Store	Advanced Store	Enterprise Store
Monthly fee	$9.95/month	$29.95/month	$74.95/month	$249.95/month
Monthly fee for eBay Store subscribers	$6.95/month	$20.95/month	$52.45/month	$174.95/month
Transaction fee (commission)	1.5%	0.5%	0.5%	0.5%
Maximum number of SKUs	20	10,000	50,000	100,000
Storage space	N/A	5GB	10GB	20GB

	Starter Store	**Business Store**	**Advanced Store**	**Enterprise Store**
Data transfer	N/A	50GB/month	200GB/month	400GB/month
Shopping search engine submittal	No	Yes	Yes	Yes
Search engine optimization	No	Yes	Yes	Yes
Inventory-based catalog control	No	Yes	Yes	Yes
Back orders and order splitting	No	No	Yes	Yes
Supply chain and vendor management—including drop-shipping	No	No	No	Yes
QuickBooks integration	No	Yes	Yes	Yes

Which level is right for you? Unless you're a very small or very big seller, I recommend the Business Store subscription. At this level, you pay just $29.95 per month ($20.95 per month if you also have an eBay Store) plus a transaction fee of 0.5%. You get most of the features of the more expensive plans, including QuickBooks integration, eBay integration, inventory tracking, and business reporting. You don't get advanced promotional or supplier management features, but then again, you can do most of the former yourself, and few stores need the latter.

Getting Started with ProStores

Getting a ProStores store up and running can be quite easy. All subscription levels let you choose from a variety of pre-designed templates; just choose the look and feel you want and then customize the features that matter to you, such as page layout, fonts, colors, and so on. Business Store subscribers (and above) can use the Design Studio HTML editor to create more unique pages.

Figure 17.1 shows a typical ProStores store, HDAccessory.com (www.hdaccessory.com). This merchant, which sells iPod accessories, has opted to include a menu system that lets customers shop for accessories by iPod model. The store also includes featured products on the home page, as well as links to bestsellers, weekly specials, new arrivals, and clearance items. As you can see, the site in no way resembles a traditional eBay Store; this is definitely the stand-alone site of an independent online merchant.

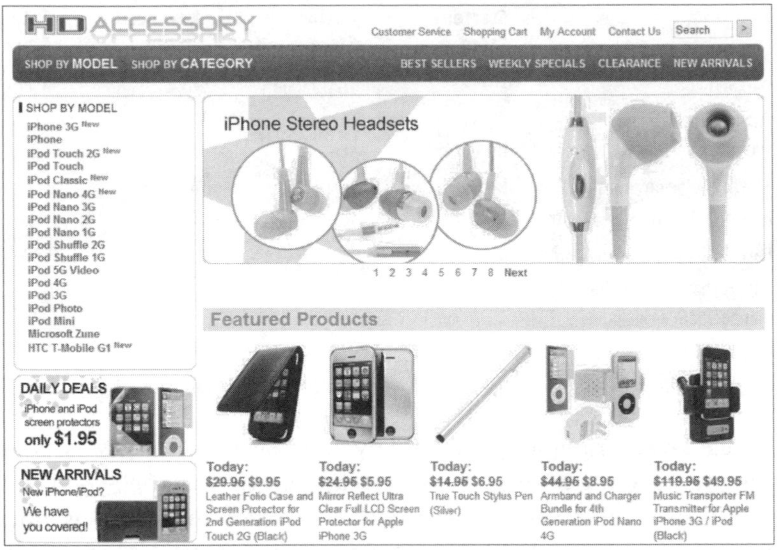

FIGURE 17.1
The eBay ProStores store for HDAccessory.com.

When you have your store up and running, you use the Store Administration page (which resembles to no small degree eBay's My eBay page) to manage all your e-commerce activities. This is also where you synchronize your store data with QuickBooks and generate all manner of business reports.

Building an Amazon WebStore Store

Amazon is another big player offering e-commerce hosting services. WebStore by Amazon (webstore.amazon.com) lets you create your own stand-alone online store—in fact you can create multiple stores if you like, all for one monthly cost.

Inside an Amazon WebStore Store

While an Amazon WebStore store has most of the same features as an eBay ProStores store, there are some uniquely Amazonian features to be found. First, you don't have to use PayPal for order processing; instead, you use the Amazon Checkout service, which is the same checkout that Amazon uses on its own website. Because of this, Amazon doesn't charge any payment processing fees. Instead, however, you get socked with a higher-than-normal 7% transaction fee on each sale.

note

Assuming that you'd be paying a 2.9% payment processing fee if you went through PayPal, Amazon's transaction fee is the equivalent of a 4.1% commission—which is quite pricey.

What do you get for your 7% per transaction? Pretty much what you'd expect, and at the level of sophistication you'd expect using Amazon's tried-and-tested e-commerce technology. This includes template-based site creation, your own domain name, a shopping cart and checkout system, and the like. You also get access to Amazon's noted fraud protection system, which is a good thing.

Amazon also provides a variety of promotional services, including automatic search engine optimization, search engine submission, and email marketing. Even better, you can incorporate into your store various Amazon site features, such as product recommendations, customer reviews, and the like. It's my opinion that Amazon lets you create the most content-rich product listing pages of any e-commerce hosting site—which, presumably, should translate into increased sales.

tip

Amazon also lets you earn referral fees (via the Amazon Associate program) if you add Amazon products to your WebStore.

In terms of hosting plans, Amazon keeps it simple, with just a single plan that costs $59.99 per month. Know, however, that items you sell in your WebStore are *not* posted to the Amazon marketplace. You can, though, choose the joint Selling on Amazon and WebStore by Amazon plan that lets you sell inventory both on your own site and on the Amazon site, via a unified inventory management interface. This plan costs $99.98 per month.

Creating Your Own WebStore

You need an Amazon seller account to open a WebStore; if you don't yet have one, you'll be prompted to create one. You then build your site using Amazon's 1-Click WebStore feature, which lets you fill in a short form (shown in Figure 17.2) to create a nice-looking set of pages. Alternatively, you can use the Setup Wizard to built a more customized storefront.

Figure 17.3 shows the kind of store you can create with WebStore. This one is for Element Jewelry & Accessories (www.elementjewelry.com). It's a nice-looking home page that stands on its own, with no obvious visual similarities to the Amazon site. The product pages, however, like the one in Figure 17.4, bear a more striking resemblance to Amazon's product pages, complete with customer reviews and the like.

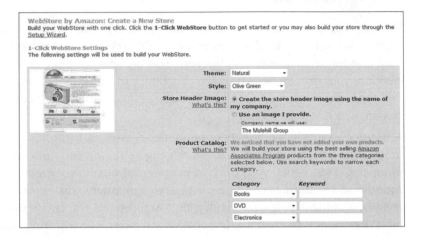

FIGURE 17.2

Creating a 1-Click WebStore store.

FIGURE 17.3

The Amazon WebStore store of Element Jewelry & Accessories.

FIGURE 17.4

A product page for an Amazon WebStore store.

Building a Yahoo! Merchant Website

The third e-commerce hosting service we'll examine comes from another big-name site. Yahoo! Merchant Solutions (smallbusiness.yahoo.com/ecommerce/) offers professional-level site design and hosting, a first-rate shopping cart and checkout service, and a variety of promotional services. It's a good choice for sellers who want a more professional online store.

Subscription Levels

Yahoo! offers three different subscription levels:

- **Starter.** This level is targeted at sellers doing less than $18,000 in sales each month. The subscription fee is $39.95 per month, with a 1.5% fee on each transaction.

- **Standard.** This level is targeted at sellers doing between $18,000 and $68,000 in sales each month. The subscription fee is $129.95 per month, with a 1.0% fee on each transaction.

- **Professional.** This level is targeted at sellers doing more than $68,000 in sales each month. The subscription fee is $299.95 per month, with a 0.75% fee on each transaction.

Each subscription level requires a $50 one-time setup fee. There is no difference between the levels in terms of how many products you can stock; each plan allows up to 50,000 SKUs per merchant. There are, however, differences between the plans aside from the monthly subscription and transaction fees. Table 17.2 details the features of each plan.

Table 17.2   Yahoo! Merchant Solutions Subscription Levels

	Starter	Standard	Professional
Monthly fee	$39.95	$129.95	$299.95
Transaction fee	1.5%	1.0%	0.75%
Setup fee (one-time)	$50	$50	$50
Maximum number of SKUs	50,000	50,000	50,000
Cross-selling	No	Yes	Yes
Gift certificate capability	No	Yes	Yes
Real-time integration with existing back-end systems	No	Yes	Yes
UPS shipping integration	No	Yes	Yes
Yahoo! Web Analytics reporting	No	Yes	Yes

As you can see, Yahoo!'s higher-end plans offer an obvious cost advantage if you're doing a large volume of sales. But they also make sense for sellers who have their own back-end systems in place and for those who want more advanced reporting and integration with UPS shipping.

Unique Features

What makes Yahoo! Merchant Services a good choice for former eBay sellers? In my mind, it's the set of professional tools offered; while still a predesigned solution, Yahoo! Merchant Solutions comes closest of the major players to providing the kind of site you'd get if you designed your own from scratch.

First, you have the choice of using Yahoo!'s built-in site development tools or of hiring your own website developer. Going the latter route, while adding some costs on your end, helps you create a site that stands out from other companies using the same provider.

Next is another choice—using PayPal for payments or establishing your own merchant account for credit card processing. That opens up a world of possibilities, especially for larger sellers who are more likely to negotiate favorable terms with their processor of choice.

Of course, you get all the expected product listing and management tools; adding products to your store is accomplished via a step-by-step wizard or by uploading inventory listings in bulk. The ability to keep up to 50,000 SKUs, even with the lowest-priced plan, is particularly appealing. And Yahoo! lets you customize your checkout pages, so that you can create a unique customer experience from start to finish.

In terms of inventory management, Yahoo! is head and shoulders above most of its competitors. You receive inventory alerts when quantities get low, and you can manage your inventory by color, size, and other variables. Yahoo! even lets you integrate your store inventory with an existing inventory system, if you have one.

I also like Yahoo!'s marketing tools. You get things like a grand opening email campaign, automatic submission to both the Yahoo! and Google search engines, a variety of credits for use with shopping comparison services, a free listing with Yahoo! Local, and a $100 credit for use with Yahoo! Search Marketing. You can also offer some unique services to your customers, including gift certificates, gift wrapping, volume pricing, and the like.

Yahoo! offers a variety of reporting tools to help you track your sales, including shopping cart drop-off, bounce rate, exit page, and keyword conversion rate analyses. And the top two plans offer free Yahoo! Web Analytics reporting in real time.

Finally, Yahoo! is one of the best-supported e-commerce hosting services out there. All plans qualify for 24/7 email and toll-free phone support, which is tough to get with other providers. It's good to have the hand-holding available, if you need it.

Creating Your Own Yahoo! Store

Creating a Yahoo! store is as easy as signing up for the service and then choosing one of the pre-designed store themes. You can select from various home page designs and color schemes and then upload your own logo to appear on the page. (Alternatively, you can use your own tools, such as Adobe Dreamweaver, to create your site—or contract with a web design firm to do the work for you.) Then you use the Add Products Wizard to upload product and inventory information to your site.

Figure 17.5 shows an example of a Yahoo! store. The simplehuman store (www.simplehuman.com) has a unique look and feel; you'd never guess that it's part of a pre-built e-commerce hosting community. What you can tell is that this is a very professional-looking site, designed with the same tools available to even the smallest seller.

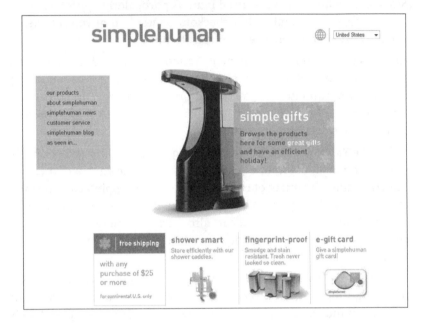

FIGURE 17.5

The Yahoo! store for simplehuman.

Exploring Other Pre-Designed Storefronts

eBay, Amazon, and Yahoo! are just three of many firms that offer e-commerce hosting services. There are lots of other providers out there worth considering, many of which—unlike the big three—don't charge any transaction fees.

When you're shopping for an e-commerce hosting service, check out these firms:

- **BizHosting.** BizHosting (www.bizhosting.com) offers two hosting plans. The Value Hosting package lets you promote up to 250 products for $21.95 per month; the Professional Hosting package lets you promote up to 1,000 products for $39.99 per month. Both plans let you create your site using either pre-designed templates or a more advanced HTML editor; there are no transaction fees or commissions. You also get a secure shopping cart and checkout system, order management, inventory management, customer management, and a variety of reporting options. Order processing is via ProPay, which charges 3.5% and a $0.35 fee per transaction.

- **CoreCommerce.** CoreCommerce (www.corecommerce.com) offers four different levels of subscriptions, priced from $39.99 (for 50 SKUs) to $179.99 (for unlimited SKUs) per month. No matter which plan you choose, there are no transaction fees or commissions. You get website creation via pre-designed templates, shopping cart and checkout services, QuickBooks integration, and integration with USPS, UPS, FedEx, and other shipping services. Customer payment is via your choice of PayPal or Google Checkout.

- **Homestead.** Homestead (www.homestead.com) is an e-commerce hosting service from Intuit. As you might expect, there is substantial integration with QuickBooks, as well as the other expected services— your choice of 200 professional site designs, extensive reporting capabilities, built-in email marketing, automatic submittal of product listings to online search engines, and payment processing via PayPal. Three plans are offered, all with an unlimited number of SKUs: Enhanced ($24.99 per month), Professional ($59.99 per month), and Enterprise ($229.99 per month). There are no transaction fees or commissions.

- **InstantEcom.** InstantEcom (www.instantecom.net) costs just $29.95 per month—even less if you pay by the year. You can create your web pages using a WYSIWYG HTML editor, or you can choose from more than 1,000 pre-designed layouts. You also get a shopping cart and checkout system, automated customer feedback forms and message boards, and payment via either PayPal or your own merchant account. You can inventory up to 500 SKUs, and there are no transaction fees or commissions.

- **Microsoft Office Live Small Business.** That's right, even Microsoft offers e-commerce hosting services, as part of its Office Live Small Business (smallbusiness.officelive.com). While you can use a basic Live Small Business website for non-retail business, you'll need to subscribe to the Store Manager service for full e-commerce hosting; this costs an affordable $14.95 per month. You get automatic product page creation (up to 1,000 SKUs), a shopping cart, checkout, invoice generation, credit card processing (via PayPal), and integration with eBay listings. There are no transaction fees or commissions.

- **Network Solutions.** Network Solutions (www.networksolutions. com/e-commerce/index.jsp) offers e-commerce services in addition to its traditional domain registration and site hosting services. You get pre-designed store templates, a shopping cart and checkout system, shipping service integration, order processing via PayPal or Google Checkout, and (of course) domain name registration and hosting. The Standard package costs $49.95 per month and lets you sell up to 300 SKUs; the Pro package costs $99.95 per month for up to 10,000 SKUs. There are no transaction fees or commissions.

- **PrestoStore.** PrestoStore (www.prestostore.com) costs $29.95 per month, with no transaction fees or commissions. You get customized site design, a secure shopping cart and checkout, unlimited SKUs, and payment processing via PayPal, Google Checkout, or your own merchant account.

- **Shopify.** Shopify (www.shopify.com) offers three different subscription levels. The Basic plan ($24 per month plus 2% transaction fee) lets you list 100 SKUs, the Professional plan ($59 per month plus 1% transaction fee) lets you list 2,500 SKUs, and the Enterprise plan ($299 per month plus 0.5% transaction fee) lets you list 10,000 SKUs. All plans include professional site design, a shopping cart and checkout system, product management, inventory tracking, built-in search engine optimization, and the like. Payment processing is via either PayPal or Google Checkout.

- **Vendio.** Vendio (www.vendio.com) is well known to experienced eBay sellers, and its online store service is an offshoot of its auction management services. There are three subscription levels: Bronze costs $4.95 per month plus a 1% final value fee; Silver costs $9.95 per month plus a $0.20 flat transaction fee; and the Gold plan costs $14.95 per month plus a $0.10 flat transaction fee. You can choose from 50 customizable store themes; checkout is via Vendio's checkout system, with payment processing via Google Checkout. As you might suspect, Vendio integrates tightly with the eBay marketplace.

- **Volusion.** Volusion (www.volusion.com) offers the expected arrange of features—pre-designed storefront templates, shopping cart, a one-page checkout system, QuickBooks integration, integration with major shipping services, and order processing via either PayPal or Google Checkout. Five plans are offered: Steel (20 SKUs for $29.95 per month), Bronze (100 SKUs for $49.95 per month), Silver (250 SKUs for $79.95 per month), Gold (1,000 SKUs for $99.95 per month), and Platinum (unlimited SKUs for $197 per month). No transaction fees or commissions are charged.

What's striking about many of these services is the total lack of transaction fees. You pay a flat monthly subscription fee, and that's it; you don't have to surrender a cut of every sale back to the site. (Except for payment processing, of course; that always costs.) Now, not all of these sites offer the full feature set you find with Amazon WebStore and the like, but still. All of these providers are used by thousands of online retailers and are worth your consideration.

Choosing Stand-Alone E-Commerce Services

Throughout this chapter, we've focused on e-commerce hosting services—companies that offer prefabricated online stores complete with all the features an average seller would need. But the prefab route isn't for every seller, especially if you want to create a unique online presence; most of the pre-built stores tend to look similar to other stores from the same provider.

When you're designing your own online store, you don't necessarily have to reinvent every possible wheel. Several third-party providers offer pre-built e-commerce modules that you can simply plug into your site's HTML code. This way, you can get features like a shopping cart without actually having to design and code your own from scratch.

The backbone of any online store is its shopping cart and checkout system; this system drives customer support, inventory management, and just about everything else you do. Here are some of the most popular providers of shopping cart and checkout software:

- 3DCart (www.3dcart.com)
- MerchandiZer (www.merchandizer.com/ecommerce-shopping-cart.html)
- Miva Merchant (www.mivamerchant.com)
- ShopSite (www.shopsite.com)
- StoreFront (www.storefront.net)
- X-Cart (www.x-cart.com)

Some of these programs are sold outright for a one-time fee; others are available via a monthly subscription (and include services hosted on the provider's own servers). Expect to pay anywhere from a few hundred to a few thousand dollars (or from $30 to $150 per month) for a quality program, depending on your sales volume and individual needs. ■

18

Managing Online Sales

In the long run, setting up an online store is the easy part. As you know from selling on eBay, managing the day-to-day operations is where the real work happens.

And, in many ways, managing your own e-commerce website isn't much different from managing your eBay sales. You have to keep track of inventory, pack and ship the items you sell, deal with customer concerns and complaints, and the like. This is where you get your hands dirty—and is the topic of this chapter.

Managing Your Inventory

Sales are important, but you can't sell what you don't have in stock. For that reason, we start our discussion with inventory management—part and parcel of any online sales operation.

Where you get your inventory, of course, is up to you. This book isn't intended as a product sourcing guide; I prefer to avoid discussions about the merits of this supplier or that, or of dropshipping versus traditional product stocking. So I'm going to assume that you have reliable suppliers for the products you sell.

That said, managing your inventory includes managing your suppliers. You need to know the desired order quantity for each of your SKUs, as well as the amount of time it takes to get an order to you after you've placed it with your supplier. This is, after all, how you calculate your minimum desired stocking levels. All you need to know is the average quantity of an item you sell per day and the number of days it takes to receive an order. Then you multiply the average sales per day by the days to receive an order, and you have the quantity that should trigger your reordering.

Let's work through an example. Assume that you sell cables, and a particular video cable sells, on average, 2 units per day. Your primary supplier takes 10 days to ship an order, so you multiply the 2 units per day by the 10-day fulfillment time, and you get a reorder point of 20 units. That is, when your inventory dips to 20 units, you reorder that product.

The math is rather simple when you stock only a handful of SKUs, but the time involved increases exponentially when you stock hundreds or thousands of different products. Each SKU has its own unique reorder point, and you probably are now dealing with multiple suppliers. You can see the headaches building.

This is why you need to automate inventory management when you build your online store. Fortunately, most e-commerce hosting services provide inventory management as part of their services; many freestanding shopping cart and checkout systems also include inventory management features.

The way automated inventory management works is simple: You enter information about a given product into a spreadsheet, database, or web form. This information typically includes the product name or model number, perhaps a brief description, your stock number, your cost, the product's selling price, the current inventory level, and your reorder point or minimum stocking level. This data feeds an inventory database, which tracks the stocking levels for all the products you sell. When an item is purchased by a customer (as noted by the checkout system), the inventory level for that item is reduced accordingly. When the stock reaches the minimum or reorder level, you're notified that you need to reorder the item, which you should then do.

note

Ordering is typically a manual process. To automate the ordering process, an inventory management system would need to integrate with your suppliers' purchasing systems, which is a daunting task.

If your hosting provider or shopping cart service doesn't provide inventory management functions, you'll have to do all this manually—or come up with your own semi-automated solution. Some sellers cope by creating their own inventory management spreadsheet or database, using Microsoft Excel or Access. They have to enter each day's sales manually into the spreadsheet or database but can still use the software to track inventory levels and generate reorder reports.

Bottom line: If you stock a large number of items, you need an inventory management system. Ideally, this should be part of your shopping list when you're searching for an e-commerce provider or shopping cart software. The alternative is to devise something on your own—or risk continually being out of stock on your best-selling items.

Managing Your Sales

I'm going to assume that your site has some sort of shopping cart and checkout system in place; that's a necessity for every online store. But a checkout system, while essential, is only part of the sales management process.

When a customer puts an item into his shopping cart and then works through the checkout system, several things should happen. First, the customer's credit card information should be sent to your payment processing service, and the payment should be processed. (At some point, these funds should be transferred to your checking account—minus the processing service's fees, of course.) The item(s) sold should be automatically subtracted from your on-hand inventory. And you should be notified of the sale.

In many ways, a good checkout system works pretty much the way eBay does, at least insofar as your interface is concerned. Just as eBay emails you when an item is sold, your checkout system should notify you of each sale made. The way you're notified differs from system to system; you may opt to receive email notification, or you may need to log into your account management module to view your daily sales. In any case, you find out when a sale is made.

What you find out is not only what was sold but who it was sold to. This information is necessary to ship the product to the buyer. You should also determine, at this point, just how the item is to be shipped—that is, what shipping service was specified, either by you or by the customer. You put this information together to process the package for shipping.

Of course, before you ship the item, you have to pack it—just as you do with all your eBay sales. Ideally, you plan for this in advance and have all the necessary boxes and packing supplies on hand. You want your packing and shipping operation to be as factory-like as possible, so that the entire process can be done quickly and without the need for skilled labor. Product A goes into box B along with packing material C and gets shipped via carrier D—that sort of thing.

Many checkout systems make the shipping process easier by automatically generating packing slips and shipping labels. It's even better if your system can generate prepaid shipping labels, so that you don't have to physically go to the post office or a UPS/FedEx store and pay for shipping. When you use prepaid shipping, you can simply hand your packages to the carrier's delivery person or drop them off at a shipping location without waiting in line; the cost of the shipping is charged to your business credit card.

Some checkout systems go even further and include tight integration with one or more carriers. This is a good thing, provided that the integration is with your carrier of choice; it's no good to have UPS integration if you ship everything via USPS Priority Mail. Still, this sort of integration greatly integrates the shipping process. When a sale is made, the system automatically generates a prepaid shipping label and enters the package in the carrier's system. When the package is shipped, it's automatically tracked within your store's checkout system. It's a nice feature, if not always essential.

Sales management doesn't end when the product is shipped. To best control your business, you need to know what you're selling—how many for how much and to whom. A robust reporting system helps you generate all manner of sales and inventory reports. Ideally, you should be able to create custom reports, on the assumption that one-size-fits-all reporting doesn't actually fit all and that you need specific reports for your specific business.

You use these reports to determine how well your business is doing. You should be able to track your sales in aggregate as well as sales by SKU. The best reports also let you segment the data by customer type, customer location, and so on, so that you can paint a better picture of your customer base. The more you know about your business, the better able you are to manage it going forward.

As part of the reporting package, you should be able to generate your business's financials—in particular, profit-and-loss reports (income statements) and balance sheets. Your accountant will need these reports to do her job; alternately, you may be able to export the raw data into QuickBooks or some other accounting package, if that's the way you do things.

Managing Your Customers

Finally, you need to be able to manage your interactions with your customers. These interactions can take many forms and can be quite time-consuming—unless you automate at least some of them.

What customer interactions do you need to plan for? Here are just the most common:

- **Product questions.** Product questions typically come before the sale, when the customer is shopping for an item. A customer may have questions about the size or dimensions of an item, the suitability to a particular task, your stocking levels, you name it. Answering customers' questions is difficult to automate because you need to give specific answers. You can ease the process by including product FAQs on your website, but you'll still get customers asking questions. So make sure your site includes either an email link or a web form that customers can use to contact you in this fashion—and be prepared to answer all questions in a timely fashion, ideally within 24 hours of submittal.

- **Order verification.** This is a communication that should happen automatically. When an order is placed, your checkout system should automatically send out an email, thanking the customer for his order and verifying the process. Ideally, the order verification email should be sent within minutes of the order being placed, and it should include all pertinent order information—including an estimate of shipping time.

- **Shipping notification.** When the item ships, the customer should be notified. Again, it's best if it happens automatically, which is possible if your checkout system is integrated with your shipping service. The shipping notification should include a link to track the shipment with the chosen carrier.

- **Customer reviews and feedback.** You're used to the feedback system on eBay, and some online marketplaces have similar systems. More likely, though, there's no way for a customer to provide feedback on a purchase—unless you ask for it. I think it's a good idea to encourage post-sale customer feedback and product reviews, if your e-commerce provider includes these features. You want to know that your customers are satisfied—and to broadcast that satisfaction to other customers.

tip

One of the things I like about Amazon's WebStore is the inclusion of customer reviews on product pages.

- **Customer complaints.** Not all of your customers will be satisfied. Some customers won't like what they receive; some will receive gifts purchased from you that they don't want; some will order items in the wrong color or size; some will receive defective or damaged items; and some might not receive anything at all. You need a mechanism to handle customer complaints, as well as a way to process product returns. At the least, you need to include a dedicated email address on your site (and in your customer emails) specifically for this purpose. You may also want to establish a phone number (toll-free, ideally) to personally handle customer concerns. In any instance, you need to be prepared for customer complaints—with both a communication mechanism and a problem resolution process.

Here's the deal: If you don't want to talk to your customers, you shouldn't open your own online store. Customer communication and satisfaction are part and parcel of running a business—any kind of business. Selling on eBay can make you lazy in this regard, as the eBay site handles most of this process. But when you're on your own, you have to handle your customers yourself. I think that's a good thing, even when customers are complaining irrationally, but in any case it's a thing you have to deal with. So deal with it!

You Need an Accountant!

Most e-commerce hosting services provide tight integration with QuickBooks, which is the accounting software of choice for most small businesses. While I think QuickBooks is great, I also think that it can never replace the services of a good accountant.

Which brings us to my final recommendation of this chapter: Get yourself an accountant! While you may have been able to handle your finances when you were selling on eBay, selling on your own website is a different kettle of fish.

Not only are you completely responsible for all your financial activities, you have more things to be responsible for—such as collecting sales tax (at least for the state in which you operate) and reporting your activity to the federal government and your state government.

While you may think that you're capable of doing all this on your own (with the assistance of QuickBooks), you're not—unless you yourself are an accountant, that is. Because most of us are not accountants, we need to enlist the services of accountants. A good accountant will know everything that needs to be done and will do it for you. Yes, you pay for these services, but it's money well spent.

I myself am not an accountant or a lawyer, so I can't give you financial or legal advice. But I can advise you to hire all the professional help you need, starting with an accountant. You'll still need a good sales and inventory management system, and you'll probably still need a copy of QuickBooks. (Your accountant will receive the data she needs from these systems and programs.) But you'll need an accountant to analyze this data, tell you how well you are or are not doing, perform all necessary filings for tax and other purposes, and provide general business advice. It's something you really can't do without. ■

19

Choosing an Online Payment System

When you do business on eBay, you typically get paid via PayPal. That is, a buyer uses a credit card to pay PayPal, and PayPal then pays you with an electronic deposit into your checking account (after deducting the appropriate fees, of course). PayPal is an online payment services that lets any seller accept credit card payments.

Many sellers, however, don't like PayPal. Either they don't like the service or they don't like the fees or whatever, but being forced to accept PayPal is one of the biggest ongoing beefs against eBay. In fact, this is the reason many sellers strike out on their own—to get out from under the PayPal yoke.

But here's the deal: PayPal is actually a pretty good online payment service. There are competitors, but PayPal's fees aren't outrageous, and PayPal does a good job for most buyers and sellers. Still, when you launch your own e-commerce website, you have a choice of which payment service you use—whether that's PayPal or someone else.

Accepting Payments with PayPal

If you've bought or sold anything on eBay, chances are you're familiar with PayPal. But PayPal isn't just for eBay sellers; online stores of all sizes contract with PayPal to provide online payment services.

The PayPal service accepts payments by American Express, Discover, MasterCard, and Visa, as well as payments via eCheck and electronic bank withdrawals. Although it's primarily a U.S.-based service, PayPal also accepts payments to and from more than 100 countries and regions in 18 different currencies.

Pros and Cons of PayPal

There are several big advantages to using PayPal on your own website. First, PayPal is a known quantity to you; you've used PayPal before, and you're just continuing the relationship, at basically the same rates you're used to. You keep your same account name and everything.

Second, PayPal is a known quantity to your customers. Even if your website customers have never shopped on eBay, chances are they've shopped at another online store that uses PayPal. They may even have their own PayPal buyer's account, which speeds up the checkout process. They know PayPal, and they trust PayPal, which means they'll be comfortable buying from you via PayPal.

Not all sellers like PayPal, however. Some dislike the (perceived) high transaction fees; some dislike the way PayPal operates; some have been dinged (or singed) by PayPal chargebacks to complaining customers.

Let's examine each of these complaints.

The sellers I meet who complain the most about PayPal tend to be the least experienced sellers. They look at the 2.9% (plus $0.30) they pay to PayPal on every transaction, and view that as exorbitant—or, if they're still on eBay, as another example of eBay nickel-and-diming them to death. In any case, they resent paying the fees.

The thing is, it costs money to process credit card transactions. No matter who handles your credit card payments, they're going to bill you for those services. And PayPal's 2.9% fee (lower if you're a higher-volume seller) isn't out of line; as you'll discover later in this chapter, you'll pay similar (if not higher) fees to a traditional credit card processing service. That doesn't mean you have to like paying those fees, but they're just a part of doing business. Factor the fees into your business's cost structure and get on with it.

PayPal, however, operates a bit differently from other credit card services. That's because PayPal isn't a traditional credit card processor; it's an online payment service. The fact is, PayPal is set up for the convenience of the online buyer, not necessarily for the convenience of sellers. Dealing with a traditional credit card processor is a little more automated than working through PayPal's one-thing-at-a-time screens; it's okay when you have a small number of transactions but a bit cumbersome when your volume increases.

As to the chargeback issue, this is a legitimate complaint. If you have a complaining customer, it's possible that PayPal will automatically side with the customer and freeze the funds in your account. (This is another reason to clear your account every day—fewer funds to freeze.) I've heard of sellers who had thousands of dollars in payments frozen for weeks on end as they tried to resolve a given situation. PayPal's attention to the customer is admirable, but retailers have some rights, too.

All this said, you may just not like PayPal. That's fair—and there are several competitors you can use instead, as you'll discover later in this chapter.

Signing Up for PayPal

Before you can use PayPal to accept payments, you must sign up for the PayPal service. You might think you're already signed up for PayPal if you've used it for your eBay business, and you're half right. If you've used PayPal on eBay, you do already have a PayPal account, but it's not the kind of account you need to use PayPal on your own website.

To sign up for a proper PayPal account, go to the PayPal website (www.paypal.com) and click the Business tab. Go to the Need to Accept Credit Cards? section and click the On Your Website link; you now see a page that details the various business services that PayPal offers.

You can choose from two different types of payment services:

- **Website Payments Standard.** This is best for small and new merchants. PayPal provides the shopping cart and checkout, but customers have to leave your site to pay via the PayPal checkout.
- **Website Payments Pro.** This is best for large and more established merchants. You have to provide your own shopping cart, but customers never leave your site.

note

The Website Payments Standard plan is similar to (but subtly different from) the Premier account you probably use for eBay.

Table 19.1 provides details on these plans.

Table 19.1 PayPal Merchant Plans

	Website Payments Standard	Website Payments Pro
Setup fee	None	None
Monthly fee	None	$30
Transaction fee (percentage)	1.9%–2.9%	2.2%–2.9%
Transaction fee (flat)	$0.30	$0.30
Checkout location	PayPal site	Retailer site
Payment buttons	Yes	No
PayPal shopping cart	Yes	No
Integrate with retailer's existing shopping cart	No	Yes
Virtual terminal for orders taken via email, phone, or fax	No	Yes
Detailed reporting	Yes	Yes
Fraud protection	Yes	Yes

My advice for retailers just starting out is to go with the Website Payments Standard service. You can upgrade to the Website Payments Pro plan at a later date if you need the additional features.

---

note

PayPal also offers two flavors of what it calls the Payflow Payment Gateway. This is a service for sellers who already have a merchant account with a credit card processing service; it integrates with your existing shopping cart and connects your store to the payment processor. You pay either $19.95/month (Payflow Link) or $59.95/month (Payflow Pro) for this service, with hefty ($179 or $249) setup fees. The Payflow Link plan lets you process 500 transactions per month, while Payflow Pro has a limit of 1,000 transactions, with additional transactions costing $0.10 each.

Understanding PayPal Fees

PayPal, like all other online payment services, charges the merchant for every transaction made. The buyer doesn't pay any PayPal fees— although he still has to pay finance charges to his own credit card company, if applicable, of course.

As a merchant, you pay a percentage of the total transaction, plus a flat per-transaction fee. Note that the fees you pay are based on the *total amount of money transferred*—that's the selling price plus any taxes and shipping/handling fees. So, for example, if you sell a $10 item and charge $0.50 tax and a $5 shipping/handling fee, the buyer pays PayPal a total of $15.50—and PayPal bases its fee to you on that $15.50 payment.

PayPal's fees range from 1.9% to 2.9%, depending on the plan you sign up for and your monthly sales volume. Table 19.2 presents PayPal's fee schedule as of January 2009:

Table 19.2   PayPal Transaction Fees (U.S.)

Monthly Sales	Transaction Fee
$0–$3,000.00	2.9%
$3,000.01–$10,000.00	2.5%
$10,000.01–$100,000.00	2.2%
>$100,000.00 (Website Payments Pro)	2.2%
>$100,000.00 (Website Payments Standard)	1.9%

note

Website Payments Pro subscribers can get a 1.9% rate if customers use PayPal's Express Checkout service—available to large merchants only.

You're also charged a flat $0.30 per transaction, regardless of your sales volume. All fees are deducted from your account with every transaction.

Let's walk through an example of a transaction. Let's say you sell a DVD player for $55, with a $15 shipping/handling fee. The total that the buyer pays is $70 (there's no sales tax involved); it's this amount on which your fees are based. Assuming that you're in PayPal's first payment tier (under $3,000 a month), you pay 2.9% of that $70, or $2.03, plus the $0.30 transaction fee. Your total fees for that transaction: $2.33.

If, on the other hand, you did more credit card volume and passed the $3,000/month level, you'd pay only 2.5% of the $70, or $1.75. Add in the $0.30 transaction fee, and you pay a total of $2.05 to PayPal.

Adding PayPal to Your Website

How you add PayPal to your site depends on the plan you choose. The integration is easiest if you choose the Website Payments Standard plan. That's because you don't have to have your own shopping cart and checkout system; PayPal supplies both.

If you sell a limited number of SKUs, you can use the Payment button method. Simply fill out a short web form with the item's name, ID number, and price, and PayPal generates a line of HTML code. Insert the code into your page's HTML, and PayPal inserts a Buy Now button onto the page, as shown in Figure 19.1.

FIGURE 19.1

Adding a PayPal Buy Now button to your product pages.

If you sell a large variety of SKUs, a better approach is to generate an Add to Cart button. This lets a customer add multiple items to her shopping cart and then use a single checkout for all her purchases. You create an Add to Cart button similarly to the way you create a Payment button.

With the Website Payments Standard plan, both the shopping cart and checkout are provided by PayPal. You don't have to add any pages to your website for these services; customers are taken from your site to PayPal for the checkout process. (You can, of course, customize the look and feel of the checkout page to some degree, so that it more closely resembles your site.)

If you sign up for the Website Payments Pro plan, you have to integrate PayPal's services with your own existing shopping cart. This means, of course, that you need to have shopping cart software installed on your site. Fortunately, most shopping cart programs are pre-integrated for use with PayPal; see the list on the PayPal site. Connecting things together is a matter of following the instructions provided with the shopping cart.

note

Many e-commerce hosting services use PayPal for their website payment services and thus seamlessly integrate PayPal into their sites. Learn more in Chapter 17, "Setting Up an E-Commerce Website."

Collecting PayPal Payments

When a customer pays for an item via PayPal, those funds are immediately transferred to your PayPal account, and you receive an email notification of the payment. This email includes all the information you need in order to ship the item to the buyer.

---

note

In most cases, the buyer's payments come into your account free and clear, ready to be transferred into your checking account. The primary exception to this is payments made via eCheck, where a customer pays PayPal from his or her personal checking account. Because PayPal has to wait until the "electronic check" clears to receive its funds, you can't be paid until then, either. PayPal sends you an email when an eCheck payment clears.

You have to manually withdraw the funds due to you from PayPal; no automatic payment option is available. You can let your funds build up in your PayPal account, or you can choose (at any time) to withdraw all or part of your funds. (I recommend clearing your PayPal account at the end of each business day; there's no reason to let PayPal hold onto your money any longer than necessary.)

You have the option of okaying an electronic withdrawal directly to your checking account (no charge; takes three to four business days) or requesting a check for the requested amount ($1.50 charge; takes one to two weeks). Just click the Withdraw tab (from the Overview tab) and click the appropriate text link.

Accepting Payments with Google Checkout

While PayPal is the most popular online payment service today, many sellers are switching from PayPal to Google Checkout (checkout.google.com). Google Checkout functions in much the same manner as PayPal, offering checkout and payment services for Internet retailers of all shapes and sizes. Your customers get a similar checkout and payment experience to what they're used to with PayPal, and you end up paying less in transaction fees than you would if using PayPal.

Pros and Cons of Google Checkout

Like PayPal, Google Checkout lets buyers pay via Visa, MasterCard, American Express, and Discover. Unlike PayPal, Google Checkout doesn't offer payment via eCheck or electronic bank withdrawal. And, at present, Google Checkout is available only to U.S. and UK merchants; it doesn't offer PayPal's international payment options.

For sellers, Google Checkout offers the same type of checkout and payment services as PayPal. But Google Checkout offers two big advantages to sellers: lower transaction fees (2.0% versus PayPal's 2.9%) and big discounts if you also advertise via Google's AdWords service. For every $1 a merchant spends on AdWords, that merchant can process $10 in sales through Google Checkout at no charge.

---

note

Google's real goal with Google Checkout—as with most of its online services—is to increase its advertising revenues. In fact, Google looks to use Google Checkout to enhance the value of its AdWords advertisements; interested users can click on a link in an AdWords ad and be offered an instant purchase option via Google Checkout. This should appeal to advertisers who can now realize a true click-to-purchase experience, and perhaps even to buyers who want to purchase the items advertised.

So if you want to reduce your order processing fees, Google Checkout is the way to go—even more so if you're an active AdWords advertiser. And while Google Checkout might not have had the same "name" value as PayPal in its early years, it's now every bit as recognizable to customers. In other words, you won't lose customers if you offer Google Checkout instead of PayPal.

Understanding Google Checkout Fees

How much does it cost you, as a merchant, to use Google Checkout? The fee structure is simple—no complex tables necessary. You pay 2% of the total sale price (that's the price of the item plus shipping, handling, and sales tax) plus $0.20 per transaction. For small and medium-sized merchants, that's significantly lower than PayPal's fee of 2.9% + $0.30 per transaction. These charges, of course, are deducted from your funds due in your Google Checkout account.

How big a savings can you realize by switching from PayPal to Google Checkout? It depends on your volume of business, of course, but let's work through an example. Let's say you sell $20 custom tee shirts with a $5 shipping/handling charge per order. If you sell, on average, 100 shirts a month, that's $2,500 in transaction volume. If you use PayPal for these transactions, you'll pay $102.50 in transaction fees (2.9% of the total plus $0.30 per transaction). If you switch to Google Checkout, you'll pay just $70 in transaction fees (2% of the total plus $0.20 per transaction), for a savings of over 30%. Obviously, if your sales volume is higher, your savings will be greater.

Setting Up a Google Checkout Account

To use Google Checkout for website payments, you first need to sign up for the service. The process is similar to what you go through when you set up a PayPal account.

You start the process by going to the Google Checkout for Merchants page (checkout.google.com/sell/) and signing in with your Google Account ID and password. (If you don't yet have a Google Account, now's the time to sign up for one.) You now see a page that lets you know what you need in order to create your Google Checkout account. You are also asked to describe your business; check the option that best categorizes the type of business you run and then click the Sign In and Continue button.

---

note

If you've already provided some or all of this information for your Google Account or AdWords account, you won't be prompted for all this information.

On the pages that follow, you fill in much the same information as you provide to open a PayPal account. You need to provide your business name, contact information, current sales volume, estimated average order size, federal tax ID (EIN) or Social Security number, and credit card information. Enter all the data as required, and you're signed up—and ready to integrate Google Checkout with your website.

Choosing a Google Checkout Service

Google offers three different ways to integrate Google Checkout with your website. Which service you use depends on the number of items you're selling and how sophisticated your site is:

- **Buy Now buttons.** These buttons are designed for small merchants and individuals selling a limited number of items. This service lets you use the checkout function on Google's website, and implementation requires only a basic knowledge of HTML.
- **Shopping cart integration.** This is useful if you're using a shopping card application supplied by one of Google Checkout's partners.
- **Google Checkout API.** This service lets you program your own shopping cart and checkout and then tie your site into the Google Checkout application programming interface (API). This option is for large merchants only.

Table 19.3 details the features of these different services.

Table 19.3   Google Checkout's Online Payment Services

	Buy Now Buttons	Shopping Cart Integration	Google Checkout API
Designed for...	Individuals and small businesses	Medium-sized and large businesses	Large businesses
Where customers check out	Google Checkout (on the Google site)	Third-party checkout service	Your website
Technical skills needed	Basic HTML	None	HTML and API programming
Setup fee	Free	Free	Free
Monthly fee	Free	Free	Free
Per-transaction fees	2% + $0.20	2% + $0.20	2% + $0.20

Obviously, there's no cost advantage to using one service over another, so which option should you choose? If you're a small merchant or an individual selling a limited number of items, the choice is simple: Go with the Buy Now buttons. If you're a larger merchant with a preexisting shopping cart and checkout system, the choice is also simple: Use the Google Checkout API. And if you happen to already use a checkout system or an e-commerce hosting service that integrates with Google Checkout, go with the shopping cart integration option.

> **note**
>
> Google Checkout integrates with more than 40 shopping cart providers and e-commerce hosting services. See the full list at checkout.google.com/seller/integrate_cart.html.

Adding Google Checkout to Your Website

For many small sellers, the quickest and easiest way to get started is to add Google Checkout Buy Now buttons to your website. When a customer clicks on the Buy Now button, he's taken to the checkout system hosted by Google Checkout, where he can pay via credit card.

To add a Buy Now button to your website, sign into Google Checkout, select the Tools tab, and then click the Buy Now Buttons link. This takes you to the Create a Buy Now Button page, shown in Figure 19.2.

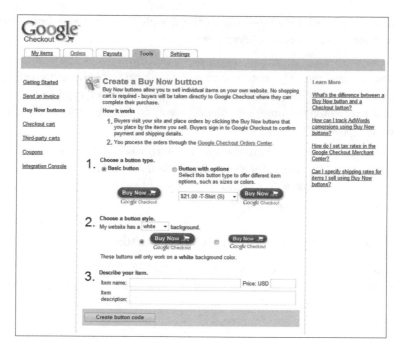

FIGURE 19.2

Creating a Google Buy Now button for your product pages.

From here, you select a button type (basic button or button with pull-down options list) and button style, and you enter your item's name, price, and description. Click the Create Button Code button, and Google generates the HTML code for the button. Copy the code from this page into your web page's basic HTML code, where you want the button to appear, and you're ready to go.

If you're a large retailer, you need to integrate Google Checkout with your existing shopping cart. This is actually easier than it sounds if you're using a Google-compatible shopping cart or an e-commerce hosting service. Just follow the instructions provided by the shopping cart or hosting service.

Collecting Google Checkout Payments

What happens when someone clicks the Google Checkout Buy Now button on your website? If you've configured Google Checkout appropriately, Google emails you whenever a new order is received. Otherwise, you can manually check the Orders tab of the Google Checkout Merchant Center. All recent orders are displayed here.

To view information about a specific order, simply click the order number. You now see the order details and have the option of choosing a shipping carrier and entering a tracking number. You also need to okay the order and charge the customer's credit card; you do this by clicking the Charge button beside the order.

When you're ready to ship the order, return to the Orders tab and click the Ship button beside the order. This will mark the item as shipped, and an email message will automatically be sent to the customer, informing him that the package is on the way.

Withdrawing Google Checkout Funds

Unlike PayPal, Google Checkout automatically deposits all funds due into your bank account. For this to happen, of course, you have to supply your bank account information to Google Checkout, which you should have done during the sign-up process.

note

On an ongoing basis, Google Checkout initiates payment to your account within two business days of a transaction. Know, however, that it might take up to three additional days for your bank to process the funds transfer. So expect payment from a purchase to show up in your bank account within five days of the original purchase.

Integrating Google Checkout with Google AdWords

Here's something that makes Google Checkout especially attractive—and, for some sellers, free. If you advertise with Google AdWords, you get a discount on your Google Checkout fees. For every $1 you spend on the AdWords program, you can process $10 in Google Checkout sales for free.

For example, if you spent $100 on AdWords in the previous month, you can process $1,000 in sales through Google Checkout at no cost. Obviously, this is an incentive for you to use AdWords to advertise your website, but it's a useful incentive—one that can save you big money over time.

And once you sign up for Google Checkout, a shopping cart icon will appear next to all your AdWords text ads. This provides a fast track for customers to click your ad and purchase your item, using the Google Checkout system.

---

note

Learn more about AdWords in Chapter 20, "Promoting Your E-Commerce Website."

Accepting Payments with Checkout by Amazon

There's a new contender in the online payment service wars, and it's a name you know. Checkout by Amazon puts Amazon.com's vaunted checkout process on your website, providing customers a familiar experience and you an end-to-end shopping cart/checkout solution, complete with credit card processing.

Pros and Cons of Checkout by Amazon

First, the good news—and there's lots of it. In general, the fees for using Checkout by Amazon are right in line with those you pay for using PayPal. There are some exceptions to the rule, but if you're selling items that cost $10 or more, you pay 2.9% of the total transaction cost plus $0.30 per transaction. That's identical to PayPal fees.

Second, Checkout for Amazon is a great shopping cart and checkout process for customers. If you've ever shopped at Amazon yourself, you know what I mean. In fact, if your customers are also Amazon customers, they can check out using their Amazon information. For these joint customers, you also have the option of offering 1-click ordering, just like Amazon does on its site. In addition, Amazon offers your customers its own purchase protection plan, which is a nice bonus.

And here's another bonus: Checkout by Amazon lets you upsell additional products within the checkout pipeline. That's something you can't do with PayPal or Google Checkout.

On the downside, using Checkout by Amazon does link you inextricably to the Amazon behemoth. I say that's a downside, as most merchants like to establish their own identity online—although some newer merchants might like the automatic authority granted via the Amazon association. But even though Amazon lets you co-brand the checkout pipeline (your logo and Amazon's), there is the risk that customers will think you're part of Amazon, which is probably not the image you want to project.

Then there's a small detail regarding those fees. While fees on orders of $10 or higher are identical to those of PayPal, if you sell something totaling less than $10, you pay a much higher fee—5% plus $0.30 per transaction. That helps to eat up what little profit you make on lower-priced items.

In addition, the standard 2.9% fee, while identical to PayPal's fee, is considerably higher than what you pay with Google Checkout. That's a minus in my book.

Understanding Checkout by Amazon Fees

Let's take a closer look at Checkout by Amazon's transaction fees. As with PayPal, the fees go down the more business you do. Table 19.4 provides details.

Table 19.4 Checkout by Amazon Fee Structure

Monthly Sales Volume (Transactions of $10 or More)	Percentage of Transaction	Per-Transaction Fee
< $3,000	2.9%	$0.30
$3,000–$10,000	2.5%	$0.30
$10,000.01–$100,000	2.2%	$0.30
> $100,000	1.9%	$0.30
Any transaction of less than $10	5.0%	$0.05

Amazon charges no setup fee or monthly subscription fee. You get charged only for transactions your customers complete. Your funds are then automatically deposited into your checking account via electronic transfer.

Setting Up Checkout by Amazon

You set up a Checkout by Amazon account at payments.amazon.com. Once your account is in place, you generate the HTML code for Amazon payment buttons for each of the products you sell. Insert this code into your product pages, and your customers see an Add to Cart button on each of your product pages, along with the Checkout with Amazon button shown in Figure 19.3.

FIGURE 19.3

Your customers see this Checkout with Amazon button when it's time to buy.

To order an item, the customer clicks the Add to Cart button. This places the product in their shopping cart; they can then order additional products or check out to place their order—which they do by clicking the Checkout with Amazon button. When they do this, several things may happen:

- If the customer is an Amazon customer and has 1-click shopping enabled, the button expands into a Buy with 1-Click widget. The customer now clicks the Buy with 1-Click button, and the order is automatically placed, no checkout process necessary.

- If the customer is an Amazon customer and does not have 1-click shopping enabled, the button still expands into a widget, but the customer clicks the Continue Checkout button. The customer now sees an order summary as a popup window on your website. To complete the order, the customer clicks the Place Your Order button.

- If the customer is not an Amazon customer, clicking the Checkout with Amazon button takes the customer to the Amazon Payments website, where she's prompted to sign in with an existing or create a new Amazon account. She then chooses a shipping address and payment method and completes the order.

At the conclusion of each process, the customer is returned to a designated page on your website, so that she can shop some more if she'd like.

As the seller, you're notified by email when an order has been placed. You then pack and ship the item and wait for Amazon to deposit your funds into your checking account.

Establishing Your Own Merchant Credit Card Account

Most small and medium-sized online retailers use one of the three online payment services just discussed. At rates ranging from 2.0% to 2.9% per transaction (plus a nominal flat transaction fee), it's not a huge burden to accept credit card payments in this fashion.

That said, higher-volume sellers may be able to get an even lower per-transaction rate by signing up for a merchant credit card account from a traditional credit card processing service. Read on to learn more.

Pros and Cons of a Merchant Account

For most online sellers, the attraction of establishing a merchant credit card account is the apparent cost savings. Most merchant credit card services have rates in the 2% to 3% range, with per-transaction fees of between $0.20 and $0.30. For many merchants, that translates into a slightly lower rate than you pay to PayPal, Google Checkout, or Checkout by Amazon. In other instances, however, the rate you pay may be slightly more, believe it or not. Obviously, it makes sense to shop around—and to compare *all* fees charged by a provider, including monthly setup and monthly subscription fees.

You see, many credit card processors charge more than just transaction fees; you may also be charged a setup fee of $25 to $400, a monthly service fee, and fees for software or terminal use. Some services also make you purchase expensive software or credit card terminals upfront. In addition, get used to paying different fees for different customer credit cards. (American Express's rate is typically higher than MasterCard's and Visa's.) In addition, transaction rates for online sales are typically higher than rates charged for traditional retail transactions—so don't get lured in by low rates that apply only to brick-and-mortar stores.

For example, Merchant Accounts Express (as of January 2009) charges 2.27% on each Internet transaction plus a $0.24 flat transaction fee and a $0.05 address verification fee; Network Solutions charges 2.16% on each Internet transaction plus a $0.30 authorization fee. While both these providers charge less than you pay for PayPal transactions, their fees are more than you pay for Google Checkout. And these processors are right in the middle of the pack, as far as fees go; ProPay, as another example, charges anywhere from 2.69% to 3.5% per transaction (plus $0.35 to $0.70 in flat transaction fees), depending on the plan you sign up for. At the high end, that's considerably more expensive than any of the major online payment services.

So going with a merchant account isn't necessarily cheaper than using PayPal, Checkout by Amazon, or Google Checkout. But even if you do the math and think you may pay a little less with a merchant account, be aware of a few issues that may come up.

First, establishing a merchant credit card account is more hassle than signing up for PayPal or Google Checkout. You may have to submit business documentation and possibly have your own credit checked, and the time it takes to set up your account may be measured in weeks instead of hours.

Second, getting everything up and running may also be more involved than simply plugging into a typical online payment service system. For example, most credit card processing services require you to either purchase and program a credit card terminal (even if you don't physically swipe any credit cards) or install dedicated card-processing software on your PC. Either option typically involves a high upfront purchase cost, which you don't have with PayPal and its ilk. (And, for what it's worth, those terminals and that terminal software are notoriously fickle in terms of operation; it's not unusual to spend a few hours on the tech support line trying to get everything set up and running properly.)

Bottom line: It may make sense to pay a little more per transaction for the convenience offered by PayPal, Google Checkout, or Checkout by Amazon. And you may not even pay more for one of these convenient services; not all merchant credit card processors offer lower rates than what you get with an online payment service.

Choosing a Credit Card Processor

Where can you go to sign up for merchant credit card processing services? Here's a short list of firms to choose from:

- Charge.com (www.charge.com)
- Chase Paymentech (www.paymentech.com)
- First Data (www.firstdata.com)
- Merchant Accounts Express (www.merchantexpress.com)
- Network Solutions Merchant Accounts (merchantaccounts.networksolutions.com)
- ProPay (epay.propay.com)
- Total Merchant Services (www.merchant-account-4u.com)

***

tip

Both Costco (www.elavon.com/acquiring/costco/) and Sam's Club (www.samsclub.com) also offer merchant credit card processing to their business members, at affordable rates. For example, Costco offers a 1.99% transaction rate (plus $0.27 per transaction fee); Sam's Club offers a 1.98% transaction rate (plus $0.26 per transaction fee). See each company's website for more information.

Before you sign up for any credit card service, ask the credit card processor to do an analysis based on your previous month's credit card business. Get the results and then compare the numbers.

When you inquire, ask about *all* applicable fees. In particular, check on software integration fees, monthly service fees, virtual terminal fees, and the like. You may also have to hit monthly minimums or pay an additional fee. And don't be surprised if your head starts swimming; most of these companies have extremely complex fee structures, based on the types of credit cards accepted (commercial cards, debit cards, private label cards, and so forth), the types of customers you have, the types of products you sell, and the types of transactions you make.

Bottom line: Check the fine print before you sign up; what sounds like a good deal may or may not be. There's nothing wrong with staying with PayPal or Google Checkout!

How Online Payment Services Make Money

It goes without saying that all online payment services are in business to make money. Just how that money is made might surprise you, however.

You might think that online payment services generate their profits from the fees they collect from sellers. While it's true that these fees generate revenue, they don't always generate a lot of profit. That's because the online payment service has to pay fees of its own to the credit card companies (MasterCard, Visa, American Express, and Discover) to use their networks. In most instances, the fees charged by the credit card companies are very close to the fees that the online payment service charges its sellers. There's a little margin for profit there, but it's slight; the payment service's fees just cover the credit card companies' fees.

Instead, PayPal, Google Checkout, and the like make most of their profits from interest. You see, there's a lag between when funds are received from the credit card companies and when those funds are withdrawn by retailers. That time lag might be only a day or two, but during that time, the funds reside in the payment service's bank accounts, where interest is earned on the money. You might think that the interest earned for a day on a $25 transaction would be so slight as to be unnoticeable, and you'd be right. But multiply that single transaction by a few million, and you can see how quickly the pennies add up.

In other words, online payment services make their money by handling your money—even if just for a few days. ■

20

Promoting Your E-Commerce Website

When you sell on eBay, you don't have to worry a whole lot about promotion. That's one of the benefits of selling on eBay—those millions of potential customers already on the site looking for stuff to buy. If you have the right stuff to sell, you'll do fine.

Running your own website is a completely different beast, promotion-wise. You have *no* built-in customer base to start with, so you have to do something to attract potential customers to your site. This is work that you didn't have to do on eBay but that now becomes a big day-to-day focus—and a big cost center. Promoting your online store takes time and money, along with no small degree of skill.

What marketing tools can you use to promote your business online? There are a lot of things you can and should do, from search engine optimization to buying advertising. Let's see what you have to work with.

Putting Together a Marketing Plan

Before you spend your first penny on promotion, you need to do a little planning. (That's right, more planning...get used to it.) You need to evaluate all the different types of promotion you can do, pick the methods you should use, and then decide how much money you need or want to spend to do it.

All these details comprise a marketing plan, and you have to write one. It's just what a traditional brick-and-mortar retailer or a big corporation would do, and it's just as important to your business as it is to them.

A good marketing plan starts with an overall marketing budget—the total dollar figure you intend to spend on promotional activities. Most companies figure this by calculating a percentage of projected yearly sales. This percentage varies from industry to industry and from business to business, but for a new retailing business, I'd advise budgeting from 5% to 10% of your sales for marketing purposes. For example, if you think you're going to do $50,000 in sales in your first 10 months, you should budget between $2,500 and $5,000 for your marketing expenditures.

note

Naturally, you should include this marketing expense in your business's budget projections. It's a necessary cost but one that you need to factor in when pricing your products and putting together your financials.

You can then take your total marketing budget and proportion it out to various types of marketing activities. For example, you might want to devote 80% of your budget to pay-per-click advertising and the remaining 20% to email marketing. Again, there's no one set way to divvy up your marketing funds; what you decide to spend your money on is your decision and your decision alone.

Of course, money is only part of the plan. Many promotional activities are essentially free or low cost in terms of monetary expenditure; instead, they require substantial time commitments. Public relations, for example, doesn't cost a lot of money but does have a big time cost. Now, time may be something you have a lot of, in which case a little hard work can have a big payback. So don't forget to include these low-cost marketing activities as part of your plan.

Finally, your marketing plan should detail your activities by month. You'll probably want to front-load your promotional activities, as you need to spend more money upfront to get customers into your new online store. After you've established a customer base, you can afford to back off of your marketing to some extent.

What activities should you include in your marketing plan? That's what we discuss throughout the rest of this chapter, so read on to learn more.

Optimizing Your Site for Search Engines

We'll start with a marketing tool that is both low cost and extremely important—search engine marketing. At its most basic, search engine marketing involves driving traffic from Google and other search engines to your website.

All About Search Engine Marketing—and SEO

Search engine marketing may be the only marketing many online retailers do for their sites. That's because, for most websites, the majority of traffic comes not from direct URL entry or even links from other websites but from queries made at Google, Yahoo!, and the other search engines. So if half or more of most sites' traffic comes from the search engines, you need to maximize your rankings at these search sites to maximize your potential site traffic—and the way you increase your site's search ranking is to optimize your site for the search engines. This is known as search engine optimization (SEO) and should be part of your site design process.

So, for most online businesses, search engine marketing and the attending SEO represent a major component of the online marketing mix. It's not the only thing you should do to market your business online, but it may be the most important thing.

With that in mind, I now present five key factors that can help you improve your search rankings. When you pay attention to these factors, you can effectively optimize your site for higher rankings with all the major search engines. This is what SEO is all about.

---

note

Learn more about SEO in my companion book, *The Complete Idiot's Guide to Search Engine Optimization* (Alpha Books, 2009).

SEO Tip #1: Fine-Tune Your Keywords

The words and phrases that users insert into their search queries are called *keywords*. These keywords should also be the most important words and phrases on your site, as they're key to high rankings with all the major search engines.

Google and the other search engines determine the relevancy of a web page to a given query by looking for those keywords on the page. The search engines not only make sure that the keywords are on the page but also examine where and how they're used on the page, to determine how important a keyword appears to be.

The search engines do this by seeing where on the page the keyword is used and how many times. A site with a keyword buried near the bottom of a page will rank lower than one with the keyword placed near the top or used repeatedly in the page's text. It's not a foolproof way of determining importance and appropriateness, but it's a good first stab at it.

Remember, the keyword or phrase is what the user is searching for. If someone is searching for "shirts," and your page includes the keyword "shirts" (or "shirt," singular) in a prominent position—in the first sentence of the first paragraph, for example—then that page is a good match for that search. If, on the other hand, your page doesn't include the word "shirts" at all, or if it includes the word only near the bottom of the page, then the search engines will determine that your site *isn't* a good match for that searcher. It doesn't matter if you have a big picture of a shirt at the top of your page (search engines can't read images, as you'll discover in a moment); unless you use the keyword prominently and relatively often, you won't rank highly for that particular search.

So the various search engines, when they examine your site, look for the most important words—the words used in the page's title or headings, the words that appear in the opening paragraph, and the words that are repeated throughout the page. The more and more prominently you include a word on your page, the more important a search engine will think it is to your site.

---

caution

Giving prominent placement to the wrong words can hurt your search rankings by providing less relevant results. If your site is about power tools but you for some reason include the words "boot" and "leather" multiple times on the page, your site will likely be viewed as a site about leather boots. This not only drives the wrong visitors to your site but also lowers your search ranking in general because you're now one of the less-useful leather boot sites listed.

So you can see that you want to make sure that each and every page on your site contains the keywords that users might use to search for your pages. If you're selling drums, for example, make sure your pages include words such as "drums," "percussion," "sticks," "heads," "cymbals," "snare," and the like. Try to think through how *you* would search for this information and work those keywords into your content.

SEO Tip #2: Tweak Your `<META>` and `<TITLE>` Tags

When calculating search ranking, most search engines not only consider the visible content on a page, they also evaluate the content of key HTML tags—in particular, each page's `<META>` tag. You want to make sure that you use the `<META>` tag in your page's code and assign important keywords to this tag.

---

note

For optimal search engine optimization, you need to know a little bit about HTML. This book isn't the place to find that information; instead, check out *Sams Teach Yourself HTML in 10 Minutes* (Deidre Hayes, Sams, 2006), a quick little guide to everything you need to know about HTML coding.

The `<META>` tag, which (along with the `<TITLE>` tag) is placed in the head of your HTML document, can be used to supply all sorts of information about your document. You can insert multiple `<META>` tags into the head of your document, and each tag can contain a number of different attributes—including the keywords used on that page. Just insert all the keywords you've identified for that page into the tag, like this:

```
<META NAME="KEYWORDS" CONTENT="keyword1, keyword2, keyword3">
```

It's easy enough for a search engine to locate the `<META>` tag and read the data contained within. If a site's metadata is properly indicated, this gives the search engine a good first idea as to what content is included on this page.

That said, the `<META>` tag isn't the only HTML tag that searchbots look for. For example, the `<TITLE>` tag is just as important as the `<META>` tag—which is why you shouldn't fall into the trap of assigning only your site name to the tag. Instead, the `<TITLE>` tag should contain two or three important keywords, followed by the site or page name. Most search engines place major importance on the `<TITLE>` tag when determining a site's content; you want to make sure that your site's most important content is listed within this tag.

SEO Tip #3: Solicit Inbound Links from Other Sites

Google was the first search engine to recognize that web rankings could be somewhat of a popularity contest—that is, if a site got a lot of traffic, there was probably a good reason for that. A useless site wouldn't attract a lot of visitors (at least not long term), nor would it inspire other sites to link to it.

So if a site has a lot of other sites linking back to it, it's probably because that site offers useful information relevant to the site doing the linking. The more links to a given site, the more useful that site probably is.

If your site has 100 sites linking to it, for example, it should rank higher in Google's search results than a similar site with only 10 sites linking to it. Yes, it's a popularity contest, but one that has proven uncannily accurate in providing relevant results to Google's users.

And it's not just the quantity of links that matters; it's also the quality. That is, a site that includes content that is relative to your page is more important than some random site that links to your page. For example, if you have a site selling NASCAR racing paraphernalia, you'll get more oomph with a link from another NASCAR-related site than you would with a link from a site about Barbie dolls. Relevance matters.

To increase your ranking, then, you want to get more higher-quality sites to link to your site. There are a number of ways to do this, from just waiting for the links to roll in to actively soliciting links from other sites. You can even pay other sites to link to your site; when it comes to increasing your site's search ranking, little is out of bounds.

SEO Tip #4: Submit Your Site to the Major Search Engines

While you could wait for each search engine's crawler to find your site on the web, a more proactive approach is to manually submit your site for inclusion in each engine's web index. It's an easy process—and one that every webmaster should master.

Table 20.1 details the URLs you use to submit your site to the major search engines.

Table 20.1 Search Engine Submittal URLs

Search Engine	URL
Google	www.google.com/addurl/
Windows Live Search	search.msn.com.sg/docs/submit.aspx
Yahoo!	siteexplorer.search.yahoo.com/submit/

Alternatively, you can use a third-party website submittal service to do all the submitting for you. These services let you enter your URL once and then submit it to multiple search engines and directories; they handle all the details required by each search engine. Given that many of these services are free, it's not a bad way to go.

These are some of the most popular site submittal services:

- 1 2 3 Submit Pro (websitesubmit.hypermart.net)
- AddMe! (www.addme.com)
- AddPro.com (www.addpro.com)
- SubmitExpress (www.submitexpress.com)

caution

Beware of services that charge a high fee for search engine submission. They don't do anything that you can't do yourself for free.

In addition to just submitting your site's URL, you should also create and submit a *sitemap* of your website. A sitemap is a map of all the URLs in your entire website, listed in hierarchical order. Search engines can use your sitemap to determine what's where on your site, find otherwise-hidden URLs on deeply buried pages, and speed up their indexing process. In addition, whenever you update the pages on your website, submitting an updated sitemap helps keep the search engines up-to-date.

Note that submitting a sitemap supplements, rather than replaces, the usual methods of adding pages to a search engine's index. If you don't submit a sitemap, your pages may still be discovered by the search engines' crawlers, and you may still manually submit your site for inclusion in each site's index.

While you could create a sitemap file by hand, it's far easier to generate one automatically. Many third-party sitemap generator tools exist for just this purpose. Some of these tools are web based, some are software programs, and most are free. The most popular of these tools include the following:

- AutoMapIt (www.automapit.com)
- AutoSitemap (www.autositemap.com)
- G-Mapper (www.dbnetsolutions.co.uk/gmapper/)
- GSiteCrawler (www.gsitecrawler.com)
- Gsitemap (www.vigos.com/products/gsitemap/)
- Site Magellan (www.sitemagellan.com)
- SitemapsPal (www.sitemapspal.com)
- SitemapDoc (www.sitemapdoc.com)
- XML-Sitemaps.com (www.xml-sitemaps.com)

For most of these tools, generating a sitemap is as simple as entering your home page's URL and then clicking a button. The tool then crawls your website and automatically generates a sitemap file; this typically takes just a few minutes.

---

tip

In most instances, you should name your sitemap file `sitemap.xml` and place it in the uppermost (root) directory of your website—although you can name and locate it differently, if you like.

Once you've created your sitemap file, you have to let the search engine crawlers know where it is. You do this via a reference in the `robots.txt` file, which should already exist in the root directory of your website.

What you need to do is add the following line to your `robots.txt` file:

```
SITEMAP: www.sitename.com/sitemap.xml
```

Naturally, you need to include the actual location of your sitemap file. The example shown here works only if you have the file in your site's root directory; if it's in another directory, you need to include that full path. Also, if you've named your sitemaps file something other than `sitemap.xml`, you should use the actual name instead.

The next time a searchbot crawls your site, it will read your `robots.txt` file, learn the location of your sitemap file, and then read the information in that file. It will then crawl all the pages listed in the file and submit information about each page to the search engine for indexing.

SEO Tip #5: Use Text Instead of Images

Today's search engines are somewhat crude, in that they parse only text content on a web page; they can't figure out what a picture or graphic is about, unless you describe it in the text. So if you use pictures or graphic images to convey important information on a page (as you might do on a typical product page), the search engines simply won't see it. You need to put every piece of information that matters somewhere in the *text* of the page—even if it's duplicated in a picture or graphic.

---

caution

Similarly, don't hide important information in Flash animations, JavaScript applets, video files, and the like. Remember, searchbots can only find text on your page—all those non-text elements are invisible to a search engine.

So when you use images on your site, make sure you use the <ALT> tag for each image—and assign meaningful keywords to the image via this tag. A searchbot will read the <ALT> tag text; it can't figure out what an image is without it.

> **tip**
>
> Here's a bonus tip: To maintain a high search engine ranking, you need to frequently update your site's content. Since most searchbots crawl the web with some frequency, looking for pages that have changed or updated content, your ranking can be affected if your site hasn't changed in a while. For this reason, you want to make sure you change the content of your home page on a regular basis.

Submitting Your Products to Comparison Shopping Sites

Search engines such as Google are separate and different from comparison shopping sites such as Shopping.com. Customers use comparison shopping sites to search for the best prices on specific products, and you can use them to drive traffic to your new online store.

When a customer searches for a product on one of these sites, she sees a list of retailers that sell that product, as shown in Figure 20.1. It's one click from this list to the product page on a retailer's own website, where the sale can be made.

How Comparison Shopping Sites Work

Consumers might be under the impression that comparison shopping sites scour the web for prices from a wide variety of online retailers. That's a false impression; instead, these sites build their price/product databases from product links submitted and paid for by participating online retailers. That's right: Most price comparison sites charge retailers to be included in their listings; that's how the sites make money.

Fortunately for retailers who have large inventories, payment isn't on a per-listing basis; instead, you pay when customers click your product listings. This is the called the *pay-per-click* (PPC) model, and the individual fee is based on a specific *cost per click* (CPC). CPC charges run anywhere from a nickel to more than a buck, depending on the site and the product category.

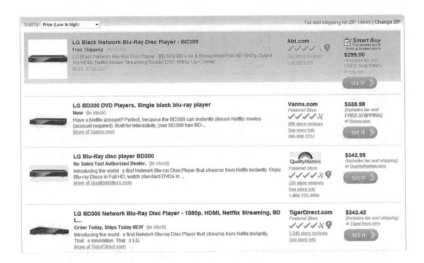

FIGURE 20.1
Comparison shopping for Blu-ray players at Shopping.com.

For most online retailers, listing with the major comparison shopping sites is an important part of the marketing mix. These sites often provide more (and more important) visibility than you get by relying on organic search results from Google, Live Search, and Yahoo! Even though you pay for the click-throughs, these clicks are likely to result in sales.

Examining the Major Comparison Shopping Sites

When it comes to comparison shopping sites, there are 10 that consistently attract the most consumer traffic:

- **BizRate** (www.bizrate.com) is one of the oldest comparison shopping sites, founded way back in the stone ages of 1996. In addition to product listings, it also offers customer reviews of the most popular products, as well as reviews of online retailers. These product and merchant reviews make BizRate an extremely useful shopping comparison site.

note

BizRate is owned by Shopzilla and shares the same product database as its parent site.

- **Google Product Search** (www.google.com/products/), formerly known as Froogle, is Google's online shopping directory. Unlike the other comparison shopping sites, Google Product Search doesn't accept payments for its listings. Instead, the site uses Google's crawler software to independently scour the web for merchants and products, free of charge. That doesn't mean, however, that you can't submit your products to Google Product Search for inclusion in its index—because you can. In fact, submitting your products ensures inclusion in the index, while relying on Google searchbot is a little dicier. But, unlike all the other shopping directories, you don't have to pay to submit or pay when your listing clicked. Like all things Google, this one is free.

- **Live Search Cashback** (search.live.com/cashback/) is Microsoft's online shopping site, a subset of its Live Search site. This site is unique in that it pays consumers to use the site. More precisely, the site offers cash rebates when users purchase from one of its listings; it's Microsoft's way of buying its way into the shopping directory market.

- **mySimon** (www.mysimon.com) was one of the first price comparison sites on the web. It's still one of the most popular, even though it doesn't include near as many merchants as some competing directories. (For what it's worth, mySimon is part of the CNET network of sites; this enables the site to include product specifications and reviews from the parent CNET site—a distinct advantage over many competing sites.)

- **NexTag** (www.nextag.com) includes listings for everything from computer monitors to airline flights. It has been one of the top five online shopping sites since it was founded in 1999, serving up product listings to more than 17 million consumers each month.

- **PriceGrabber** (www.pricegrabber.com) is one of the most-trafficked shopping directories on the web, with more than 26 million users. In addition to traditional product listings, it offers an online storefront service for smaller merchants and individual sellers.

- **Pricewatch** (www.pricewatch.com) specializes in computers and consumer electronics products. It's not the directory for you if your business sells clothing or other soft goods, but if you offer any sort of electronic gadget for sale, it's a good place to list.

- **Shopping.com** (www.shopping.com) is my personal favorite comparison shopping site. From a consumer's perspective, Shopping.com provides more than just simple price comparisons; it also offers customer reviews of both products and merchants, to help people make better purchase decisions. From a merchant's perspective,

Shopping.com hosts 1.5 million customers per day—and delivers 17 million sales leads to participating retailers each month. If you're an online merchant, it should definitely be at the top of your online shopping directory hit list.

note

Shopping.com was acquired by eBay in 2005—but there is very little interaction between the online shopping directory and eBay's online auction site.

- **Shopzilla** (www.shopzilla.com) offers consumers a more streamlined interface than the category-heavy sites of many of its competitors. That said, it operates from the same product database as its related BizRate site, which is a nice two-fer for participating merchants.

- **Yahoo! Shopping** (shopping.yahoo.com) is Yahoo!'s online shopping directory. Previously a simple directory of online merchants, the site was revamped several years ago into one of the leading price comparison sites on the web, complete with numerous product comparison features for consumers.

note

DealTime product listings are also incorporated as part of the Shopping.com site.

Submitting Your Listings to Comparison Shopping Sites

Now that you know which are the most popular comparison shopping sites, how do you get your products listed on these sites? While the detailed listing process differs somewhat from site to site, the general principles are the same.

Each comparison shopping site operates a consumer front end (for shoppers) and a merchant front end (for retailers). You can typically find the link to the merchant page at the bottom of the site's consumer home page.

Before you submit any listings to a directory, you have to sign up for the site's merchant program—sometimes called an advertiser program. This is normally a simple process, with no upfront charge. During this process, you have a chance to review the site's CPC rates, any additional listing features you can pay for, and the site's data submission process. Make sure you know what you're signing up for before you commit and send your first data file.

As noted previously, most comparison shopping sites don't charge you to submit your product listings—which would be cost-prohibitive if you had a large number of SKUs. They do charge you, however, when a customer clicks on a product listing to go to your website; you pay whether that customer buys anything or not.

How much will you pay? The CPC rates differ from site to site and from category to category but typically run from a nickel to a buck per click. Check with each site to get the precise pricing schedule.

Creating and Uploading a Data File

How do you get your products listed on a comparison shopping site? Fortunately, almost all of these sites accept bulk uploading of all the items in your inventory. You can therefore submit all your products to a site in a single file.

The first step of this process is to create a data file of the products you have for sale. Check the requirements for a given site, but expect most sites to accept information in either tab-delimited text, spreadsheet, or XML (RSS or Atom) formats.

For most online retailers, the easiest approach is to use Microsoft Excel to create a spreadsheet file that contains all the required data. You can then save this file as a tab-delineated TXT file, if that's what a given site requires. While the specific requirements differ from site to site (and you should check with each site to find out exactly what it needs—and in what format), most such files include some or all of the following information about each product:

- URL for the product page on your site
- Product name
- Item number or UPC (bar code)
- Price
- Quantity available
- Product category

In your spreadsheet, create one column for each type of data required. Create one row for each product you offer. If the site accepts Excel format XLS files, you're done—save for uploading the file, of course. If the file requirements are different, you'll need to save this file in the required file format.

> **tip**
>
> If you have a large number of SKUs, look into automating this process by export-ing your inventory listings directly into the spreadsheet file.

Once you've created your data file, you have to upload it to each of the comparison shopping sites you work with. This process differs from site to site (of course), so you'll need to consult the precise instructions for each site. In general, however, it's typically a simple matter of clicking an "upload file" link on the site and then selecting the file to upload.

> **tip**
>
> Even though Google Product Search doesn't accept paid listings, it will accept your product data file (for free). You submit your product inventory to Google Product Search via Google's related Google Base service; learn more at www.google.com/base/help/sellongoogle.html.

How often you upload a file depends on the site's requirements and how often your inventory levels change. You may be able to get by uploading a file once a week, or you may need to upload an updated data file daily. Again, check the site's requirements.

Buying PPC Advertising

Improving your ranking in a search engine's search results isn't the only way to reach the millions of potential customers who use search engines each day. You can also purchase ad space on the search results pages—text ads that look a lot like the organic search results.

For this type of pay-per-click (PPC) advertising, you purchase specific key-words or phrases. Your ad appears in the "paid results" section of search engine results pages when a user searches for that particular word or phrase. You don't pay for the ad itself; you pay only when a customer clicks the link in your ad to go to your website.

Many companies combine organic search marketing with PPC advertising in a holistic online marketing campaign. They're closely connected, after all—and the combination of the two increases your chances of reaching potential customers through a given search engine.

How Important Is PPC Advertising?

Because you only pay when someone clicks on an ad (and then hopefully purchases something on your site), many online retailers, large and small, integrate PPC into their marketing mix. But how much of *your* mix should you devote to PPC advertising?

It depends. While it's unlikely that PPC ads will drive as much traffic to your site as will organic search engine results or submissions to the price comparison sites, it can still be an effective part of your mix. There will always be some percentage of searchers who either confuse paid results with organic results, thus benefiting PPC advertisers, or who trust the paid results much the same way they trust display ads in traditional Yellow Pages directories.

Purchasing Keywords

Pay-per-click advertising isn't like traditional display advertising, which we'll get to in a moment. PPC advertising doesn't buy discrete space on a given web page, nor does it allow for graphics-intensive advertisements. Instead, it's all about getting a text ad onto a specific search results page.

A PPC advertiser purchases a particular keyword or phrase from the ad network—or, more precisely, ad space that appears on search results pages and other websites that relate to the keywords in question. The advertiser's text ad is linked to that keyword in two different ways.

First, when a user enters a query on that ad network's related search engine site, the advertiser's ad is displayed on the first page of the search results, typically in a "paid results" or "sponsored links" section either on the top or side of the page. As you can see in Figure 20.2, this type of ad is designed to look kind of like an organic search result.

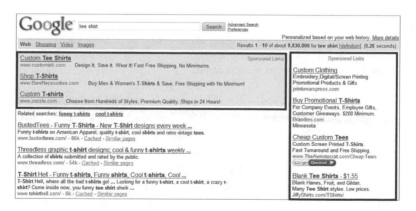

FIGURE 20.2

PPC ads from the Google AdWords network—the "sponsored links" at the top and right side of a Google search results page.

The second place the ad appears is on third-party sites that belong to the ad network. The ad is placed on specific pages that contain content related to the purchased keyword. These ads, also text only (as you can see in Figure 20.3), can appear anywhere on the page; the ad placement is up to the owner of the web page.

FIGURE 20.3

Google AdWords PPC ads on a third-party web page.

So, for example, if you sold printer ink cartridges, you might purchase the words "printer," "ink," and "cartridges." When a consumer searches for any of these keywords on the ad network's search engine, your ad appears. Your ad also appears when a consumer goes to a third-party website that features content containing these keywords.

Paying by the Click

Of course, the reason it's called *pay-per-click* advertising is that an advertiser pays the ad network only when customers click on the link in the ad. (The link typically points to the advertiser's website—or, most commonly, a special landing page on the website.) If no one clicks, the advertiser doesn't pay anyone anything. The more clicks that are registered, the more the advertiser pays.

note

PPC advertising is in contrast to traditional cost-per-thousand-impressions (CPM) advertising, where rates are based on the number of potential viewers of the ad—whether they click through or not.

Ad rates are on a cost-per-click (CPC) basis. That is, the advertiser is charged a particular fee for each click—anywhere from a few pennies to tens of dollars. The actual CPC rate is determined by the popularity of and competition for the keyword purchased, as well as the quality and quantity of traffic going to the site hosting the ad. As you can imagine, popular keywords have a higher CPC, while less popular keywords can be had for less.

Advertisers typically bid on the most popular keywords. That is, you might say you'll pay up to $5 for a given keyword. If you're the high bidder among several advertisers, your ads will appear more frequently on pages that contain that keyword. If you're not the high bidder, you won't get as much visibility—if your ad appears at all.

> **note**
>
> Here's something important to know about PPC advertising: Your ad probably won't appear on every search engine results page for the keyword your purchase. The page inventory is limited, while advertisers are theoretically unlimited. The big PPC ad networks rotate ads from multiple advertisers on the search results and third-party pages.

Evaluating the Big PPC Ad Networks

Which are the most important PPC ad networks today? Not surprisingly, they're the same companies that run the three largest search engines:

- Google AdWords (adwords.google.com)
- Yahoo! Small Business Search Engine Marketing (sem.smallbusiness.yahoo.com/searchenginemarketing/)
- Microsoft adCenter (adcenter.microsoft.com)

Let's look at each separately.

Google AdWords

Just as Google is the largest search engine, Google AdWords is far and away the largest PPC ad network. Google sells ads on its own search results pages, throughout its entire network of sites, and on participating third-party sites. Google claims that its AdWords program reaches more than 80% of all Internet users; most advertisers confirm that AdWords generates the overwhelming majority of PPC traffic to their sites.

> **note**
>
> The Google Network includes all of Google's sites (Google Maps, Gmail, YouTube, and the rest), the hundreds of thousands of small and medium-sized sites that participate in the Google AdSense program, and a number of major websites, including Amazon.com, AOL, and About.com.

Advertising with Google AdWords isn't like a traditional advertising buy; there are no contracts, deadlines, and such. You pay a one-time $5 activation fee and then are charged either on a CPC or CPM basis. (You can choose either payment method.) You control your costs by specifying how much you're willing to pay (per click or per impression) and by setting a daily spending budget. Google will never exceed the costs you specify.

How much does AdWords cost? It's your choice. If you go with the CPC method, you can choose a maximum CPC click price from $0.01 to $100. If you go with the CPM method, there is a minimum cost of $0.25 per 1,000 impressions. Your daily budget can be as low as a penny, up to whatever you're willing to pay.

If you go the CPC route, Google uses AdWords Discounter technology to match the price you pay with the price offered by competing advertisers for a given keyword. The AdWords Discounter automatically monitors your competition and lowers your CPC to $0.01 above what they're willing to pay.

Creating an AdWords ad is as easy as following these steps:

1. Write the ad (a title line and two lines of text).
2. Enter the URL of the part of your site you want to link to.
3. Choose the keyword(s) you want to purchase—up to 20 keywords or phrases.
4. Set the maximum you're willing to pay per click.
5. Set your monthly AdWords budget—Google recommends a $50 monthly minimum.

Once your ad campaign is started, you can monitor performance from the main AdWords page. From here, you can view your campaign's performance, generate various reports, create new ads, and access Google Analytics for additional performance tracking.

Yahoo! Small Business Search Engine Marketing

Yahoo! Small Business Search Engine Marketing (sem.smallbusiness. yahoo.com/searchenginemarketing/) is a distant number-two in the PPC advertising game. It works pretty much like Google AdWords: You purchase specific keywords, and your ad appears in Yahoo!'s search results for that query, on related sites in the Yahoo! network, and on third-party pages that participate in the Yahoo! Search Marketing program.

Once you sign up for Yahoo! Search Marketing, you can start creating your ads. As with AdWords, the process is fairly straightforward:

1. Choose the keywords you want.
2. Specify your maximum bid per click ($0.10 minimum).
3. Set a daily budget.
4. Write your ad (title, description, and URL).

Yahoo! then matches your keywords with keyword queries of its search engine users, and it displays your ad on those search results pages. Your ad also gets displayed on third-party pages that contain content similar to the keyword(s) you've purchased.

You monitor your Yahoo! campaigns through the Dashboard. You can track multiple campaigns, view campaign performance, generate various reports, and create new campaigns.

Microsoft adCenter

Most advertisers designate the bulk (75% or more) of their PPC ad budgets to Google AdWords, with the remaining amount split between Yahoo! and Microsoft. Microsoft adCenter (adcenter.microsoft.com) is Microsoft's answer to Google and Yahoo!, and it's currently the number-three player in the PPC ad space.

After you sign up for the program, you start creating your adCenter ads the same way you create similar ads with Google and Yahoo! You can create both Search Ads and Content Ads; the former appear in Live Search results pages, the latter on editorial pages on the Microsoft content network.

note

The Microsoft content network features some pretty big sites, including the main MSN web page, MSN Money, MSN Entertainment, FOX Sports, and other similar pages.

The process of creating an ad is similar to that with the other PPC ad networks:

1. Write the ad, including a title, one-line description, and URL.
2. Pick your keywords—up to 100.
3. Set the maximum CPC rate ($0.05 minimum).
4. Set a monthly budget.

When you're done, your ad appears on relevant search and content pages. You manage your account via adCenter Analytics, where you can view all sorts of data about your ad campaigns as well as manage your existing ads and create new ones.

Creating a PPC Campaign

Okay, you think that you need a PPC component to your online marketing plan. What do you need to do to get started?

The first step is to select which ad network or networks to use. If you're just starting out, I recommend going exclusively with Google AdWords; it's easy to use and will far and away deliver the most traffic of all the current ad networks. Once you get the hang of the PPC thing, and if your budget allows, you can expand to include Yahoo! Search Marketing and Microsoft adCenter. But it's okay to start simple, and AdWords is as simple as it gets.

Choosing keywords for PPC advertising is exactly the same as choosing keywords for SEO. In fact, if you've already selected your SEO keywords, these are the keywords you want to purchase for your PPC campaign.

Now we come to the money part of the equation. Most PPC networks require you to bid on the keywords you select, typically in the form of a maximum CPC price you're willing to pay. How do you know how high to go?

Here's where a little research and performance tracking are in order. Basically, you have to determine what a lead—a single click-through—is worth to you.

Start by determining how much profit you make off a sale from your website. For example, let's say you sell an item for $100 retail that costs you $60 to purchase or manufacture; you generate $40 profit on each sale.

Next, determine your conversion rate from your PPC campaign; you can find this metric in the reports section of most ad network dashboards. For most sites, expect your conversion rate to be in the low single digits. For our example, let's say that your conversion rate is 1%, meaning that 1 out of every 100 people who click your ad end up buying your product.

Now it's math time. Each sale you make is worth $40 to you, and it takes 100 clicks to make one sale. Divide $40 by 100, and you discover that each visitor you attract costs you $0.40. This means you can afford to spend a maximum of $0.40 per click before you start losing money on each click. So, in this example, you'd set your maximum price per click to $0.40.

Of course, the effectiveness of the ad you write will, to some degree, determine your conversion rate, and thus your maximum CPC rates. It takes a lot of talent to drive sales from a simple three- or four-line text ad, but that's what you need to develop.

Buying Display Ads

PPC ads are text ads, which should not be confused with more traditional display ads. Display ads are those banner ads that you see at the top (and sometimes along the sides) of web pages. These banner ads combine text and graphics (and sometimes videos and Flash animations), much the same way that display ads work in printed media.

The problem with display advertising, as compared to search engine marketing or PPC advertising, is that the click-through rates are much, much lower. Most people see a display ad and move right past it. Even if the ad registers, they don't bother to click through, which results in click-through rates in the low single digits. Of course, if you purchase space on enough high-traffic websites, even that low click-through rate can generate significant traffic.

That said, display advertising is one of the fastest-growing parts of the online marketing mix, especially for large advertisers. If you have big plans for a big website—and a corresponding big budget—this may be a way to go. But for most smaller online retailers just starting out, it's too expensive, ineffective, and inefficient to be practical.

If you do opt to include display advertising as part of your online marketing mix, you can purchase banner ads directly from some major websites or go through an advertising network. Some of the most popular online ad networks are AdReady (www.adready.com), Casale Media (www.casalemedia.com), Motive Interactive (www.motiveinteractive.com), and ValueClick Media (www.valueclickmedia.com).

tip

Both Google AdWords and Yahoo! Search Marketing offer display advertising as part of their mixes. If you already do PPC advertising with either of these services, you might want to check out their offerings.

Engaging in Email Marketing

After you get your website off the ground, a good way to spend your time and money is on email marketing. An email marketing campaign involves the sending of targeted email messages to your existing customer base; these emails can advertise upcoming promotions, new products, and the like.

note

Don't confuse email marketing with spam emails. Legitimate email marketing is sent only with prior approval by the customer; spam is unsolicited and typically unwanted email.

Most email marketing is a form of direct marketing. You're using the emails not to increase brand awareness or simply drive traffic to your website but rather to solicit direct sales of a particular product. For most online retailers, that means using email to put today's promotions in front of customers and get them to click through and order specific products.

Compared to other parts of the marketing mix, email marketing has several advantages, including the following:

- It's low cost; it costs nothing to send 100,000 emails, compared to the tens of thousands of dollars it would take to send an equivalent number of postal mails.

- It's fast; you can get an email into the hands of a customer within seconds, compared to the days or weeks it might take to place an offer with traditional media.

- It's easily trackable; all you have to do is create a distinct landing page for the URL in the email and then track traffic coming to that page.

- It's proactive; compared to search engine marketing, which waits for a user to find you, you're pushing your message to your customer base.

- It's targeted; you can send email promotions to specified customers in your company's database.

Successful online merchants use email marketing to entice more sales from their existing customer base. If you offer goods or services for sale over the web, email marketing should be an essential part of your marketing mix.

---

tip

Many e-commerce hosting services offer the capability to create and send email promotions to your site's customers. Look for this feature when you're shopping for a website host.

Marketing on YouTube

Here's a new and relatively low-cost way to market your business and products—via videos on YouTube. As you're probably aware, YouTube (www.youtube.com) is the largest video sharing community on the Web, with more than 35 million viewers each month. If you play your cards right, you can create a YouTube video that is seen by thousands if not hundreds of thousands of potential customers—some subset of which can then be persuaded to visit your website for more information or to purchase whatever it is you're selling.

YouTube videos are by nature inexpensive to produce; you don't need anything more than a typical consumer camcorder to do the shooting. And YouTube doesn't charge anything to upload and host your videos. This combination of high potential and low cost makes YouTube marketing ideal for small businesses on a tight budget.

Know, however, that the most effective YouTube business video isn't a blatant advertisement; if all you do is post a 30-second ad online, no one will watch it. Instead, you need to create a video that YouTubers want to watch—something entertaining, educational, or informative. That may be a funny video promoting your product, a how-to video demonstrating how to do something that people really need to do, or a video packed with useful news or information. In fact, the most effective YouTube business videos are rather like infomercials: They use a light sell to get their message across and entice viewers to ask for more.

For example, if you sell auto parts, you may want to produce a series of educational videos showing potential customers how to do things like change their oil or check their brake fluid. If you sell crafts, you may want to produce a series of informational videos showing how you make the items you sell. Make sure you include your website's URL in your videos, and interested viewers can then visit your site for more information—and hopefully to buy something.

note

Learn more about using YouTube videos for marketing in my companion book, *YouTube for Business* (Que, 2008).

Marketing to the Blogosphere

Blogs are becoming more important to savvy online marketers. The goal here is to get your company or product in front of influential bloggers. When a well-read blogger mentions your company or product, it's free advertising to all of that blogger's readers. In fact, it can be even better than that; in some readers' eyes, it's tantamount to a celebrity endorsement.

This type of social media marketing typically utilizes traditional public relations methods; you "work" influential bloggers much as you'd work reviewers at traditional print newspapers and magazines. But there are also some blogs that let you pay for a mention or review. This sort of paid placement is similar to product placement in movies or TV shows, and it is becoming more common in the blogosphere.

> ### tip
>
> If you're interested in exploring product placement in the blogosphere, check out Blogitive (www.blogitive.com), a network of bloggers that accept paid placement.

The key is to do your research and find out which blogs your customers read; typically these are industry- or topic-specific blogs. You can then find out who the bloggers are behind these blogs and start up the necessary email correspondences. Make friends with the bloggers—and then make them aware of all your new products and promotions.

Conducting Online Public Relations

Blog marketing is just one type of online PR; when you cultivate relationships with influential bloggers, you're engaging in a public relations activity. You get your best results not by sending out an electronic press release but by making friends with individual bloggers and actively participating in targeted online communities.

In some ways, online PR is no different from traditional PR: You're trying to get as many outlets as possible to mention your latest product or promotion. But online PR involves many new and different channels you need to address, from blogs and social networks to topic-oriented communities and message boards. It's not as simple as sending out a hardcopy press release.

Another way that online PR differs from traditional PR is that results are more easily tracked. With traditional PR, about the only thing you can track is actual mentions in the media. With online PR, however, you can track actual sales that result from mentions on various websites; all you have to do is provide the solicited media with their own dedicated URLs to link back to your site.

It goes without saying that public relations is always a key part of a company's marketing mix. That remains so when we're talking about the online marketing mix—which has to include online PR.

Where Do You Start Your Promotional Efforts?

In this chapter I've presented a lot of information about possible promotional activities. It can all get a bit confusing, especially if you don't have a background in marketing or advertising. Given a limited budget and the time constraints of a typical entrepreneur, just where do you start?

The one essential thing every website owner must do is optimize his site for search. While you can pay a consultant or service to do SEO for your site, most site owners do their own optimization. That's free marketing, which is always a good thing. (In addition, many e-commerce hosting services offer rudimentary SEO tools; if they exist, use 'em.)

Next, I recommend taking advantage of the major comparison shopping sites. That means creating and submitting product lists on a regular basis, and it also means allocating a portion of your budget for CPC results. But there's no better place to be than in front of customers searching for what you're selling.

Along the same lines, I like reserving a part of the budget for PPC advertising. I'd start with Google AdWords and purchase a few keywords for the main products you sell. Evaluate the results on an ongoing basis to see whether you want to increase or decrease the money you spend on this type of advertising.

As to the other types of promotion, they're interesting but not necessarily essential—at least at the outset. Yes, you probably want to get the word out about your site launch (that's online PR), but beyond that, it may not be a good use of your time to be shooting YouTube videos and working the social networks. SEO, comparison shopping site submittals, and PPC advertising—those are the essential components of a starting marketing mix. Concentrate your efforts and your money there. ■

21

Migrating Your eBay Business to Your Own Website

Okay. You've read all the preceding chapters in this section and think that opening up your own e-commerce website makes sense. If you're ready to make the move, what do you need to do to make it happen?

Migrating existing eBay sales to your own online store is not the easiest thing in the world to accomplish. In fact, you're likely to experience some decrease in sales if you attempt a full and immediate transition. You need to be prepared for what lies ahead, which is what this chapter is all about.

Does Migrating to Your Own Online Store Make Sense?

Now is a good time to once again ask the question: Does it really make sense to open your own online store? I know, I know, it sure is tempting, especially if you're really peeved at eBay's latest anti-seller shenanigans. But it isn't the best thing for all sellers, as we'll examine.

Comparing Costs

Let's look first at the costs of running your own website versus selling on eBay. It's tough to do an apples-to-apples cost comparison because the operations are so different. But we can make an attempt.

For this comparison, let's assume that you're selling fixed-priced items on the main eBay marketplace, and you do not have the monthly costs associated with running an eBay Store. Let's also assume that the comparative online store is based at a typical e-commerce hosting company with associated typical costs—$30-per-month subscription plus a 1.5% commission rate. We'll also assume that you budget 5% of your sales for marketing, use Google Checkout for online payments, and didn't have to pay a setup fee to the hosting service. Most importantly (although perhaps less likely), we'll assume that you can maintain the same volume of business in your new online store as you were experiencing on eBay.

We'll compare three different business models. In model A, the business sells tee shirts; the average transaction price is $20, and there are 100 transactions per month. In model B, the business sells video games; the average transaction price is $40, and there are 200 transactions per month. In model C, the business sells DVD players; the average transaction price is $60, and there are 300 transactions per month.

Table 21.1 plays out each scenario.

Table 21.1   eBay vs. E-Commerce Website: Three Scenarios

	Sales Revenue (per Month)	Listing Fees	Transaction Fees	Online Payment Fees	Monthly Fees	Marketing Costs	Gross Profit
Model A (eBay)	$2,000	$35	$240	$88	$0	$0	$1,637
Model A (e-commerce website)	$2,000	$0	$30	$60	$30	$100	$1,780
Model B (eBay)	$8,000	$30	$1,200	$260	$0	$0	$6,510
Model B (e-commerce website)	$8,000	$0	$120	$200	$30	$400	$7,250
Model C (eBay)	$18,000	$105	$1,335	$486	$0	$0	$16,074
Model C (e-commerce website)	$18,000	$0	$270	$420	$30	$900	$16,380

In each of these scenarios, you make slightly more money with your own website than you do selling on eBay. Of course, different scenarios may produce different results, depending on the types of products you sell and your sales volume. Other variables are the online payment service you use and the fees you pay your e-commerce hosting service. Based on the choices you make, you could end up making more or less money than estimated here.

---

note

This comparison changes completely if you opt to create your own website from scratch, as opposed to going the pre-built hosted route. When you start from scratch, you have lower ongoing fees (you don't pay a commission to any- one) but much larger upfront costs.

Importantly, the assumption that you can maintain your sales level when you move off eBay may not be valid—especially during the early months. Remember, you're moving from a site with tens of millions of visitors each month (eBay) to a site that has zero customers on day one. You have to build up your customer base over time, so it may take six months or a year before you realize similar sales numbers. Don't expect comparable sales when you first launch the site.

Comparing Effort

So you might be able to generate more profits on your own website than on eBay. Are those profits commensurate with the increased effort you'll be expending?

Listing on eBay is a relatively low-effort endeavor. You take some digital photos, write a few item descriptions, and post your listings. That's it until an item sells, when you have to do the requisite packing and shipping. Not a big deal; many big eBay sellers operate their businesses effectively part time.

Running your own website, however, requires a lot more—and a lot differ- ent—work. Yes, you create product pages, but you need to do this only once, not on an ongoing basis as you do with eBay's listings. Instead, you have all the effort associated with keeping a website up and running, per- forming all your own customer service, and promoting your site. That's in addition to the normal packing and shipping, of course.

All in all, it takes a lot more effort to run your own website than it does to sell on eBay. This may be the biggest change most sellers face—and for which many are totally unprepared.

Which Items Should You Migrate?

Here's something else to consider. Not every item you sell on eBay may be ideally suited for selling on your own website. That's right, eBay is the bet- ter marketplace for some types of items.

In general, a freestanding online store is a good place to sell commodity items or items that you sell in large quantity. That is, an online store is a great place for selling the same items day in, day out. You spend your marketing efforts promoting the same items that you sold last week and that you will sell next week.

Conversely, if you sell rare items and collectibles, you may be better off selling on eBay. That's because it's tough to efficiently promote single items on your website; if you have a rare 1940s copy of *Action Comics*, how do you let all potential buyers know that you have it? That's a much easier proposition on eBay, which remains a robust marketplace for collectors of all stripes and sizes. Post your *Action Comics* listing on eBay, and potential buyers will find it.

Equally importantly, collectors will bid up the price of your items when you list them in eBay's auction format. You have no similar mechanism for conducting auctions on your own website; you can sell fixed-priced items, but not auction items. So if you want the upside of auction bidding, staying on eBay is the only way to go.

That's not to say that you can't sell used or one-off items on your own website. In fact, many sellers embrace these types of products—and do a good job with them. What they do is sell their sites as the place to find used clothing, let's say, or refurbished power tools. Their selection changes almost daily, but customers know that if they're looking for those types of items, that website is the place to go.

All of which brings us to the inevitable conclusion that you don't have to completely move your business from eBay to your own website. You can sell some types of items in your online store and other types of items on eBay. For that matter, if you're careful, you can sell the same items on both sites. In fact, it may make sense to keep your eBay sales rolling while you try to get your own website off the ground; this way, you'll keep a steady revenue stream while you're building your new customer base.

note

Learn more about selling on more than one site in Chapter 22, "Selling in Multiple Channels."

Changing Your Business Model and Processes

It again bears repeating: Selling on your own website is completely different from selling on eBay. You have to learn some new skills and change some old ones; your entire business model changes, in fact.

Take your normal selling process. In the world of eBay auctions, it became a weekly routine: Create and post your listings on day one, wait a week, collect your money and pack and ship the items on day seven, then repeat.

On your own website, this type of dependable schedule simply doesn't exist. You create new product pages only when you add new items to your inventory mix. Otherwise, you post your items *once* but then update your inventory listings continuously. Sales can happen any time, so you have to be prepared to pack and ship five or six days a week. (You get Sunday off, by default.) You also have to manage your online payment service account on a daily basis and offer seven-day-a-week customer service. Then there are the challenges of designing (and redesigning) your website, revamping your home page on a regular basis, and doing ongoing website maintenance—all activities you never had to worry about on eBay.

And don't forget marketing. Many online sellers spend a large part of each day managing their PPC ad campaigns, doing online PR, tweaking their site for SEO, submitting updated inventory listings to comparison shopping sites, you name it. Promotion takes a lot of effort—and a unique skill set that you may or may not possess.

All in all, running your own website is more work—and different work— than selling individual items on eBay. You need to think through everything you need to do on a daily basis, make sure you've scheduled the proper amount of time, and then prepare yourself for the work ahead. It's an eye opener.

Making the Move

Preparations made, it's now time to make the move. What's the best way to get from eBay to your own website?

Before you do much of anything else, you first have to decide what you'll be selling on your website—and for how much. You'll want to have a stable source of product, a place to store all your inventory, and an inventory management system in place so that you won't run out of your bestsellers. If you're selling different items than you did on eBay, just finding suppliers will require some homework; it may also require some upfront expenditure to purchase your starting inventory. For that, financing may be necessary—so be prepared to put together the required actual and projected financials and make a trip to your local bank.

As to product pricing, remember that you're now selling items at a fixed price; you can no longer rely on the eBay auction marketplace to decide the final price for you. That means doing some market research, searching other online stores for similar products to discover the most competitive pricing. As a newcomer to the game, you don't want your products to be overpriced, or you won't be able to draw customers from established sellers; and while undercutting the competition makes good sense, you don't want to price so low as to be unprofitable. Take your time to set the best price for both your customers and your business.

While you're doing this, you also have to decide how you want to create and host your online store—and then get started putting things together. You also need to set up a shopping cart, a checkout system, and an online payment service, so that you'll be ready to take orders on day one.

During the site setup process, you create product pages for the items you're selling. This typically requires taking one or more photos of each product, as well as writing all the text for the product page. You should also employ SEO techniques to optimize each product page for search engine placement.

When the product pages are created, you have to upload details of your starting inventory—all the individual items you have in stock and ready for sale. Once your inventory is registered on your site and all your support services are in place, you're ready to take the site live.

note

While you're doing all this, I'm going to assume that you're still selling on eBay—which will probably make for some very long days (or nights!). You want to keep one business going while you're launching the next one, which means pulling double duty. Prepare for it.

You're ready to go live, that is, if you've already done some pre-launch promotion. You can't just create a few web pages and say you're in business. You have to let customers know of your new site, which means doing a little PR (getting the word out to sympathetic bloggers, for instance), sending an email out to your existing eBay customers (assuming that you have their email addresses—you do, don't you?), and uploading your inventory listings to the major online shopping sites. You may also want to launch a PPC advertising campaign, targeted on keywords for select products. And all this promotional activity has to be ready to go on day one.

When the big day finally comes, you can activate your shopping cart system and let visitors start making purchases. That's the fun—and profitable—part. More work will come as you manage your burgeoning sales, but don't dwell on that just yet. Take pride in the first sales made on your very own website—and consider yourself a real businessperson.

Choosing Your Domain Name

One of the benefits of running your own online store is having your own unique domain name. No longer will you be stores.ebay.com/*yourstorename*/; you can now be www.*yourstorename*.com instead.

This assumes two things, of course. First, that your e-commerce hosting service lets you use your own domain name (most do), as opposed to tacking your name onto their domain, as eBay does. And, second, that the domain name of choice is available for your use—which it may not be.

With millions and millions of sites on the Web, lots of the potential domain names are already taken. If you sell large-sized tee shirts and want to be known as Big Shirts, you may find that www.bigshirts.com is in use by another website. In fact, it's likely that the most simple and direct domain names haven't been free for a number of years.

If the name you want isn't available, what do you do? Well, you could try registering the same name but in a different top-level domain—.net or .biz instead of .com, for example. But that may not be a satisfactory solution; most customers type ".com" by default, and thus you'll lose business to whomever has the .com version of your name.

A better solution is to alter the name of your store. Instead of calling yourself Big Shirts, maybe you can be The Big Shirt Store and use www.bigshirtstore.com or www.thebigshirtstore.com as your URL. If you think about it, there are probably several variations on your desired name that you could use.

It's also possible that the domain you want is taken but not in use. Enter the URL into your web browser and see where it takes you; if you see a "parked" page rather than an active one, you may be able to pay the domain holder to transfer the domain to you. Go to www.networksolutions.com/whois/ to see information about the current domain name owner and, if you want, make an offer to buy the domain. ∎

22

Selling in Multiple Channels

Throughout this book, we've discussed various ways for you to sell your products. You can sell via eBay auction, eBay fixed-price listings, an eBay Store, eBay's Half.com site, craigslist, the Amazon marketplace, and even on your own e-commerce website. But these channels aren't mutually exclusive; many sellers choose to sell in two or more online marketplaces.

Should you sell in multiple channels? Doing so could be a good way for you to increase your sales—or create an unmanageable mess. Read on to find out if it's a good fit with your business.

What Is Multichannel Selling—and How Does It Work?

Put simply, multichannel selling is selling in more than one channel or marketplace. This may involve selling in two or more online marketplaces, such as Amazon and eBay; an online marketplace and your own online store; or an online marketplace and a brick-and-mortar storefront.

A retailer can sell exactly the same items in multiple marketplaces or sell a different mix in each channel. For that matter, a seller can go by the same retail name in both channels or use a different name in each marketplace. There are no rules; multichannel selling simply means selling in more than one place at the same time.

How does multichannel selling work? It all depends on the approach you take.

For example, some sellers maintain the same inventory on multiple sites. That is, they offer the same SKUs on both eBay and Amazon, or on Amazon and their own website. This takes a bit of organizational expertise, as it's relatively easy to sell the same item twice if the inventory is not constantly updated across sites. You also have to deal with the issue of whether you price items the same in different marketplaces; you don't necessarily want to compete with yourself on price on different sites.

Other sellers opt to sell different items in different channels. This lets you play to the strengths of each marketplace. You may, for example, sell collectible and hard-to-find items on eBay, where there is a large built-in customer base for these types of items (and the ability to price-to-market via the auction process), but sell commodity items at a fixed price on your own website.

In other words, there are no rules when it comes to multichannel selling. You can do it if you sell only a single SKU or if you sell thousands of SKUs. You can do it if you sell clothing or printer cables or auto parts. You can do it if you're a small independent seller or a large company. It simply doesn't matter.

Pros and Cons of Multichannel Selling

However you choose to do it, multichannel selling has its own unique set of benefits and challenges. It's definitely not as easy to do as selling in a single marketplace.

Benefits of Multichannel Selling

Why would you want to sell in more than one marketplace or channel? There are a number of reasons, all of which boil down to making more money:

- **You can reach more potential customers.** It's simple. You sell on eBay, you reach only eBay customers. You sell on both eBay and Amazon, you reach both eBay and Amazon customers. Now, the customer bases of two different marketplaces may have some overlap—that is, some customers may shop on both sites—but in almost all instances, you'll increase the number of potential customers for your products if you sell on both. This increased exposure should result in increased sales.

- **You can tailor your product mix to the strengths of different marketplaces.** We all know that eBay is good for selling some types of items but less good for others. So why not sell eBay-friendly items on eBay and other types of items on another site? There's no reason for you to artificially limit your SKUs because the single channel you sell in isn't friendly to some types of merchandise. Instead, sell some items in one place and other items in another—and play to each channel's strengths.

- **It's cost-efficient.** Just because you sell in two channels doesn't mean you double your costs. In fact, many of your fixed costs don't change at all if you sell in more than one channel. Your rent, utilities, warehousing costs, and the like are the same whether you sell in one channel or three. You can effectively spread these fixed costs over multiple channels when you opt for multichannel selling.

- **It's operationally efficient.** While there are some operational challenges for selling in multiple channels, which we'll discuss in due order, there are also some operational efficiencies to be gained. For example, you need to shoot only one digital photo and write a single description that you can then use in multiple product listings across multiple sites. There's a lot of work you need only do once for multiple marketplaces.

The end result of these advantages is that you should be able to achieve greater sales with not much extra effort—which should increase your profits correspondingly.

Drawbacks of Multichannel Selling

In addition to the benefits, there are some definite drawbacks to selling in multiple channels. These include the following:

- **Inventory management is more difficult.** Imagine this scenario: You have one rare baseball card in stock, but have it listed on both eBay and your own website. You sell the item on your website, but then later that day you receive a notice that the item has also sold on eBay. Since you can't sell the same item twice, you're in trouble. This is the challenge of multichannel inventory management—keeping the inventory for each channel either discrete or up-to-date with your master inventory. Somehow, you have to link all your inventory and marketplace listings together, so if something sells in one channel, your inventory is correspondingly reduced in all other channels. It's not easy, and if you're sloppy with it, you can end up with a boatload of headaches—and unhappy customers.

- **Pricing decisions are more difficult.** If you sell the same item on multiple sites, the easy and tempting thing to do is to price that item the same on all sites. But what if competition is more intense on one site than another? Maybe you need to price the item a little lower on that site. But then why give away profit on the other sites? So you price it lower here and higher there, and before long, you have customers price shopping between your two sites—and you find yourself competing with yourself. But if you leave the price the same across all marketplaces, you may lose sales on the most competitive site. Confused yet? You should be; pricing decisions get a lot more complex when you're selling in multiple marketplaces.

- **Different channels have different requirements.** Multichannel selling is not as easy as creating a single product listing and then posting it on different websites. Each marketplace has its own rules, regulations, and requirements, and you have to meet them all. This can be difficult to keep track of—and even more difficult to do.

- **You can create channel conflict.** Not all sellers believe that you can maintain a presence in multiple channels. Sooner or later, you start to compete with yourself, just as the different channels compete with each other. This is called *channel conflict*, and it's a big deal, even among the largest retailers. Eventually, you find your business in conflict with itself, unsure of where you want to concentrate your efforts.

- **You can confuse your customers.** Channel conflict leads to customer confusion. Are you the retailer who offers great service on his own website, or the one who has bargain prices on another marketplace? If you try to be all things to all people, you'll end up being nothing to no one.

In short, selling in multiple channels, while potentially financially rewarding, is challenging. The extra work and concentration on details can throw you off your main business and make any additional sales only marginally attractive. If your customer service in all channels begins to deteriorate, you'll end up with long-term lower sales. Is that what you want?

When Does Multichannel Selling Make Sense— and When Is It a Recipe for Disaster?

To effectively sell in multiple channels, you have to be at the top of your operational game. If you're sloppy or just inexperienced operationally, you will screw it up—no doubt about it. There are just too many details to keep track of; you'll eventually end up double-selling items and ticking off your customers.

So multichannel selling is only for the pros—or for sellers who operationally have their act together. What else is necessary to be successful selling in multiple channels?

First, you need to adequately access the upside for your business—as well as the challenges. Will you double your sales by selling in two marketplaces? (Probably not.) How much more effort do you need to expend—and will you increase your sales enough to make it worth the effort? Sometimes you don't know until you try it, so is the second marketplace one you can easily get in and out of, or does it require a big time or money investment? If it's easy to do and you're likely to see a significant uptick in sales, then by all means, go for it. But if the upside is iffy and the effort and cost are great, why bother?

Another equally important factor is what you intend to sell where. Some businesses sell the same products in all channels and appreciate the increased potential customer base—and increased sales—that result. Other businesses see no point in competing with themselves in multiple channels and refuse to sell the same product in more than one marketplace.

To me, it makes more sense to sell different products in different channels—if that's how your business works. If you're used to selling a variety of items on eBay, for example, you may want to continue selling some of those items on eBay but move other items to Amazon or your own website. This way, you can take advantage of the strengths and weaknesses of each channel; you can sell commodity products on your own site while still selling collectibles on eBay. Or maybe you can sell larger items on your local craigslist site while offering smaller, more easily shipped items on Amazon. You get the idea.

In any case, you need to really think through the issue of multiple-channel selling before you commit to a new marketplace. It isn't as simple as porting existing listings to a second site; there's a lot of management work involved, and you need to plan for it.

Managing Inventory Across Channels

Let's take a moment to discuss the trickiest part of multichannel selling: managing your inventory across channels. It's tricky because, in many cases, you're using the same inventory to stock multiple channels.

Now, this isn't much of a problem if you sell completely different products in different channels. For example, you might sell rare comic books on eBay and used textbooks on Amazon; that makes it easy to separate your inventory for the different channels.

But if you sell the same SKUs in more than one channel, inventory management gets complicated. If you have three units of a given SKU in stock and sell in two channels, do you have three units available in both channels, or do you have two units available for one channel and one unit available for the other, or what?

The most inventory-efficient way to manage multiple channels is to create a single pool of inventory—so those three units of that one SKU are available for purchase in all the channels you sell. When a purchase is made in one channel, the inventory level is reduced accordingly.

Single-pool inventory works okay under a few conditions. First, all of your sales channels have to tie into that inventory; when a sale is made in one channel, it has to be reflected in the inventory available for the others. This requires tight inventory management processes, which probably means advanced inventory management software designed for use with multiple channels.

Second, you need to have more units on hand than you have channels. That is, if you sell in two channels, you need to have two or more units on hand at all times—enough to show availability in each channel.

Things become problematic if you have fewer units on hand than you have channels. Let's say, for example, that you sell rare baseball cards and have one unit available of a particular card but that you post that card as "available" in two different channels. If your inventory management is tight, you should be able to sell the card in one channel and immediately register an "out of stock" situation in the other channel. Since not all inventory management systems operate in real time, however, it's more likely that when you sell the card in channel one, it will still show "available" in channel two for a period of time—minutes, hours, maybe even days. And if it appears to be in stock, the possibility exists for a second customer to purchase it—even though it really doesn't exist.

This, then, is the challenge behind managing inventory across channels. Different retailers handle this challenge in different ways.

One solution is to simply keep on hand as many units as you have channels. If you sell on eBay, Amazon, and your own website, for example, you always keep three units of each SKU on hand. This works well for commodity items but not for used items, collectibles, and other one-of-a-kind items.

Another solution is to physically assign inventory units to different channels—that is, to not work with pooled inventory. If you sell in three channels, you manage three separate inventories. While this helps to keep each channel fully stocked, it eliminates one of the beneficial efficiencies of multichannel selling.

Yet another approach is to not sell certain types of items in multiple channels. If you sell commodity items, offer the same SKU across all channels and use the pooled inventory approach. But if you sell one-of-a-kind items, sell those items in a single channel only. That way, you'll never end up selling the same item twice—and having to deal with the angry customers that result.

Creating a Multichannel Marketing Plan

An important facet of multichannel selling is multichannel marketing. That is, you need to figure out how to promote the same (or different) products across multiple channels.

If you sell the same items for the same price under the same business name in multiple marketplaces, you may be able to promote all your channels at once. That is, when you run an ad or seek product placement, you mention all your online storefronts, thus driving business here, there, and everywhere. It theoretically shouldn't matter to you whether a customer buys your product on eBay or Amazon or on your own site, as long as you make the sale; a customer can gravitate to the site with which he's comfortable. This provides a bigger bang for your marketing buck, as you're promoting multiple channels on the same budget.

On the other hand, this type of "everywhere" retailing can be confusing to customers. Is this business an eBay retailer, or an Amazon seller, or does it run its own website, or what? When confused, customers will typically not buy—or they'll buy elsewhere. (And the confusion reigns supreme if your pricing differs from site to site—it's the old bugaboo of channel conflict.)

Promotion gets more difficult if your product mix varies by marketplace. Well, it's not necessarily more difficult, but it's certainly not easier. That's because you need to promote each product mix separately; you can't combine marketing efforts between sites. So you'll need to create a discrete marketing plan for each channel in which you sell. There's no efficiency in effort or expense with this approach.

In any instance, you probably want to look at your marketing for each channel separately, even if you sell the same stuff everywhere. Ideally, you want to drive the most possible business to each channel—which requires focusing your marketing efforts for each channel. Marketing for the Amazon marketplace is a lot different from promoting your own online store, and you need to make the best effort for each channel. For this reason, you may in fact end up spending *more* marketing funds than you would if you sold in only a single channel, but that's the nature of the beast. Maximize each channel's sales, and you maximize your overall sales.

Selling Online 2.0—The Time Is Now

Multichannel selling is the logical extension of what I call Selling Online 2.0. This is truly next-generation selling, worlds beyond traditional eBay auctions.

The 1.0 version of online selling was essentially listing placement. You didn't have to do much more than create a product listing and upload it to the eBay site; eBay did everything else for you, save for managing inventory, packing, and shipping. You didn't have to worry about site design or promotion or channel conflict or anything else. You didn't even have to worry about pricing, as the auction process took care of that for you. In short, selling online was so easy, practically anyone could do it.

As we move to the 2.0 model, online selling requires more effort, more skills, and more professionalism. Not everyone can do it; there's a lot more involved. You need to learn how to evaluate different channels, structure and design websites, promote and advertise products, manage large inventories, and evaluate your selling success. It's like running a real business—because it now *is* a real business.

Not everyone can move to the new model. Casual sellers will find the process much more difficult and may be forced back to the 1.0 world of eBay auctions. But if you have the knowledge and the diligence and the right skill set, you can move your selling to the next level. And the next level is a lot more profitable, if you do it right.

With all the changes happening on the eBay marketplace, now is the time to migrate your business to the 2.0 model. It's not for the faint of heart, but if you're in it for the long run, this is the only viable way to go. Selling on eBay will never go away, but smart sellers—next-generation sellers—will migrate to selling on craigslist, on Amazon, and on their own websites. Multichannel selling is next-generation selling. Are you ready for it? ■

Index

D

E

F

M

N

O

Q–R

S

More Titles By Michael Miller

Googlepedia: The Ultimate Google Resource, Third Edition

ISBN: 9780789738202 | 744 pages

Googlepedia is not just for searching! Did you know that over the years Google has added a variety of features, services, tools, and businesses that make it a one-stop-shop for virtually any web user? This book takes you way beyond web searches by exposing you to Google's tools, services, and features. *Googlepedia* provides comprehensive information that will benefit every Google user.

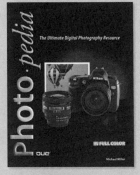

iPodpedia: The Ultimate iPod and iTunes Resource

ISBN: 9780789736741 | 528 pages

iPodpedia is the first book to show you everything that iPod and iTunes has to offer—from music to movies and beyond. Whether you want to get the most out of your iPod's music playback, create your own playlists, edit your music info and album art, convert your home movies and DVDs to iPod videos, listen to audiobooks and podcasts, or just unfreeze a frozen iPod, *iPodpedia* will tell you how to do it.

Photopedia: The Ultimate Digital Photography Resource

ISBN: 9780789737250 | 624 pages

Photopedia is a comprehensive A to Z guide that includes instruction in both basic photographic techniques and advanced digital image manipulation. This is a full-color guide to all aspects of digital photography—from composing the shot to editing, printing, or sharing the photograph. *Photopedia* is perfect for those new to digital photography and for traditional photographers who face a learning curve when switching to digital.

YouTube for Business

ISBN: 9780789737977 | 288 pages

To any businessperson or marketing professional, YouTube's 20 million viewers are a tempting target. How can you tap into the potential of YouTube to promote your business and sell your products or services? The answers in *YouTube for Business* show you how to make YouTube part of your online marketing plan—and drive traffic to your company's website.

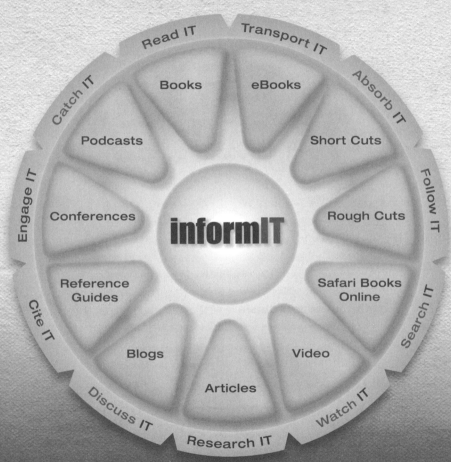

FREE Online Edition

Your purchase of *Selling Online 2.0* includes access to a free online edition for 45 days through the Safari Books Online subscription service. Nearly every Que book is available online through Safari Books Online, along with more than 5,000 other technical books and videos from publishers such as Addison-Wesley Professional, Cisco Press, Exam Cram, IBM Press, O'Reilly, Prentice Hall, and Sams.

SAFARI BOOKS ONLINE allows you to search for a specific answer, cut and paste code, download chapters, and stay current with emerging technologies.

Activate your FREE Online Edition at www.informit.com/safarifree

> **STEP 1:** Enter the coupon code: WFBFGDB.

> **STEP 2:** New Safari users, complete the brief registration form. Safari subscribers, just log in.

If you have difficulty registering on Safari or accessing the online edition, please e-mail customer-service@safaribooksonline.com